# DRESSING YOUR INNER DRAMA QUEEN

Master the Art of Outfits That Scream and Whisper Style, While You Juggle Toddlers and Life!

VIVIAN ABREU

All rights reserved. Photography © 2025 by Vivian Abreu. No part of this book may be reproduced in any form or by any means including electronic, mechanical or photocopying or stored in a retrieval system without permission in writing from the publisher except by reviewer who may quote brief passage to be included in a review.

Cover Design by Vivian Abreu
ISBN: 979-8-218-74031-3
First Printing: 2025

Published by SAM D'MONES LLC
P.O. BOX 896
Westwood, NJ 07676
www.samdmones.com

Printed in the United States

# CONTENTS

Acknowledgements ................................................................. 1
Chapter 1   Embrace Your Inner Drama Queen ............................. 2
Chapter 2   The Power of Color: Your Personal Palette ................ 16
Chapter 3   Dress For Your Body Type: The Ultimate Guide ...... 27
Chapter 4   From Diapers to Designer: Fashion Through
            Motherhood ................................................................. 39
Chapter 5   Statement Pieces: Making a Bold Impression ........... 52
Chapter 6   Everyday Chic: Effortless Style Tips .......................... 64
Chapter 7   Sustainable Style: Fashion that Cares ........................ 76
Chapter 8   Accessorize Like A Pro: The Finishing Touch ........... 87
Chapter 9   How to Shop Like a Superhero ................................. 99
Chapter 10  Zodiac Styles: Fashion Based on Your Star Sign ...... 111
Chapter 11  Creating Outfits for Every Occasion ....................... 130
Chapter 12  The Art of Layering: Style and Function .................. 142
Chapter 13  Fun Fashion for Moms On the Go .......................... 154
Chapter 14  Pajamas to Party: Dressing Up and Down ............... 166
Chapter 15  Wardrobe Essentials: Building Your Fashion
            Foundation ................................................................. 179
Chapter 16  Glam Up: Transitioning Seasonal Styles ................... 191
Chapter 17  Mommy and Me: Matching Styles for Family Fun . 202
Chapter 18  Fashion Faux Pas: What to Avoid ............................. 215
Chapter 19  Confidence is Key: Owning Your Style .................... 227
Chapter 20  Your Style Journey: Embrace and Evolve ................. 239

# ACKNOWLEDGEMENTS

In crafting this book, I am profoundly grateful to my beloved family. To my husband Jeyson Rivera, whose unwavering support and belief in me have been the cornerstone of my journey—thank you for giving me the time and space to bring this dream to life. Your encouragement has been invaluable. To my twin boys Maximus and Jaxon, and my daughter Samantha, who inspire me every day, this book is as much yours as it is mine. Thank you for being my greatest source of strength and motivation. Without you all, this endeavor would not have been possible.

## CHAPTER 1
# EMBRACE YOUR INNER DRAMA QUEEN

**The Power of Self-Expression**

The glorious world of self-expression! It's like stepping onto a stage wearing a sequined tutu, a feather boa, and a tiara-because why not? In the grand production of life, we all star as the lead actors, and our clothing is the costume that reflects our inner drama queens. Self-expression is not just a whimsical idea; it's your superpower, the ultimate accessory, and an invitation to showcase the fabulous being you are. Fashion is like a language; it speaks volumes without uttering a single word. Just ask my four-year-old twins, Maximus and Jaxon, who express themselves daily by mixing pajama bottoms with superhero capes. Who knew an outfit could be both charming and utterly confusing?

When you wear something that resonates with your spirit, it's like declaring to the universe, "Here I am! Take me as I am, preferably in this gorgeously polka-dotted dress!" It's an instant confidence boost, a small but mighty act of defiance against those days when the laundry hamper threatens to consume your last clean pair of yoga pants. From flared jeans that scream 70's disco revival to a power suit that says I mean business... and I can out-bargain you at any clearance sale,' each article of clothing is an opportunity to channel your inner diva. And believe me, darling, you have an inner diva just waiting to burst forth like a confetti cannon.

Now, let's talk about the sacred ritual of getting dressed each morning.

## EMBRACE YOUR INNER DRAMA QUEEN

You've faced kids throwing breakfast on the wall, the dog having an existential crisis over his food bowl, and an ever-intimidating pile of laundry glaring at you. After surviving that, making a sartorial choice feels like a triumphant victory! Picture this: you waltz into the kitchen, still wearing the remnants of yesterday's mascara, and you catch a glimpse of yourself in the toaster. Suddenly, an epiphany strikes — today's the day for that fiery red blazer! It's time for the world to recognize that you are more than just a "toddler wrangler" or a "mom in sweatpants." You are a fashion icon on a mission! But what if you're feeling a little less than chipper? Here's the beauty of self-expression; it works both ways. Are you in the mood to channel your inner rock star? Go for the oversized band tee, acid wash jeans, and combat boots. Feeling a bit more conventional? A tailored pencil skirt and blouse can do wonders. That's the magic of style; you can create an ensemble that serves as both a protective shield and a badge of honor. It's that duality of fashion. Like a superhero's cape, it empowers you while simultaneously making the chicken nuggets you're frying for the kids feel a bit less tedious.

Let's not forget; embracing self-expression means you can also explore those hidden aspects of your personality. We've all seen those quirky outfits that make you say, "What were they thinking?" Those are bold statements, my dear friend! You may just find that a whirlwind of mismatched prints can celebrate your eclectic spirit better than any plain cotton t-shirt ever could. And here's a fun fact —being unique ain't just stylish; it's also an excellent conversation starter. You can proudly declare, "Oh, these are my vintage flamingo overalls! They really capture my love for tropical vacations, even on a Tuesday!" You'll find laughter and connections that form through shared creativity and humor.

Ultimately, donning outfits that mirror your spirit cultivates a profound connection with your identity. Worthy moments of self-discovery often sneak in, like an uninvited guest trying to steal your cheese platter at a party. Why wait for a special occasion to dress fabulously? Each day that you stride into the world clad in attire that embodies your unique flair is an excellent opportunity to showcase your individuality. So, let's cast aside the mundane and embrace the illustrious art of self-expression through fashion.

Remember, my dear readers, in a world full of copies, be an original-a sassy, dazzling, and unapologetically expressive original. Rock that tutu, feather boa, and tiara with pride because darling, the world deserves to see the fabulous you!

## Identifying Your Unique Style

Identifying your unique style is akin to embarking on a scavenger hunt for buried treasure, except instead of gold coins and jewels, you're sifting through racks of clothing and discovering pieces of brilliance that scream, "This is YOU!" In the chaotic landscape of motherhood, where toddler tantrums and bedtime stories dominate the stage, it can be easy to lose sight of who you are beneath the superhero cape of "Mom." But fear not, fellow fashionistas! Your unique style is patiently waiting to strut down the runway of your life, and together we will coax it out of hiding. Let's face it: identifying your style can feel as daunting as trying to assemble a piece of IKEA furniture while blindfolded. Don't let that frighten you! Instead, grab a cup of coffee — or a stiff drink (no judgment, I'm here for you, darling) — and think about what draws you in. What makes your heart go pitter-patter like a seven-year-old meeting their movie star crush? Is it the grace of bohemian maxi dresses swirling in the breeze, or perhaps the sharp lines of a classic trench coat that makes you feel like a power-wielding executive? Make a list of those fashion items that make your heart sing, and avoid the noise of trends that don't resonate with you. After all, as thrilling as a fleeting trend may be, it might not fit your unique voice like your favorite pair of worn-in self-distressed jeans.

One of the most essential steps in unearthing your unique style is to look through your closet like a detective on a fashion mission. Pull out every piece of clothing, no matter how long it's been since you wore it- yes, even that suspiciously sequined sweater from your college days. Ask yourself: "Does this spark joy, or is it bringing shame to my wardrobe?" If it's been living in the closet like a hermit for longer than six months, it can safely be retired (or donated, if it

# EMBRACE YOUR INNER DRAMA QUEEN

has some semblance of decency). The pieces that truly shine with your essence should bring a smile to your face and remind you of who you are— not who your aunt Ethel thinks you should be.

Drawing inspiration from your lifestyle is also integral to discovering your unique style. Are you knee-deep in toddler drama, sprinting from playdates to grocery stores? Perhaps the effortlessly chic "playground fashionista" look is calling your name, favoring athleisure wear that can transition from kicking a soccer ball to grabbing a quick latte without missing a beat! Or maybe you're a #BossBabe who needs daring attire that commands respect in the boardroom while allowing space for a spontaneous dinner date afterward. Juggling motherhood while trying to express your unique style isn't just possible; it's downright essential!

Another delightful path towards discovering your unique style is to explore fashion muses— those inspiring figures whose looks resonate with your spirit. Don't be shy! Go on an online rabbit hole exploring Pinterest boards, Instagram feeds, and mood boards until something stops you in your tracks and screams, "That's me!" Maybe it's the effortless elegance of Audrey Hepburn or the daring boho vibes of Sienna Miller. Channel that energy into your wardrobe! Just remember — while emulating someone's vibe can spark inspiration, the goal is to mix their aesthetics with your quirks and twist until you find your authentic style.

Keep in mind that your style is not set in stone; it's a swirling, growing entity-like the pizza dough you tried to toss that one time and ended up in a gluten catastrophe. It evolves, transforms, and adapts as you continue to grow. Embrace the idea of experimenting; try the bright florals that you've never dared to wear or the bold prints that seem to leap out of the rack when you walk by. Fear of judgment? Toss it out the window, my darling! Wearing something that doesn't fit you or look right? That's a fashion faux pas, but it's also a steppingstone on the incredible path of style exploration. Remember, identifying your unique style is a quest for the fabulous version of you hiding beneath all those layers of self-doubt and cluttered laundry. So as you embark on this glorious journey, celebrate every misstep and every triumphant fashion find. Trust that your wardrobe will lead you to the radiant, authentic you that is simply waiting to emerge. Now, let's hang that fired sequined sweater back in the closet, because it's time for the emergence of the dazzling you —let's shine bright, my fashion-forward friend!

## Dressing for Your Mood

Dressing for your mood —the sartorial equivalent of fine-tuning a delicate violin. How you feel on any given day significantly influences what you wear, and let's be honest, life as a busy mom can oscillate between "I've got this!" and "Help! I've lost my sanity under a pile of laundry!" So, let's dive into this psychological robe party and explore the magical connection between your wardrobe and your inner emotional landscape—because life is simply too short to wear boring mom jeans when you can wear your fabulousness like a crown!

Imagine waking up on one of those glorious mornings where everything feels just right. You sip your coffee, and even the kids' breakfast choices appear for the first time to be untouched by melted crayon disasters. On days like these, why not channel your inner fashionista with a chic outfit that radiates positivity? Picture a bright yellow sundress, sparkly sandals, and a pair of oversized sunglasses. You'll feel like Beyoncé strutting through the grocery store, teeth gleaming with confidence, even as you pile boxes of cereal that would send a nutritionist into a tizzy! Choosing to dress for joy sets the tone for the day, positively influencing how you perceive each moment. Every step feels like a mini catwalk, and every smile exchanged feels like an affirmation of your fabulousness!

Now, let's flip the script because we all know those days happen, too-that day when you're stuck in a marathon meeting with a toddler who's transformed into a whirling dervish. You wake up to chaos, and your matching socks— and even your sanity— are nowhere to be found.

Let's talk about how to dress when you just can't even. When that mood strikes, embrace the power of casual chic. You want an outfit that says, "I'm here, I'm hazy, and I may or may not be sporting a

## EMBRACE YOUR INNER DRAMA QUEEN

spit-up stain in disguise". Grab those high-waisted comfy leggings that you can pretend are "stylish" and pair them with an oversized graphic tee that has "Messy Mama" written all over it. A structured blazer over that can transform this sartorial nonchalance into "I might own a Fortune 500 company" vibes, depending on how much caffeine you've managed to consume!

And oh, the power of soft fabrics! Whether it's an oversized cardigan that feels like a cozy hug or a velvety one-piece that you can slide into like it's a magic carpet, the right fabrics can elevate your mood exponentially. Choose your textiles like you choose your friends— go for those that lift you up and make you feel like you're floating on a cloud! Of course, this can sometimes lead to a tragic steamy sweater fiasco when the twin tornadoes start to feel like they need a snack and you immediately start sweating from the sheer effort of being a "put-together" goddess. But hey, even sweat deserves to shine in the right mood.

What about those days when you feel a little spicy, flirtatious, or filled with positive rebellious energy? Take a moment to find your inner rock star! Go for the spikes, the studs, the leather jackets, and the fierce statement pieces that tell the world you're here to conquer it like the fierce lioness you are! A flashy red lip to match, and you're ready for playdates that turn into impromptu dance parties with the aisles of the toy store as your stage. Let that mood cascade into your outfit selection- never underestimate the power of a bold accessory or fierce footwear! Nothing says "I'm fabulous!" more than a pair of dramatic heels that tower over the usual shoes you wear — just make sure your feet still remember how to navigate the world in them!

And while we are on the subject, let's think about practicality. Some moods come with a side of chaos (hello, motherhood). When you feel moody after sleepless nights, embrace fabrics and cuts that first and foremost tell the world you will not be wrestling with your wardrobe today. An easily layered outfit allows you to adapt to any situation, like taking those twins to the park or racing against time to meet the school bell. And if you happen to trip on a rogue toy while rocking that adorable dress? Fear not, because confidence will always be your best accessory, turning even the most tragic of spills into moments of fashionable grace— a fabulous moment for your Instagram feed!

At the end of the day, darling, dressing for your mood means honoring and embracing who you are at that moment. Life's a colorful tapestry, and like a painting in progress, your style evolves as your emotions ebb and flow. Remember, whether you're flowing in fabulousness or hiding under stretchy pants, your wardrobe should reflect your emotions and spark joy.

So, paint the world in all your glorious hues, and know that you're rad regardless of which mood you choose to don today! Now go out there and dress like the rock star that you are— because you deserve to own every mood, one fabulous outfit at a time!

**Overcoming Fashion Fears**

Overcoming fashion fears is an exhilarating journey that's bound to lead you down the rabbit hole of self-discovery, think of it as a high-stakes adventure, with high heels and a sprinkle of glitter at the center of it all! Picture this: you're standing in front of your closet, facing a fluffy avalanche of outfits that have been anxiously lurking behind your everyday essentials.

Your eyes dart from the vibrant banana-yellow dress you've been eyeing but never had the courage to wear to the classic "go-to" ensemble that says, "I gave up—please hand me a snack". Sound familiar? Fear not, my fabulous friends, for we are here to dismantle those daunting fashion fears, one laugh and stylish tip at a time!

Let's kick things off with the number one fashion phobia I've encountered: the paralyzing fear of standing out. Cue the dramatic music! The thought of being the only one in neon leopard print juxtaposed against a sea of monochrome outfits can induce sweaty palms and a hasty retreat to the safety of your go-to black leggings. I get it- it feels like showing up at a party dressed as a disco ball in a room full of boring gray walls. But here's the twist: standing out is your superpower! Your quintessential banana-yellow dress can brighten an entire room —kind of like a sunbeam, but with a lot

## EMBRACE YOUR INNER DRAMA QUEEN

more pizzazz! When you lean into your unique style, you inspire others to do the same. Remember that you're not just wearing an outfit; you're setting an example. Embrace your vibrant vibe and strut into the world; consider it a public service for fashion!

Next on the list of fashion fears is the old belief that certain styles are "off-limits" after motherhood. What? Who invented this fashion faux pas? As if motherhood comes with an automatic drip of frumpiness steeped in sweatpants and oversized tees! Let's crush this myth together! Fashion knows no age, body shape, or roomfull-of-children chaos. Your body is a canvas that deserves to be draped in the fun, flirty, and fabulous. Want to channel your inner rock star at the next PTA meeting in a daring leather jacket? Go for it! Fancy that striking midi skirt that twirls like a dream.

Wear it with pride! Motherhood is not an excuse to bury your inner goddess; it's an opportunity to embrace it! Donning your unique style can comfort your spirit while simultaneously keeping your toddlers entertained during playdates. So, let's toss that frumpiness out the window like a deflated beach ball!

Now, we must address the fear of weird fashion combinations-those outfits that seem like the fashion equivalent of an unorthodox recipe. "Can I really wear polka dots with stripes?" you wonder, feeling like a fashion rebel. Why, yes! Why not? Look, if Pinterest can come up with sour cream frosting and bacon cupcakes, you can mix prints like nobody's business!

The truth is, style is about experimentation, and feel it or not, backlashing is part of the glamorous journey. Maybe it's the oversized vintage sweater thrown over a sleek dress or wacky accessories that make people wonder if you're a part-time circus performer. Playful combinations allow you to express your creativity and play with your unique aesthetics, so dive right in and show the world what whimsy looks like!

And then there's the ever-persistent fear of judgment. You know, that nagging little voice in your head that shrieks "What will people think?" whenever you consider wearing that bodacious purple jumpsuit or your trusted fuchsia high heels? Newsflash: those who judge are often grappling with their own insecurities! People are too busy worrying about themselves to focus on your fabulousness. So why should you care? The reality is, every time you rock that look you've been eyeing, you obliterate others' expectations and redefine beauty on your terms. So, wear that outfit that brings you joy, and two-stepping away from the haters! Who knew that rocking the socks off your style could turn you into a beacon of joy and self-expression?

Finally, let's chat about practicality. Some days, you may feel like you'd rather pull a full-on Julia Roberts "Pretty Woman" moment and shout, "I'm a mess!" as you change the fifth diaper of the day. In those moments, pick a signature look that makes you feel powerful— even if it's just comfy jeans and a slouchy tee paired with an outlandishly glam pair of shoes! Even as you're navigating life as a busy mom, that one stellar outfit can be all you need to remind yourself of your fabulousness, even in the trenches.

Ultimately, overcoming fashion fears means embracing the delightful chaos of life while wearing what makes you feel like you —amplified! Each of us deserves a unique style that empowers, uplifts, and resonates with our vibrant spirit. So kick those fears to the curb and step forward with flair!

Remember, life's too short for boring fashion-dare to express yourself, embrace your splendid quirks, and strut your stuff like the fabulous human you are! Now go out there and rock the world with your style-because you're a true fashion warrior, and fear has no business in your fabulous life!

**Embracing Fashion Flaws**

Embracing fashion flaws—the glorious art of wrapping your arms around your idiosyncrasies like a warm, fuzzy cashmere blanket on a chilly morning. Let's face it, no one, and I mean absolutely no one, is perfect, and neither is our wardrobe! Each of us has those quirky little fashion traits that make us uniquely fabulous, and I'm here to make a case for celebrating them! So grab your proverbial glasses, put on your fiercest attitude, and let's dive into the world of fashion imperfections— because spoiler alert: they make you, you!

## EMBRACE YOUR INNER DRAMA QUEEN

First and foremost, let's discuss that age-old battle with body image. In a world that often cultivates the illusion of "perfect" bodies adorned in "perfect" outfits, it can be easy to feel like you're operating in a perpetual state of fashion failure. But guess what? The truth behind a well-crafted wardrobe isn't a mere figure; it's personality and flair! If you're rocking a few extra curves or flaunting that post-baby tummy, wear them with pride! You're a vibrant canvas painted with experience and love. Fashion complements your unique body; it doesn't define you. Embrace those so-called imperfections as attributes that add depth to your style. You want to play up a specific trait? Go for it! Or find that perfectly tailored piece that hugs your curves just a tad tighter — it's called owning your fabulous self!

Let's move on to something that I know too well; poor garment fit. Let's say you've found that dreamy dress, but the sleeves fit like a nervous squirrel climbed in and forgot to leave. Or perhaps, the hem grazes your ankles while your confidence takes a nosedive. Rather than allowing that to ruin your day, remember this, every outfit is a work in progress. If something doesn't fit quite how you imagined, consider it an opportunity! That squirrel-burdened dress might simply need a quick trip to the tailor - like a makeover for your wardrobe! Unleash your inner fashion surgeon and cut it just right. And yes, I'm talking about wearing clothes that feel as great as they look. Layer up and style up with statement pieces that creatively mask any fit woes while still letting your personality shine!

Then there's the relentless issue of fabric choices that turn a simple task — like sitting down — into a potential wrestling match! There's nothing worse than sporting a glamorous silk skirt that becomes a battle of wills every time you're attempting to slide into a chair. Not only that, who knew that a fabric could turn jeans into a fast track to a sauna experience? As fabulous as they are, certain fabrics require a disclaimer much like a roller coaster ride:

"May induce discomfort and flash dance moves." But fear not; embracing fabric "flaws" can foster creative layering! Combine that unforgiving silky goodness with a cozy cardigan, and voilà-fashion triumph! Add your favorite statement necklace to distract from the intricate balancing act of comfort and style.

And oh, the lovely world of fashion trends — those fickle beasts that sometimes pull us into scary terrain. When you try that new trend and realize too late that it's not your thing, it's natural to feel defeated. Worrying because "everyone else seems to be doing it" is a slippery slope. Trends come and go like playground swings! Why not strut your own version? Mix and match trends that appeal to you and create a uniquely wild concoction of pieces that showcases your flair. Embrace not only the "in" and trendy, but throw your pre-loved vintage jacket on top of the latest fashion fad to create a fusion that turns heads while simultaneously giving your wardrobe a nap!

Moreover, let's take a stroll down memory lane. Some of the most cringe-worthy fashion choices are often the ones we learn from. Remember that phase when you thought chunky highlights were "the way forward"? I do, and they haunt me to this day! But get this- those moments can mold your fashion sensibility! Celebrate those cringe-worthy throwbacks as milestones. They've shaped your journey and are merely stepping stones on your road to master the alluring tapestry of style that you weave. It's through our fashion blunders that we ultimately find clarity amid the clutter of trends and societal expectations. Embracing fashion flaws means treating them as parts of your vibrant mosaic instead of ugly cracks in your grand portrait. Life isn't about perfecting style; it's about crafting a journey adorned with quirks and expression. So toss aside the idea of flawless dressing, because that's a fashion myth we refuse to believe! Instead, wear your "flaws" with unapologetic confidence; with sass, charm, and humor, you'll make them shine. At the end of the day, let your unique style tell the world: "I'm fabulously imperfect, and I wouldn't have it any other way!" So go forth, dear readers, and embrace your fashionable flaws— they are the sequined embellishments of your style story!

# EMBRACE YOUR INNER DRAMA QUEEN

## Creating Your Personal Style Manifesto

Creating your Personal Style Manifesto is like crafting the perfect recipe for your fashion identity; it requires a dash of passion, a sprinkle of self-awareness, and a generous serving of unapologetic flair. Ah, a manifesto-not just for political movements or revolutionary causes-but a delightful blueprint for dressing your authentic self! As we dive into this joyous undertaking, think of it as crafting a personal love letter to your wardrobe, filled with exclamations of joy, quirks, and a few absurdities that make you, well, YOU!

First things first, let's grab a cup of your favorite beverage — coffee, tea, or something with an unfortunate amount of whipped cream — and find a cozy spot where creativity can flow like a wide river. Now, think about your values and how they align with your fashion choices. What does style mean to you? Is it about confidence, comfort, or individuality? Perhaps it's a stunning mixture of all three, like a perfectly blended smoothie! Maybe fashion symbolizes the ability to express your feelings on that day when you simply don't want to wrestle with expression through words. Jot down these reflections; they'll serve as the foundation for your personal style manifesto!

Now, let's get specific! Make a list of words that resonate with your fashion ethos. Are you feeling whimsical, daring, eclectic, or classic? Your personal style manifesto should embody your essence like that perfectly fitted pair of jeans hugs your curves. So, here's where you can infuse some personality: break out the markers and craft a vibrantly colored, oversized document that highlights your favorite style descriptors. Don't shy away from including borderline absurd terms like "loud and proud" or "glamorous potato." This manifesto is about representing your spirit, quirks, and the delightful unpredictability that defines you!

Once you clarify your values and descriptors, it's time to explore some inspirations-those glamazons or fashion renegades who fuel your creativity. Perhaps it's a mix of iconic figures across eras — think the classic elegance of Audrey Hepburn, the rebellious flair of Cyndi Lauper, and the quirky artsy vibe of Lady Gaga! Look for images that resonate with you, print some out, and create a vision board that reflects your style inspirations. This is a visual reminder of who you admire and what aspects of their style speak to your heart. Who doesn't love a good dose of inspiration while sipping on your perfectly crafted caffeinated concoction?

Next up, it's time to let go of the layers that don't resonate with your vision. Yes, my lovely friend, we're diving into the always-challenging area of decluttering! Rummage through your closet like a fierce warrior ready to conquer the fashion battlefield. As you sift through the myriad of pieces, hold onto those that spark joy and confidence while placing those "What was I thinking?" items into the "donate" pile. This revolutionary clearing brings you one step closer to aligning your wardrobe with your unique personal style manifesto. Trust me; once you decide to let go, it feels as liberating as strolling through a park in a flowy sundress on a sunny day — totally refreshing.

With that decluttering battle behind you, it's now time to curate outfits that truly represent your manifesto! Challenge yourself to create looks that infuse your values and descriptors. Think of fashion as a form of art — allow yourself to mix and match pieces in unexpected ways that express your quirky personality. Assemble outfits that speak to your unique style in joyous, playful declarations: "Today, I am whimsical with a side of boss lady!" Remember that each outfit is an opportunity to embody your manifesto and create a personal jewelry box filled with your sartorial narrative.

Finally, don't shy away from celebrating your style journey! Craft an affirmation around your manifesto, and each time you step out in something that encapsulates your essence, recite it like a cheerful mantra.

Think: "I am unapologetically me, and I embrace the fabulousness of my personal style!" This affirmation serves as a grounding reminder that your uniqueness is your greatest strength, and that every outfit is its own celebratory step towards authenticity.

Creating your Personal Style Manifesto is about embarking on a splendid fashion adventure that evolves alongside you. It's a

## EMBRACE YOUR INNER DRAMA QUEEN

celebration of individuality, creativity, and embracing every quirk that makes you who you are. So prepare to wear your manifesto proudly, infusing each day with confidence and flair because darling, your style is your art, and the world deserves to bask in the brilliance of your uniquely crafted fashion journey! Now go forth and dazzle them all— self-expressive fashion awaits, and you're ready to shine bright like the fabulous star you are!

## CHAPTER 2
# THE POWER OF COLOR: YOUR PERSONAL PALETTE

**The Psychology of Color: How It Affects Your Mood and Style**

When it comes to fashion, it's not just about looking good-it's about feeling fabulous! Today, darling, we're diving deep into something that may shock you: the psychology of color in your wardrobe! Oh yes, those colors you choose to wear can actually affect your mood, influence how others perceive you, and, dare I say, even impact your life choices! So put away those gray sweats, and let's talk about the magical world of hues!

Think about it for a moment. Have you ever slipped into a bold red dress and felt like you could conquer the world? Or perhaps you donned a soft lavender top and suddenly wanted to curl up with a cup of chamomile tea and binge-watch all your favorite shows? The colors we wear can not only express our personalities but also send powerful messages about our emotions. Red can evoke passion, ambition, and that inexplicable urge to take over the office, while blue can offer calmness and an overall Zen-like vibe, as if you've just left a yoga retreat and are now ready to tackle the toddler meltdowns waiting for you at home.

But beware! The color wheel is not always a straightforward thought process. Wearing orange might make you feel like a radiant sunbeam, but to others, you might resemble a traffic cone! Yes, darling, color is subjective, and sometimes the most fabulous shades can clash with personal associations.

# THE POWER OF COLOR: YOUR PERSONAL PALETTE

You might adore the checky brightness of yellow, but if your Aunt Bertha wore it the last time she invited you over for a home-cooked meal (only to burn the roast), it might trigger a visceral emotional reaction, leading you to believe that yellow is as bad as a Monday morning without coffee!

Now let's enjoy a particularly juicy fact— did you know that the power of color extends beyond just you? That's right! How you see yourself in an outfit can change how people react to you. Choose colors wisely, and you'll feel as confident as Beyoncé strutting through the village with her entourage. Studies have shown that people often perceive you based on the colors you wear, believing that those draping your fabulous figure define your competencies, or maybe even your baking skills (I'm still waiting for someone to give me a baking color range!). Want to look trustworthy on date night? Go for the classic blues! Seeking to radiate approachability during a networking event? Rock the soft pastels! Just remember to steer clear of chartreuse unless you're auditioning for a role in a monster movie.

Speaking of monstrous disasters, let's chat about occasions where color can go awry. Have you ever investigated your closet, faced a sea of colors, and felt paralyzed —like Dorothy with no idea how to get back to Kansas?

Trust me, you're not alone! Sometimes we have an entire wardrobe of vibrant shades and somehow still manage to wear our beloved "dark cocoon" (a.k.a. the ever-dependable black). After all, black has been the go-to for people who want to avoid making any statements— like when your toddler launches spaghetti sauce onto your favorite top, and suddenly you're a walking art installation! Let's keep it real; sometimes we all need to embrace the dark side while juggling toddlers and messy meals.

What's delightful about understanding the psychology of color is how we can wield it like a sword. We can take control of our images and moods, shifting the colors we drape ourselves in to align with how we want to feel or how we want to be seen. Ready to tackle a chaotic playdate? Let's throw on those sunshiny tones! Or perhaps you want to command the room in your next big meeting— hello, power red! Remember, if you're feeling the chaos inside, just find the hue that matches your inner drama queen's vibe.

Color truly is fascinating, and I hope today's hue to revolutionize your outlook and your wardrobe while tackling those toddler tornadoes has opened your eyes to the colorful universe swirling around you. So let's embrace our inner rainbows and sprinkle those delightful shades all over our fabulous lives. Whether it's confidence, calmness, or a little extra pizzazz you seek, it's all in the color! Now, go forth and transform that wardrobe into a canvas of self-expression that would put even Picasso to shame!

## Finding Your Perfect Palette: A Step-by-Step Guide

The quest for the perfect color palette— like hunting for the holy grail but with more sparkle and fewer dragons. Finding the hues that make you feel alive, bold, and just the right amount of sassy is crucial in the vast universe of fashion. As the queen of color, I, Vivian Abreu, am here to help you uncover your unique palette in a playful step-by-step guide that makes this journey feel less daunting and more fabulous. So, grab a cup of tea (or a glass of wine, because we're in this for the long haul) and let's get started!

First things first, you need to establish your skin undertones. And no, I don't mean that weird sunlight-in-the-face, squinting type of undertone.

We're talking about whether your skin leans toward warm, cool, or neutral. If you look fabulous in gold jewelry, you might fall under the warm category. If silver is your shining armor—and you can pull off rock star vibes in icy blues— then you're likely in the cool camp. But fear not if you can swing both sides of the pendulum, darling, you're a lucky neutral! Once you've identified your undertone, it's like receiving a secret treasure map leading you to your color paradise. Who knew skin could hold such power? Now that we know the foundational aspects, let's venture deeper into the color spectrum. Go grab some colorful swatches or head to your favorite fabric store.

# THE POWER OF COLOR: YOUR PERSONAL PALETTE

Feeling overwhelmed? Don't panic! Just remind yourself that swatches are there to help you, not haunt you like your Aunt Berth's rogue social media posts. Hold different hues next to your face and see how they interact with that radiant visage of yours. Do bright oranges make you look like a pumpkin that rolled out of a bad Halloween scene? Can you rock that nostalgic 80's teal like you were born for it? Pay attention to how these colors interact with your skin and lift your spirits!

Speaking of spirits, grab a glass of bubbly and let's head on to the next step: narrowing down the color palette that complements your dreamy self. Choose five to seven colors that give you life. Sounds easy, right? Just like separating your toddlers at a birthday party! But hold onto your hats, because it's not just about your personal favorites. Consider practicality and versatility here; can you mix and match these hues with items already inhabiting your closet like it's a fashionable reunion? If your palette can create outfits for yoga class, playdates, and spontaneous date nights, you know you've hit the jackpot!

Ah, next steps! Once you have your curated color collection, it's time for outfit styling — my favorite part! Mix and match your color selections to find combinations that make you feel like a divinely inspired fashionista.

Prepare for your closet to evolve rapidly like a hermit crab in search of a new shell. You might find that pairing your soft pastel pink with a crisp white or vibrant royal blue makes you feel as radiant as you did on your wedding day... or maybe just slightly less chaotic than chasing twin tornadoes through the park.

Now comes the fun part, my dear stylish warriors — test it out in the wild! Yes, venture into public with your newly discovered palette as if you were strutting down the runway of life! Whether you're at grocery shopping or plucking stray tantrums from your toddlers, see how these colors make you feel when paired with various accessories, patterns, or statement pieces. Keep note of which outfits earn you compliments, and which stylish combinations make you feel like you lost a battle with a pack of wild raccoons. Adjust your palette accordingly, because nothing says "fashion disaster" is like a color combination that leaves you at odds with your own reflection.

Finally, remember that finding your perfect palette is a journey, not a race. As with everything in life, style evolves, and so can your favorite hues. Stay open to discovering new shades and combinations, and don't forget — humor is a key ingredient in this colorful concoction! Wear each hue with pride, embrace the laughter, and be the fashion superhero of your own story. So let your palette shine brighter than your toddler's tantrum meltdown, and make sure you're ready to tackle those daily adventures in looks that inspire you. After all, darling, life is too short to wear colors that don't make you feel utterly fabulous!

## Color Combinations: Creating Outfits That Sing

Color combinations - the intricate dance of hues that can take your outfit from "meh" to "majorly fabulous" in a heartbeat! Just like that time you accidentally spilled coffee all over your guest's fancy white tablecloth and managed to pass it off as abstract art — color combinations are all about making bold statements and leaving a memorable impression. So, let's slide into the delightful world of color pairings and explore how to create outfits that make you feel like you're strutting the runway — with your toddlers in tow!

First things first, let's forget everything you thought you knew about the proverbial "rules" of matching color. Gone are the days of strictly pairing hues that are only adjacent on the color wheel. Rule-breaking is how we create magic, darling! The vibrant clash of pinks, reds, and oranges can ignite your ensemble like fireworks on the Fourth of July! So, grab your favorite flamboyant pieces and get ready to explore combinations that defy the fashion police. After all, life is too short to be color-coordinated like an overzealous kindergarten class!

Now, let's dig into some classic color pairings that enhance your style pizazz. Neutral bases, such as black, white, or beige, are like your cute bestie who invests in a neutral wardrobe. They pair beautifully with almost any pop of color.

## THE POWER OF COLOR: YOUR PERSONAL PALETTE

Got a pair of vibrant emerald, green pants? Fantastic! Team them with a crisp white top and then add a tan cardigan for a touch of sophistication, a look that says, "I might be a mom, but I can totally drop it like it's hot at PTA meetings!" Make sure to accessorize wisely; a bold statement necklace or playful earrings can elevate your entire outfit and earn you bonus points. Don't forget — sometimes the loudest colors speak the most softly, so rock those playful accessories with style.

Let's not forget the fun of complementary color combinations. You know, those hues that sit across from each other on the color wheel: think blue and orange, red and green, or purple and yellow. These pairings are like the unexpected plot twist that bumps up the excitement of your outfit! Picture yourself in a fabulous plum dress that's cinched at the waist with a striking golden belt. How dramatic and beautiful is that? You might feel like royalty walking into a crowded room, channeling your inner Rihanna while leaving others wondering if they accidentally stumbled into a fashion show.

And remember, even if your toddler spills juice on you mid-strut, just laugh it off! Juicy stains are the new black, at least for us stylish superheroes.

And now, let's delve into the magical realm of monochromatic outfits! Yes, darling, we can channel our inner art teacher with different shades of a single color. Think of it as stealing the spotlight at a concert where you're the main act, radiating waves of elegance. Who said wearing all one color wouldn't make everyone stop in their tracks? The creation of texture is key here; bring on the frills, the fabrics, the layers! A deep indigo blouse paired with soft navy trousers, both topped off with a light azure scarf can create such an effortlessly chic look that even your in-laws might forget they were ever critical of your sartorial choices. Who knew monochrome could be such a crowd-pleaser!

But what about those days when you want to create an outfit that does more than just "sing", you want it to perform a full Broadway number (Yes, my dream moment)?

Layering can turn your wardrobe into a performance of color. Start with a base of subtle tones and layer vibrant pieces on top. Picture a muted lavender tunic topped with a crimson blazer, finishing off the look with a pair of cozy lavender fats. It's an outfit that not only makes a statement but could also double as your go-to attire for picking up dry cleaning or running from a toddler tantrum-you know, the regular shenanigans of mom life!

Finally, embrace the importance of having fun with your color combinations. Fashion should be joyful, a canvas for self-expression, so feel free to experiment like a toddler with finger paints! Don't worry about clashing; embrace it! Throw on that striking fuchsia shirt and those dazzling mint pants you've been eyeing and make it your masterpiece! Remember, the ultimate rule of color combinations is that there are no rules-only adventures waiting for you to embark upon. So, gather your rainbow wardrobe, channel your inner fashionista, and create outfits that not only sing but burst into a full-blown, glittering musical number! After all, life is way too exciting to stay muted!

## Dressing for the Season: Seasonal Color Trends and Their Impact

The changing seasons: a chance to update our wardrobes and embrace new color trends! Just when you think you've mastered your palette, Mother Nature throws us a plot twist that could rival the biggest blockbuster-colors that ebb and flow like the tides, leading you to wonder if last year's vibrant hues are now as outdated as neon leg warmers. But fear not, fashionistas! In this section, I'm here to untangle the web of seasonal color trends and help you navigate the glorious array that comes with each changing season.

First up, let's talk about the warm, glorious embrace of spring. As the flowers bloom and the world awakens from its winter hibernation, so do our wardrobes! Spring is like that chipper friend who always insists you invite them to brunch, and boy, do they bring the best news. Soft pastels and bright florals are the themes of the season, and they transform your wardrobe into a breath of fresh air. Think sumptuous shades of blush pink, lilac, mint green, and

## THE POWER OF COLOR: YOUR PERSONAL PALETTE

sunny yellow — perfect for those delightful brunches that seem to magically turn into all-day wine tasting sessions! Ha! (I should know) But remember, darling, while we layer a few pastel pieces together, you still want to avoid resembling an Easter egg rolling down a grassy hill!

Then comes summer, with its relentless heat and the opportunity to trut around like the sun-kissed goddess you were destined to be. Think vibrant colors that could make even a parched cactus jealous! Bright corals, vivid teals, crisp whites, and zesty lemons are calling your name, perfect for those mountains of ice cream you'll inevitably indulge in under the sweltering sun. Plus, these daring shades can help create a striking contrast against the vibrant green scenery and the ever-elusive vacation vibe — because nothing says "I really should be on a sandy beach right now" like a flamboyant sunset orange maxi dress! And let's not sidestep the importance of using these colors as shields against those pesky summer selfies; wear them, and you'll shine brighter than that neon pink flamingo in your pool!

Now, with autumn waving its colorful leaves in our direction, it's time to start shifting towards earthier tones that mirror nature's miraculous transformation. The shades of deep burgundy, burnt orange, mustard yellow, and rustic browns create a delicious canvas, making your wardrobe feel like a cozy, chic café on a crisp autumn afternoon. Layering is your best friend here as you mix rich colors with textured fabrics — hello, cozy sweater weather! This is the season where dressing becomes an art, and you can throw in scarves, cute boots, and ankle wraps that would make even the chicest scarecrow in the pumpkin patch weep tears of joy.

And then, winter arrives with its frosty chill, beckoning us to adventurously pile on layers. Suddenly we're in a wardrobe fight: how do we stay warm without resembling the Michelin Man? Fear not! Enter the realm of jewel tones, colors that are as bold and rich as your strategies for tackling holiday chaos. Think luxurious emerald greens, royal blues, and iridescent reds — you want a color palette that screams, "I might have just singlehandedly mastered holiday parties, but I've also eaten a whole plate of Christmas cookies!" Jewel tones paired with neutral palettes allow you to fan your chic fame while maintaining the level of warmth required to face icy gusts without looking like a yeti.

Remember that while seasons dictate trends, staying true to your character is equally important! Feel free to play with the seasonal palettes-dare to mix and match colors from different seasons to express your divine style. Who says you can't wear that dreamy pastel lavender in fall? Or those luscious earth tones in the height of summer? Mixing seasonal trends allows you to break the rules while keeping your wardrobe fresh like the aroma of freshly baked cookies— sweet, delightful, and oh-so-tempting!

In this fabulous journey through seasonal color trends, let yourself shine like a disco ball. Each color unravels stories and possibilities waiting to be curated in your wardrobe. By tuning into the vibrant hues of spring, summer, autumn, and winter, you can engage in a delightful fashion dance that brings out your unique style while keeping up with seasonal changes.

So go ahead, embrace those colors, strut your stuff, and remember that the seasons are merely guides, while you are the fashion maestro conducting your fabulous ensemble symphony!

## The Confidence Boost: How Wearing the Right Colors Changes Everything

Confidence - the elusive potion that every woman seeks while juggling toddlers, errands, and the occasional existential crisis about what to make for dinner. But fear not, fellow fashionistas! One of the most underrated secrets to unlocking that confidence resides in the magical world of color.

Yes, darling- what you wear can be a fabulous booster shot that transforms your attitude from "I've lost my last caffeinated sanity" to "I am a fierce fashion warrior, ready to conquer the world!" So let's chat about how the right colors can turn your mood from drab to dazzling in no time flat!

Picture this: you wake up to a gloomy Wednesday, and after several attempts at securing your sanity through the usual routines

## THE POWER OF COLOR: YOUR PERSONAL PALETTE

of caffeine and cartoon negotiations, it's clear today will be a challenge. How about we unleash the ultimate power of color? Rushing to get dressed in a muted wardrobe of grays and blacks? Honey, resist that temptation! Instead, grab a fiery red top or a vibrant cobalt blue dress that embraces your inner diva.

The moment you adorn your fabulous self in colors that suit and uplift you, you'll begin to feel a rush of energy. It's as if a pep squad of enthusiastic cheerleaders has appeared from nowhere chanting your name and instilling you with confidence!

But wait, let's not underestimate the influence that color can have on how others perceive you. When you walk into a room draped in shades that resonate with your personality, you radiate more than just good vibes - you radiate authority! Think about it: slip into a bold emerald green blouse that complements your skin, and suddenly you're an unstoppable force, looking the part of the confident boss babe you were born to be. Research shows that people associate certain colors with emotions: blue for tranquility, red for confidence, and yellow for cheerfulness. Now, as you strut into the office with that bright canary yellow dress, others will see you as an embodiment of happiness-and who wouldn't want that? You might even find someone handing over their workload, utterly mesmerized by your sunny charisma.

Let's not forget that color can work wonders in social scenarios as well! Maybe you have a big playdate coming up, and you know-not convinced-your toddler is going to launch themselves into a meltdown over sharing toys. Instead of a subdued "I give up" outfit, banish that idea!

Slip into something outrageously fun and colorful! Choose bright pinks and daring oranges that announce, "I am here, I am lively, and I can handle whatever chaos unfolds!" Not only will you feel uplifted, but other moms will take notice. They may even begin to doubt their color choices, silently thinking, "Wow, I should have worn that brilliant raspberry top instead of my usual frumpy gray!" Cue the confidence, darlings!

There's also the undeniable, thrilling fact that wearing the right colors can birth an undeniable sense of self-worth! What we wear shapes our self-image, and when you adorn yourself in hues that flatter and empower you, you're reminding yourself of your strength and beauty! Imagine zipping up a gorgeous fuchsia dress that makes you feel like a million bucks. Suddenly, the reflection that stares back at you may no longer feel like the frazzled mom juggling three snack bags and a sippy cup. Instead, you see a beautiful individual-capable, thriving, and fiercely unique! Color has this glorious power over our perception and how we present ourselves to the world. Why not harness it to boost that confidence and redefine your identity?

And let's talk about the delightful phenomenon when you begin to wear colors that excite you. It's as if you transform into a superhero, complete with your own color palette! You'll find joy in selecting combinations, mismatching and layering until you arrive at that perfect outfit that screams "you" louder than a four-year-old at a candy store. Wearing bright colors encourages spontaneity and creativity. So, as you dive headfirst into a world of fun patterns and daring mismatches, you'll feel that vibrant energy inspiring confidence to step beyond routine and embrace unpredictability!

In the end, it's not just about colors, it's about how those colors impact you, darling! The right shades can elevate your mood, empower you, and radiate a magnetic charm that makes life's challenges feel more manageable.

So, shake up your wardrobe, unleash those fabulous colors, and let your confidence shine like the dazzling diamond you are! Remember: fashion is not merely about looking good, it's about feeling unstoppable. So, go ahead and make the world your runway, one fabulous hue at a time!

## CHAPTER 3
# DRESS FOR YOUR BODY TYPE: THE ULTIMATE GUIDE

**Understanding Your Body Shape: The Basics**

When it comes to fashion and style, understanding your body shape is like finding the secret sauce in a perfect recipe-once you get it right, everything just clicks! I mean, let's face it; trying to fit your fabulous self into something just because you saw it on that supermodel-influencer-dressed-in-gold-leaf-on-a-beach photo is like trying to squeeze a toddler into last summer's swim trunks something I've embarrassingly tried myself.

It ain't pretty, and someone will definitely cry. So, let's dig into the basics of body shapes, shall we?

First, let's get down to the nitty-gritty: we women come in all shapes and sizes, and each one is equally spectacular (and occasionally prone to awkward outbursts when faced with a bad hair day). These body shapes can generally be categorized into five main types: apple, pear, hourglass, athletic, and rectangle. Each type has its unique attributes that deserve to be celebrated. So, if you ever catch yourself gazing into your closet —cue the melodramatic music— and lamenting that you have "nothing to wear," it's time to tune into your fabulous figure instead, darling!

The apple shape—let's start with this one, shall we? If you find that your waist tends to make a grand entrance before your actual legs do, and you have beautiful curves at the bust and a somewhat undefined waistline, you might be dancing on the apple-shaped side of things. You're like a well-proportioned fruit salad-filling, luscious, and generally delightful in crowded brunch scenarios. The secret here lies in choosing styles that highlight your lovely neckline while draping elegantly over your midsection. Think flowy dresses or tops with A-line silhouettes that play up your curves without making you feel like you're trapped in a sausage casing. Now, if you've got hips that could practically meet the neighbors in a dance-off at any family gathering, you're likely rocking a pear shape! Oh, my fabulous pears, you've been blessed with a defined waist and fabulous curves around the hips. You're like the star of a rom-com, always twirling your way into the spotlight! To embrace your divine silhouette, you'll want to focus on drawing attention to your upper half without overshadowing your glorious lower half. Tops with intricate designs or bold colors are your go-to, while skirts should flow, but never fight against that exquisite shape!

Next up, we have the hourglass figure, a classic siren of geometry. Picture Marilyn Monroe, and you've got the visual! Those balanced curves mean you're adorable no matter what you wear — yes, even those polka-dot pajamas your kids insist are a fashion statement. To accentuate your fabulous waist-to-hip ratio, opt for fitted clothing that shows off those hourglass assets. Wrap dresses are your friend, and don't shy away from high-waisted pants that'll ensure everybody knows you're not just a treasure in the waistline department; you're a whole chest of gold!

And then comes our athletic beauties-yes, you, the ones who can probably outrun your toddlers when they make a beeline for the cookie jar! If you're a bit more straight up and down or your arms and legs are toned popsicle sticks, it's time to adorn those fabulous limbs. You may think, "What's my shape?" and wonder how the fashion gods could have overlooked your fabulousness. But darling, your shape is stunning in its own right. Create the illusion of curves with playful layers, ruffles, and designs that scream "I'm here for a party, and let's make it fabulous!" Remember, you've got the physique to tackle any obstacle— and even the most challenging jumps into a stylish outfit.

# DRESS FOR YOUR BODY TYPE: THE ULTIMATE GUIDE

Lastly, we can't forget about the rectangle-shaped wonders out there who are the epitome of chic linearity. You glide smoothly through life with minimal curves, channeling that sleek goddess energy. Tailored pieces will be your saving grace— they'll add structure and create beautiful lines that hug your body in all the right ways. Seek those pieces that can create the illusion of curves, like peplum tops or voluminous skirts that flare out, making your style pop like a firework on the 4th of July.

Understanding your body shape is essential in navigating your unique style journey, but more importantly, it's about honoring your wonderful self and dressing accordingly. When you embrace who you are, you become unstoppable, and every outfit choice will feel like a standing ovation from your closet. So, dear friends, follow those body shape guidelines, put your own glamorous twist on them, and let your inner drama queen shine-after all, the world deserves to see your fabulousness in all its delightful forms!

## Flattering Styles for Apples: Accentuating the Right Curves

My apple-shaped beauties! If you're part of this esteemed group, you'll know that dressing to highlight your stunning curves can be both a thrilling adventure and a comedy of errors. Let's be honest: navigating through racks of clothing with the grace of a runaway shopping cart can feel like attempting a circus balance act while juggling a toddler and your latte! But fear not, my lovely apples; I'm here to guide you through the dizzying world of fashion choices that flatter your fabulous body shape and will have you strutting out like a runway model-minus the attitude and with a little more "where did my coffee go?"

First things first, let's talk about silhouettes; they're the key to unlocking your style potential. Think of your body type as a charming pear tree planted in an orchard of goodies. Unfortunately, you're often mistaken for a fat pancake (gasp!). That's why the goal here is to create the illusion of a defined waist and draw attention to the lovely attributes you possess.

A line dresses, which beautifully flow from the waist down, are like magic carpets that whisk you away into realms of comfort and chicness. You have permission to twirl, and I insist you maximize that twirl factor when wearing A-line dresses that accentuate your narrowest point while allowing the skirt to elegantly cascade down.

Tops are your best friends in this styling saga, too! Peplum tops and wrap-style shirts are the fairy godmothers of your closet — they'll give you that hourglass look you crave without any hocus pocus. The lovely flounce of a peplum creates curves in all the right places, while a wrap top cinches in at the waist, showing off your luscious shape. Don't be afraid of prints either! A bold print or beautiful texture can be a fun way to draw the eye up and away from any unwanted midsection drama. Just be wary of large patterns; you don't want to look like a walking quilt come to life! Moderation is key, darling.

Speaking of drama, let's have a moment of silence for those notorious elastic waistbands. Yes, my fellow apples, while the comfort of an elastic waistband is a siren song that beckons you on a shopping spree, they can often lead to disaster if you're not careful! You definitely want to avoid falling into the trap of loose, baggy shirts that can make you look like you're embracing a potato sack aesthetic — unless that's the vibe you're going for, and in that case, you do you, darling! Instead, opt for fitted tops that grace your body like an attentive waiter at a five-star restaurant, and steer clear of anything that resembles a tablecloth gone rogue!

Now, let's talk bottoms! When it comes to pants and skirts for apple shapes, the right choices can truly unveil your magnificent allure. High-waisted styles are your allies — they not only hold you in (you're welcome) but also create length in your legs and maintain that precious waist definition that we all adore! Pair high-waisted trousers with a fitted cop for an effortless ensemble that oozes chicness. Flared jeans are another winning choice, as they balance out your beautiful curves and enhance your silhouette.

DRESS FOR YOUR BODY TYPE: THE ULTIMATE GUIDE

And can we talk about skirts? A swing skirt that hits just below the knee will have you feeling like the queen you are- just don't attempt to palm off your precious cookies to the kids while wearing it; those are a tragedy waiting to happen!

Let's not forget the power of layers! A tailored blazer or long cardigan slung over your fitted top can bring elegance to your outfit and can seamlessly conceal any "oops" moments from that third cookie at your child's playdate. Remember, darlings, tailoring is where it's at! You wouldn't show up to a black-tie event in an un-ironed tuxedo, so why ever consider wearing poorly fitted clothes that don't enhance your fabulous properties?

With accessorizing, it's all about distraction— a quick sleight of hand, if you will! Statement necklaces or earrings can easily draw attention upward, while lovely belts placed just under the bust can highlight your beautiful curves without drawing attention to any areas you'd rather not focus on.

And when it comes to shoes, choose ones that elongate your legs— hello, fabulous heels! Just remember to break them in before engaging in that playful chase back to the cookie jar. So, there you have it, my apple-shaped wonders, flattering styles that accentuate your gorgeous curves while keeping you stylish and chic.

Embrace your figure with confidence and remember that you can literally laugh in the face of that fashion faux pas-because life is just too short, and the only drama we should embrace is the inner drama queen that lives within us all!

## Dressing Pear-Shaped Bodies: Embracing Your Beautiful Curves

The glorious pear-shaped goddess! If you find that you possess beautifully defined hips and a lovely waist that would make even the most skilled sculptor nod in approval, then congratulations! You are part of a fabulous club that has been blessed with a magnificent silhouette reminiscent of a classic masterpiece. Dressing as a pear-shaped wonder is not just about covering up; it's about embracing those divine curves and showcasing your feminine flair like the confident queen you are. So grab a glass of your favorite wine (or juice box-it's all good!), and let's delve into the art of dressing that oh-so-glorious pear body!

First, let's embrace this fabulous shape with open arms (or stylish sleeves, if you prefer). The secret to your success lies in balancing proportions, and luckily for you, there are countless styles that will have you and your lovely curves dancing in perfect harmony. Start with the top half, this is where you can really draw attention to your gorgeous upper body and create that stunning hourglass silhouette, we all pine for! A fitted blouse with fun patterns or embellishments will do the trick beautifully. Not only will those fabulous designs catch the eye and create conversation, but they'll also cleverly guide the gazes away from the hips when needed. Trust me! You'll be turning heads at the grocery store in no time, and you might even distract the kids from their snack requests!

Next up, we're diving into the magnificent world of dresses! Oh, my dear pears, if you're looking for an effortless outfit that ensures you make an entrance, I implore you to try out A-line and fit-and-flare dresses. These beauties are, quite frankly, the holy grail of pear fashion. The way an A-line dress flows from the waist down to create a gentle cascade, all while cinching you in at the waist, pure magic! You'll feel like you've stepped straight into a fairy tale, and bonus points if you practice your twirl while you're at it. Fit-and-flare dresses take it up a notch, giving you that flattering fit through the bodice and flaring out over those fabulous hips. Perfect for any occasion — be it a wedding, brunch, or simply a midweek grocery run where you end up in a casual standoff for the last avocado. Who wouldn't want that?

Now, let's not hide those beautiful curves under a bushel basket! When it comes to bottoms, don't shy away from embracing all the loveliness your hips have to offer. Opt for high-waisted trousers or skirts that show off your narrow waist and give a slight flare to the legs — this creates that enchanting hourglass look that makes heads turn. Imagine this: you're wearing high-waisted pants that fit like a glove, and you walk into a room with the elegance of a gazelle but

DRESS FOR YOUR BODY TYPE: THE ULTIMATE GUIDE

with the hearty giggle of a mom dodging spilled juice at the same time. You'll radiate confidence and charm, which is precisely how everyone should approach their fashion game!

If you have the perfect pair of jeans, you'll know that the right pair will lead to endless compliments. Choose bootcut styles or slightly flared jeans that balance out your silhouette while ensuring maximum comfort for those all-too-familiar tag-team toddler chases. Do not underestimate the power of pockets— those ingenious creations that can hold snacks, toys, or even a small stuffed giraffe, because let's face it, there's rarely a time when that doesn't come in handy, right?

Let's sprinkle in a little bit of layering magic! A tailored blazer or a cardigan that gently smooths over your hips is a powerhouse choice! Think of it as your fashion shield, keeping you warm while enhancing your shape—plus, it offers an elegant vibe. Just remember that when wearing layers, keep the top fitted to avoid looking like a refrigerator left unattended at a family picnic. No one wants that!

And fashion wouldn't be complete without the pièce de résistance: accessories! When it comes to pearls of wisdom for our pear-shaped ladies, I suggest big, bold earrings or statement necklaces that draw the eye upward, adding flair while keeping your fabulous curves intact. Choose chic belts to accent and define your waist further, creating the illusion of those luscious curves we love while keeping your outfit polished and stylish.

So, dear pears, gather your confidence, embrace your curves, and let go of the old ideals of what fashion "should" be. Revel in the beauty of your shape and let your sense of style shine through— your unique essence will undoubtedly leave everyone around you in awe. After all, life is too short for boring outfits! Remember, the world deserves to see your fabulous curves strutting with confidence, grace, and a dash of sparkle, just like the true pears you are! Now go out there and let your style blossom!

## Hourglass Figures: Highlighting Your Natural Balance

The hourglass figure! The iconic shape that graced the pages of countless fashion magazines and probably caused more than a few double-takes on the sidewalk. If you possess this marvelous physique - where your waist is the star of the show and your curves are on point — then congratulations! You're the living embodiment of "back to the future" fashion that will never go out of style. But sweetie, with great curves comes great responsibility, and I'm here to help you highlight that glorious balance with flair, laughter, and a sprinkle of sass!

First things first— let's admire your waistline! If the hourglass were to be turned into a real-life sculpture, you would definitely be the centerpiece that people stop to admire. To embrace your enviable curves, the key is to accentuate that waist while ensuring your top and bottom are in harmony with each other. Fitted tops are your best friends; think wrap shirts, peplums, or those glorious bodysuits that hug you in all the right places without triggering a wardrobe malfunction whenever you reach for your child's snack stash. Wrap tops are particularly magical, as they not only showcase your bust but cinch at the waist, creating that stunning hourglass silhouette that will leave onlookers floating in a fashion daze.

Now, let's talk about those fabulous bottoms! A tailored pencil skirt is like a secret weapon in your dress-up arsenal—it showcases the curves while enhancing your shape without being too clingy or giving off "I'm auditioning for a second season of Real Housewives" vibes. If you want to bring more drama to your outfit without the need for overemphasized reality-show theatrics, opt for knee-length skirts with a slight flare or those chic skirts that hug you up top and flutter down below. The fluttering of the material around your legs adds a touch of whimsical flair that might even convince your kids that you went to fashion school (despite your extensive background in snack distribution).

When it comes to denim, let's talk bootcut and flared jeans! Both styles work wonders for hourglass figures, creating balance while honoring the curves you possess. You can strut confidently into any

## DRESS FOR YOUR BODY TYPE: THE ULTIMATE GUIDE

room knowing full well that your jeans are enhancing those gorgeous legs. They can elongate your silhouette, and let's be honest, everyone could use a touch of visual elevation before dashing through the amusement park or navigating an obstacle course created by your toddlers. And don't forget high-waisted styles — these jeans will sculpt your waist beautifully and allow for maximum fashion-forwardness while cleaning up after a toddler tornado.

In the realm of dressing up for special occasions, I must shout out the magic of fit-and-flare dresses! They practically scream "I'm ready for anything," all while giving you a princess vibe. With a fitted bodice and flowy skirt, this style will have heads turning faster than you can search for the nearest changing room (because heaven knows shopping with multiple kids requires superhuman strength). Add a statement belt to ramp up the waist definition, and voilà! You're a fashion-forward goddess who can also effortlessly navigate the chaos of family life.

Speaking of chaos, layering can be a game changer for your hourglass figure. A well-tailored blazer or sleeveless duster can give structure to your stunning proportions while allowing you to channel your inner corporate warrior or red-carpet superstar. Just remember, if you're going to layer, keep the outer garments fitted so you don't resemble a snowman who forgot to put on pants! Balance is key; it's an art form just waiting for you to master it!

When accessorizing, be bold-it's your fashion stage! Opt for statement earrings or chunky necklaces that bring attention to your face rather than overwhelming your fabulous curves. The right accessories can elevate any outfit, and they also serve as brilliant distractions when you're busy navigating the playground or hunting for lost toys with one eye on the prize (and the other glued to your stylish handiwork).

Ultimately, my hourglass darlings, it's time to honor your stunning figure and wear your outfits like you mean it! Whether you're sipping coffee at the park or dining at a delightful little restaurant (while praying that your littles won't stage an impromptu meltdown), own your style with confidence!

You have the innate ability to turn heads and change hearts, so let your wardrobe reflect your vibrant spirit. Strut that hourglass shape like it's a runway and embrace the balance that comes with it— because darling, you are inherently beautiful, and the world should know it!

## Transitioning Between Body Types: Adapting Your Style

The marvelous journey of transitioning between body types - where clothing becomes a personal metaphor for life's constant changes, much like rescheduling playdates or rushing after an elusive toddler with ice cream.

As women, we know that our bodies can shift like a chameleon trying to find the best hide-and-seek spot. Our shape may alter from pregnancy to weight changes, stress-induced cupcakes, or life-altering moments. The important thing to remember is that no matter where you land on the body shape spectrum, there's an incredible wardrobe waiting to be curated just for you — because, darling, your style journey only gets more fabulous with each transition!

One moment, you might find yourself representing an athletic figure, and the next, your body may be singing a different tune as it embraces a curved silhouette. The key to successfully navigating these changes is flexibility paired with an understanding of your evolving shape. It's like doing the cha-cha of fashion! Embrace the fun of reinventing how you dress and feel empowered to flaunt whichever shape you find yourself rocking today.

Embrace those curves like they're an affectionate friend who will always have your back (even if your kids sneak off with the snacks)!

First things first: if a transition happens to you-be it due to motherhood, diet changes, or an unexpected affinity for pizza crust in the middle of the night (don't we all?), it's crucial that you reassess your wardrobe. While we adore our beloved pieces, there's a time and a place to let go and invite new friends to our closet party! Take a moment to sift through your clothing collection as if you're

## DRESS FOR YOUR BODY TYPE: THE ULTIMATE GUIDE

auditioning them for a talent show. The last time you wore something might have been during a "skinny jeans era" that has since vanished from your life! It's out with the old and in with the fabulous. Trust me, you'll feel like a fashion phoenix rising from the ashes of last year's wardrobe!

As you embrace your body transformation, recognize which pieces accentuate your changing form. For athletic shapes adding curves, for instance, using layers and fitted styles can create that hourglass illusion- even if you're resorting to bringing out the dust bunnies hiding in the nooks of your closet! For curved silhouettes, you'll want to discover styles that provide a soft drape without adding bulk. Seek out flattering fabrics that hug in all the right places — nobody needs to feel like they're trapped in a sausage casing, darling!

If you're transitioning to or from an apple shape, A-line dresses and fitted tops could become your new best friends. Conversely, return to those high-waisted wonders if you're leaning toward a pear-shape, because nothing quite says "I love my curves" like a pair of tailored trousers accentuating your waist! The beauty of transitions is that you can blend the best of each world. Perhaps you fall somewhere in-between; that's perfectly normal too! Fashion is all about personalization and creativity, so take the time to experiment with different styles until you find what feels uniquely you, even in moments of uncertainty.

Don't underestimate the joy of layering! As you ebb and flow between body types, embracing the art of layering pieces can be a lifesaver, especially during seasons of change. An open cardigan or a trendy long vest can add depth, texture, and excitement to your ensemble without sacrificing comfort. You'll find that layering allows you to play with both fitted and flowy garments together, serving both style and functionality as you navigate life's demands— or, shall we say, the delightful chaos that ensues when dodging flying toys and negotiating snack rations!

And let's talk about accessories - they don't just bring an outfit to life; they also act as your personal cheerleaders. A chunky belt can help define your waist— whether you're embracing curves or finding balance in a straighter figure. A fabulous statement necklace has the magical ability to distract onlookers and create focal points around your lovely face, ensuring you're always dressed to impress. So, remember, accessorizing is a strategic play for wardrobe warriors transitioning through body types!

Finally, dear readers, embrace the reality of change! With each phase of your life, your body might feel different, but that doesn't mean your fabulousness has to suffer. You're wonderfully complex, and your style should adapt and reflect your journey. Whether you're transitioning to life events, or simply because you want to embrace your changing tastes, enjoy the roller coaster of fashion. It's all about celebrating who you are right now, because, sweetie, you deserve to strut your stuff in style, regardless of how your body evolves! So, raise a glass to your personal style journey; it's bound to be full of laughter, a few dress mishaps, and oh-so-much fabulousness!

## CHAPTER 4
# FROM DIAPERS TO DESIGNER: FASHION THROUGH MOTHERHOOD

**Navigating Fashion Choices After Motherhood**

Motherhood! That beautiful roller coaster ride where your life takes a complete detour from "me, myself, and I" to "Mommy, can you wipe my nose?" In a blink, you go from sipping lattes in cute café corners to swigging cold coffee while searching for the elusive left shoe that somehow found its new home in the depths of the toy box. With the arrival of these little bundles of joy, one may wonder where fashion fits in. Fear not, dear reader; I am here to help you navigate your post-motherhood fashion choices— even if it means occasionally wearing a superhero cape made of stained cotton!

First things first, let's address the elephant in the room— or perhaps it's the chubby-cheeked toddler playing with your purse. Your body changes after having kids, surprise! It's like going from a glamorous runway model to a jiggly jelly. But here's the kicker: you are now a fabulous jelly! So, let's embrace those curves, rolls, and stretch marks. The key to navigating fashion choices post-motherhood is to say goodbye to the "ideal" body image and, instead, celebrate your unique shape with outfits that flatter and celebrate you. Channel your inner drama queen, and wear what makes you feel like royalty— crown not included, but it absolutely should be!

Next up, practicality is your new best friend in the battle of the wardrobe.

Kindly ditch the idea of donning a floor-length gown for an afternoon at the park. Sure, you might look like a fairy-tale princess, but I guarantee a kid on a swing will swing right onto your hemline. Embrace chic yet practical choices: versatile dresses that can be worn to lunch with friends and still allow you the range of motion required to chase a rogue toddler — bonus points if it has pockets (because, let's face it, where else are we going to stash the granola bar for a moment of patience?).

And let's talk about fabric. Is this a conversation we're having? Absolutely! If you think you can keep up with the demands of motherhood in delicate silk, you might be living in a dream world where unicorns prance and laundry magically do itself. Instead, steer your cart toward stretchy fabrics like jersey or, my personal favorite-denim with a little give. These materials hug your curves without redefining the world of uncomfortable, and when you wipe off that inevitable toddler sneeze, you'll thank the fashion gods for their contribution to the world of easy care.

Then, there's the issue of choosing the right print. People often ask, "Vivian, how can I dress stylishly while parenting?" and my answer is simple: choose prints that can hide the chaos! Say it with me: florals, polka dots, and, my all-time favorite, patterns that look shockingly modern but hide ravioli stains! You'll feel like you're stepping straight out of a fashion magazine, even if you just spent the last three hours wearing baby food like it's a new kind of luxurious face mask.

However, do not forget the accessories! Trust me when I say that a killer pair of statement earrings can elevate any outfit from "I woke up late" to "I may have conquered the world today" in seconds flat. Choose pieces that reflect your vibrant personality without the frustration of intricate buckles and annoying clasps — because we all know that when you have two toddlers running in every direction, the last thing you need is to fight with your jewelry like it's a game of tag. Simplicity is the key; bold, beautiful, and easy-to-wear will give you the fashion wizardry you crave.

Finally, and this might just be the best advice I can offer, remember to invest in self-confidence. Fashion choices post-motherhood can

## FROM DIAPERS TO DESIGNER: FASHION THROUGH MOTHERHOOD

be a humbling journey, but let's not lose sight of the fiery woman inside you.

Confidence is the best outfit you can wear, and when you strut your stuff-whether it's in an athleisure set at the grocery store or that daring little black dress on date night— own it! Your unique style is as beautiful as your chaotic daily life, and I won't have it any other way.

So, there you have it! Navigating fashion choices after motherhood can be as thrilling as a wild toddler chase and as rewarding as finding a long-lost piece of chocolate that you thought was gone forever. As you embrace your new wardrobe that accommodates small messes and embodies fabulousness, may all your outfits survive the whirlwind that is motherhood—and make you look stunning doing it!

### Practical Tips for Dressing Stylishly on the Go

The art of dressing stylishly on the go— the ultimate balancing act between style and survival in the unpredictable circus that is motherhood! As a mom constantly on the move, I've navigated the intricate dance of fusing practicality with a dash of fabulous flair. Thus emerged the inspiration behind SAM D'MONES, my fashion line crafted with passion and precision. Here at SAM D'MONES, I've handpicked a collection that perfectly marries comfort, elegance, and style. Our line is tailored for those who crave effortless chic, offering pieces like the sophisticated pinstripe navy and grey two-piece pant set and the snug cotton sweat pant ensemble. And when date night calls for a touch of glamour, our vegan leather set matched with a chic tweed crop top jacket delivers a look worthy of Chanel. Whether you're wrangling a toddler or juggling errands, I'm here to reveal my ultimate guide to mastering on-the-go fashion, ensuring you shine like a star amid life's delightful chaos!

First, let's talk about the timeless power of layering. Picture this: you wake up, and the weather is indecisive, much like your kids during breakfast. One minute it's warm, the next minute a breeze that makes you wish you had put on that sweater you're eyeing. Enter layering! A light, stylish cardigan is your best friend. Not only does it provide endless outfit possibilities, but it also acts as a security blanket when you need to wrap yourself in comfort (because we all know that some days, a cozy hug is the best accessory). You can easily whip it off if you overheat while chasing your kids or slide it on for an instant put-together look when dashing off to drop the kids at school.

Next up, let's have a heart-to-heart about pre-planning outfits. Trust me, I know that the sheer thought of laying out your clothes the night before can feel like a Herculean task, especially when you know you must hide the butter stains from breakfast. But consider this: setting aside a base outfit the night before can save you precious minutes in the morning—minutes you could spend scrolling through your phone apps in a glorious moment of silence or brewing that caffeine fix that will make you feel alive! Opt for something versatile; a well-fitted pair of jeans and a chic top can be dressed up or down. And on the rare occasion that you have a minute to spare, throw on a pair of stylish flats or some statement earrings, and voilà! You're off and looking fabulous.

Let's not forget about the magic of accessories. Oh, how I adore them! They hold the power to transform any basic outfit into a fashion statement-like a crown on a queen. As much as I love my kids, nothing says "I'm not in a perpetual state of chaos" like a statement necklace that catches the eye of another mom who may be solely wearing sweatpants and a T-shirt. A colorful scarf can be your go-to style rescue to cover up spills (or the remnants of last week's toddler craft) while also adding a pop of personality. And remember, bags aren't just vessels for holding half-eaten goldfish crackers; they're the ultimate accessory! Opt for a chic tote bag big enough to fit all your essentials without playing the dreaded game of "Where's My Lipstick?" Oh yes, you can say goodbye to that dark abyss known as the bottom of your purse!

Comfort is key, darling! I still remember the days when I wore high heels effortlessly while doing groceries. Ah, the naivety! But alas, comfort reigns supreme in my world now. Flats and fashionable

## FROM DIAPERS TO DESIGNER: FASHION THROUGH MOTHERHOOD

sneakers are your ticket to being trendy while keeping that pep in your step. Brands are embracing stylish styles that don't scream "I'm a mom living a life of sweatpants," and you should take full advantage of that!

Choose shoes that let you dance, sprint, or leap effortlessly as you chase after a runaway shopping cart or dash to help a child avoid an unscheduled faceplant. I can't stress enough the importance of fabrics. You want to ensure that your clothes are breathable and functional yet resonate with your personal fair. Look for wrinkle-resistant materials that don't scream, "I wrangled my kids into chairs for this slideshow." Fabrics like modal or bamboo blends have that delightful softness but also help you conquer numerous tasks without looking like you dove straight from the laundry basket. Because let's face it: there's a fine line between effortlessly chic and desperately disheveled, and you want to stay on the right side of that line!

In short, never underestimate the art of embracing spontaneity! There may be days when your carefully planned outfit goes awry because your toddler decides to take a detour into the nearest mud puddle (cue dramatic sigh).

In moments like these, simply embrace the chaos, and remember you are the woman wearing whatever you want, and you're doing it fabulously! IF you find yourself wrangling a spilled juice box or whatever your child just discovered under the couch, channel energy into the sheer delight of your unique journey and wear your outfit with pride, even if it's clashing with an unexpected splash of grape juice.

So, there you have it! Dressing stylishly on the go is as much about practicality and preparation as it is about flaunting your fabulousness. As we embrace our lives filled with toddler shenanigans, throw in bursts of risky colors, keep comfort in mind, and layer with love. Remember, you're not just a mom; you're a fashion superhero, conquering the frenetic tornado of daily life with a chic flair!

## Balancing Comfort and Style

Comfort and style — the eternal duel that every mom knows all too well.

It's as if we are living in our own "Game of Thrones," except instead of epic battles, we find ourselves torn between putting on the perfect outfit and the overwhelming desire to wear pajamas all day long! Who can blame us?

After sleepless nights and high-speed toddler chases, suddenly "comfort chic" has taken on a whole new meaning. As a fashion aficionado and founder of SAM D'MONES, let me guide you through the fine art of balancing comfort and style without sacrificing your dignity (or your sanity).

First, let's acknowledge the unsung hero of modern motherhood: athleisure. I mean, who knew we could look both chic and polished while running after toddler tornadoes? Athleisure has become the crème de la crème of dynamic dressing. Imagine sleek yoga pants that allow you to do everything from a sun salutation to wrestling a small child out of a snack smorgasbord. Pair these with a stylish oversized sweatshirt that doesn't just say "I'm a mom", it exclaims, "I'm a fabulous mom who might just crush you in a racing game!" In essence, athleisure allows us to fulfill our destiny of being fashion-forward warriors, not to mention the fact that spandex is more forgiving when negotiating snack-induced mid-afternoon bulges.

Of course, there lies the challenge of turning the comfy joggers you rely on into something that doesn't scream "I've given up." This is where accessorizing comes into play! Statement jewelry, even if it's as simple as a few layered necklaces or kooky earrings, can elevate an outfit faster than you can say "sippy cup." The key is to find accessories that speak your style with confidence and flair. Think about how a stunning pair of earrings can instantly add that "wow" factor when paired with a simple white tee — like a cherry on top of a sundae, if you will. The cherry might occasionally end up in your toddler's hand, but you get the picture.

## FROM DIAPERS TO DESIGNER: FASHION THROUGH MOTHERHOOD

While we're discussing accessories, let's not forget the must-have oversized tote bag. This constitutes both style and functionality, kind of like the Swiss Army knife of handbags. An oversized bag gives you the freedom to stuff it full of all life's necessities: a change of clothes for the kids, a pack of wipes (or a small forest of them), your ever-elusive lipstick, and-oh yes, a snack for yourself (cue the angels singing). Your bag should scream "I mean business" while still having the capability of holding an entire toddler wardrobe. You'll not only look fabulous hauling that bag around, but you'll also feel like a veritable superhero versus the evils of morning chaos.

Then there's the trifecta of favorite fabrics: cotton, modal, and jersey. These fabrics are the epitome of comfort while allowing your skin to breathe and move. One minute you're at the playground, and the next you're running into the grocery store. You want to ensure you're wearing clothes that won't leave you feeling like a stuffed sausage. Imagine walking around with pits of sweat stains! No, thank you! Look for tops that are loose, flowing, and breathable— after all, nobody needs a reminder that you are not the creator of the world's tightest girdle. Comfort should be your guiding mantra!

Now, let's have a moment of honesty about footwear. Ladies, the classic "I can't walk in heels anymore" dilemma? It's real! Yes, fashion shoes are mesmerizing, but we know that running after a child is like being part of a high-stakes Olympic event. Thus, the age of the fashionable sneaker has dawned upon us! Brands are now catering to our need for stylish comfort, creating options that make you look effortlessly chic. Picture yourself trotting around in a pair of sleek, modern sneakers, feeling as if you've just walked off a fashion runway while simultaneously avoiding a toddler-sized pile of snacks. A miracle? Absolutely!

As we navigate this choppy sea between comfort and style, let's not overlook our best weapon: confidence! Confidence is what carries the day.

When you put on an outfit that makes you feel amazing — be it joggers with a bold print or floaty cotton dresses—it's contagious! You radiate a sense of style that transforms casual into chic. Remember, being comfortable in your skin and your clothes is of utmost importance. When you believe you look fabulous, the world will mirror that energy.

So, here's to all the moms striving to balance comfort and style: let's wear our leggings with pride, indulge in our oversized totes, and walk with the confidence that we are fashion visionaries who are also keeping small humans alive! Embrace the glorious juxtaposition of sitting on the living room floor while draped in a flowing tunic — because fabulous isn't just how we look; it's also how we carry ourselves through this beautiful, chaotic life of mothering, dreaming, and slaying it one outfit at a time!

## Kids and Clothes: The Art of Non-Staining

The delightful (and often chaotic) world of kids and their clothes! If you're a parent, you know that children possess a superhuman ability - the power of transforming even the cleanest outfit into a canvas for a Jackson Pollock masterpiece. The moment you put on a fresh, pristine outfit for your child, you may as well be waving a red flag in front of a hungry bull, inviting the inevitable chaos that's about to unfold. Let's dive into the art of non-staining clothing, because if I could bathe my children in protective bubble wrap, I would. But instead, allow me to share some comical yet practical tips to keep those stains at bay while maintaining that fashion-forward flair!

First, let's talk about fabric choices that act as your shield against stains.

Some materials, bless their hearts, are kind enough to laugh in the face of mashed peas or the latest "art project" that ended up smeared on a shirt. Opt for fabrics that are inherently stain-resistant or have the power to be easily cleaned. Enter poly-blend fabrics! These amazing materials not only give your darling offspring some long-lasting durability but also demonstrate power against stains, much like an invisible superhero cape. Next time you shop, look for

## FROM DIAPERS TO DESIGNER: FASHION THROUGH MOTHERHOOD

blends of polyester and cotton; they're your durable saviors in a world filled with unexpected messes.

And what about colors? The world of fashion has taught us countless lessons, but the most vital ones when it comes to kids. Dark colors reign supreme. Remember that saying "Don't wear white after Labor Day"? Well, I'd add, "Also, don't wear white while parenting." You'll uncover stains that you didn't even know existed! Instead, lean toward deep blues, rich reds, or even funky patterns that could camouflage the minor mishaps-think of it as your child's very own form of camouflage from the stain police! Floral prints, stripes, and abstract designs serve the purpose of holding the focus away from the inevitable ketchup explosion and allowing your little one to flourish in fashionable, stain-distracting style.

Next on our stain fighting quest is the brilliant idea of layering. Now, before you roll your eyes, hear me out! A simple T-shirt layered over a long-sleeve shirt not only adds style but also provides protection. Think of it as a fashion shield! The inner layer catches the primary onslaught of whatever gooey concoction your child decides to launch their food towards-hopefully, this works like a charm while you sip your lukewarm coffee. Plus, if you channel your inner fashionista, you can always peel away the soiled T-shirt and reveal a pristine, stylish long-sleeved underneath, a magician's reveal fit for the finest of art performances, even if the show revolves around finger paints!

Speaking of protections, let's not overlook the power of aprons. I know, I know-it may sound like I just suggested avoiding high couture but hear me out! An adorable apron can save the day while your little chefs endeavor to whisk flour into a masterpiece that would normally cover more than just the table. Choose aprons that are chic enough to double as part of the outfit— they are quite possibly an overlooked accessory that fights stains while ushering in the beautiful world of culinary creativity and chaos. Remember that your kids can channel their inner Picasso, and with a fashionable apron, they'll look the part too!

Of course, we must acknowledge the ever-elusive perfect washing technique. I remember my first dousing of a stain-removing soap that I thought could cleanse the world— it didn't. Instead, I relied heavily on good ol' said-prestigious washing powder and mixed it with a little magical water (and prayer). But seriously, don't throw clothes into the washing machine and hope for the best. Pre-treat those stains with appropriate concoctions recommended by experts until your child's clothing resembles the rebirth of a lava lamp after a spin cycle. You must develop parental skills that borders on superstitious when it comes to laundry, and this is where true art lies!

Finally, let's embrace the reality that kids will be kids. They'll stumble, spill, and create memories— usually on their outfits. Instead of dwelling on the inevitable discovery of magical mystery stains, consider viewing them as badges of honor! Those little remnants are simply a testament to exploring their creativity. As a mom, you have the extraordinary power to embrace the chaos and find joys hidden amongst the painter's palette that has formed on your dear child's shirt.

So, here's to the noble quest of raising stylish children in a world where non-staining is seen as both an art and a battle! As you navigate tricky choices, remember that it's all part of the grand design. Whether it's sporting polyblends or channeling your inner fashionista with well-placed layers, you'll be a master of parenting and style! Remember, darling, that even amidst the mess, the fabulous lives on and laughter remains the ultimate non-staining accessory.

### A Case for Mom-Approved Accessories

Accessories! The unsung heroes in the realm of mom fashion! While we often focus on the main sections of our wardrobe, let's not underestimate the power of those little adornments that could transform an entire outfit from "I just rolled out of bed" to "look at me, I could totally be in a magazine!" As a seasoned mom navigating the whirlpool of playdates, tantrums, and grocery lists, I stand firmly in my conviction that accessories can make all

# FROM DIAPERS TO DESIGNER: FASHION THROUGH MOTHERHOOD

the difference. They not only allow us to express our personalities but also serve some rather important practical purposes that can make our chaotic lives just a dash more fabulous. So, grab a donut and a cup of coffee (because we both know you deserve it), and let's dive into the delightful world of mom-approved accessories!

First and foremost, let's talk about statement jewelry. Consider that statement necklace an ethereal force that instantly elevates your outfit. A basic tee and jeans? Yes, please! Toss on a chunky, colorful necklace, and voila! Suddenly, you've morphed into a fashionista ready to conquer the mall while quietly navigating the depths of toddler land. But let's be real: statement jewelry isn't just designed to make you look fabulous; it's also brilliant at distracting from remnants of that rogue smear of mashed banana on your shirt.

If you can't beat them, confuse them! Nothing says, "I've got it together" like wearing a bold accessory while simultaneously sporting a night's pasta sauce on your elbow.

Next up, we have scarves — oh, how I adore them! Scarves may seem like simple accessories, but they are truly the superheroes of the accessory realm. Multifunctional and fashionable, these lovely pieces can work wonders with just a flick of the wrist. A scarf is perfect for adding a splash of personality to any outfit, transforming plain into pizazz! Need a quick shield against an impromptu splash battle during a snack time crisis? Genius! Want to offer a touch of bohemian chic while running errands? Boom! Our trusted scarf covered that too! And let's not forget, they also function as the ultimate tool to hide our "sweaty messes" after racing up a flight of stairs during a toddler revolt.

Then we arrive at the always essential handbag. Your handbag is not merely a container; it's your mobile command center! A well-chosen bag can put the finishing touch on your ensemble while simultaneously having the ability to transform into a bottomless pit of snacks, toys, and half-eaten lollipops. Opt for a stylish tote or a sophisticated crossbody bag that is spacious enough to hold an arsenal of toddler necessities but chic enough to make you feel like you're holding a golden chalice-because, darling, you're a queen! A well-structured bag can do wonders for your confidence, reminding you that you're more than just a vessel for diaper bags and juice boxes.

Footwear is another essential category that deserves proper accessory. A fashionable pair of shoes can drastically change the energy of your outfit. Kick off those tired old sneakers, step out of the mom shoes, and embrace shoes that exude charisma. Opt for chic flats or ankle boots that feature a fun print or color. This small adjustment can make you look effortlessly put together! Besides, they'll allow you to chase those pint-sized tornadoes without sacrificing style. Never underestimate how a good shoe can make you feel ready to take on whatever the day — or your little ones- throw at you!

Let's not forget the power of hair accessories! Hair ties are no longer just a bland tool for giving up and slapping your hair into a bun; they can be fun, stylish, and functional. Think embellished hairpins, colorful scrunchies, and trendy headbands that add flair to any hairstyle. When your toddler has other plans for styling your hair like a crafty makeover with their oatmeal, simply pop on a cute hair accessory to cover the chaos. This will also allow you to maintain that ever-illusive "I woke up like this" aesthetic while simultaneously proving that you're an unyielding force of nature!

In closing, the ultimate accessory: confidence! When you're sporting those mom-approved accessories, own it. Stand tall, showcase your unique style, and rock those statement pieces like the fashion icon you are! Confidence is incredibly contagious and can set the tone for the day's adventures. You are not just a mom; you are a multifaceted superhero capable of conquering the world while looking utterly fabulous-even when you might not feel like it.

So, there you have it! Accessories are your powerful allies in navigating the often-chaotic landscape of motherhood in style. Embrace the statement pieces, scarves, handbags, chic footwear, and hair tools that tell you the truth.

## FROM DIAPERS TO DESIGNER: FASHION THROUGH MOTHERHOOD

Together, they combine to build your unique tapestry of self-expression, turning the everyday into extraordinary. With your newfound accessory wisdom, go forth and create legendary looks that let the world know that being a mom can be as stylish as it is rewarding.

## CHAPTER 5
# STATEMENT PIECES: MAKING A BOLD IMPRESSION

### Understanding Statement Pieces: What Are They and Why They Matter

When you hear the term "statement piece," do you envision a glittering necklace that stops traffic or a bright red handbag that practically screams, "Look at me!"? Well, darling, you're on the right track! A statement piece is that magical, show-stopping item in your wardrobe that turns heads faster than a toddler on a sugar rush at a birthday party. It could be a jaw-dropping jacket, a flamboyant piece of jewelry, or an audacious pair of shoes that declares your very essence in ways words can't. Trust me, in the world of fashion, wearing a statement piece is like announcing your arrival to the universe with a fireworks display while the audience collectively gasps in delight.

Now, why do they matter, you ask? Good question! In a society where the grind of everyday life (hello, toddler tantrums and endless dishes) can dull your glorious sparkle, statement pieces serve as your very own favorite superhero cape. They empower you to reclaim your identity amidst the chaos of motherhood and the mundane daily routine. Think about it: splurging on that fabulous hot pink blazer? It's like putting on a magic cloak that transforms you from mom-who-forgot-where-she-put-the-iPad to fierce-fashionista-strutting-through-the-grocery-store. You don't just wear a statement piece; you embody it. And let's face it,

## STATEMENT PIECES: MAKING A BOLD IMPRESSION

who doesn't want to channel a little extra confidence while trying to juggle twins and a shopping cart?

The beauty of a statement piece lies in its versatility. It can elevate an otherwise basic outfit to extraordinary levels, bank vault levels of fabulous—no intricate capes or ridiculous spandex suits necessary! Picture this: a pair of classic black leggings paired with a towering pair of blue cobalt heels and a simple white tee. Voila! You're now the envy of all sidewalk strollers while you casually navigate through life. Yes, the grocery store becomes a runway, and that questionable stain on your legging is simply a badge of courage— proof of the life you lead

But let's not kid ourselves; sporting a statement piece can be a delicate art. Much like trying to convince some toddlers to eat broccoli, it takes a few well-timed adjustments to get it just right. You'll want to ensure that your statement piece doesn't overshadow your entire ensemble. Nobody wants to be that person resembling a walking carousel, spinning with layers of sequins and noise pollution radiating from your very being. When incorporating statement pieces into your outfit, remember the golden rule: Everything in moderation. Let your statement piece do the talking while the rest of the ensemble plays a supportive role. Think of it as a well-rehearsed theatrical performance, where the leading star shines brightly, yet the ensemble cast stands proudly - everyone knows their role.

Besides making you look fabulous, adorning a statement piece gives you an added layer of fun to your dressing routine. Think of it as adding a pinch of glitter to your favorite mom hairstyle, or to put it another way, transforming a plain diaper bag into a designer dream (yes, those do exist). The joy of curating an outfit around your statement piece becomes a delightful treasure hunt. Each day becomes an opportunity to express your whimsical spirit, allowing the universe to witness every nuance of your fabulous self. Who needs a fairy godmother when you have statement pieces?

Overall, let us not forget the power of community. When you strut into a room adorned with a statement piece, the energy shifts. It sparks conversations, friendships, and maybe even a little envy!

You may notice heads turning, compliments raining like confetti, and conversations evolving around the creativity that is your outfit. In a world where fashion often feels like a competition between moms opting for yoga pants and kids-themed sweatshirts, your statement pieces proclaim: "I'm a mom, yes, but I'm also a fierce warrior of style!"

So, put on that statement necklace, slip into those fabulous shoes, and strut your stuff, love! Embrace the beautiful chaos of motherhood, make a lasting fashion statement, and show the world that even while juggling toddlers, you are a fierce, fashionable queen! Remember, when it comes to statement pieces, the world is your stage, and darling, you are the star!

## Choosing the Right Statement Piece for Your Personal Style

Choosing the right statement piece for your personal style is akin to finding your soulmate — only instead of swiping right on an app, you're navigating a dizzying array of options while simultaneously wrangling toddlers in a store. If you've ever seen a toddler let loose in a candy store and thought, "That's exactly how I feel when I walk into a boutique," you're not alone!

Finding that one fabulous item that resonates with your inner diva while also being practical enough not to require a trip to the ER is no small feat, my friend. So, buckle up as we embark on this fabulously chaotic journey together!

First things first, let's talk about your signature style. Are you a boho goddess with flowing dresses that exude peace, love, and a strong aversion to dry cleaning? Or maybe you're a structured minimalist who thrives on crisp lines and neutral tones — think crisp white shirts and sleek blazers. Whatever your flavor, identifying your unique style sets the foundation for choosing the right statement piece. When you're standing in front of your closet, ask yourself: "What do I want to say to the world today?" Do you want to convey confidence? Playfulness? Or perhaps a gut-wrenching need for extra caffeine? Identifying your emotional

## STATEMENT PIECES: MAKING A BOLD IMPRESSION

needs for the day can provide clarity and direction as you select your dazzling piece.

Now, let's address color. Oh, glorious color! Color can be as intoxicating as a good cup of espresso-irresistible and uplifting. When selecting your statement piece, don't shy away from vibrant hues that reflect your personality. If you love to stand out, go for bold colors that even a traffic cone would envy. If you're feeling a tad more introverted, consider softer tones that whisper elegance with just a hint of intrigue. Remember, the right color can complement your skin tone while injecting a burst of vibrancy into your life. So, when you're eyeing that neon green faux fur coat that is admittedly an acquired taste, ask yourself, does it resonate with your inner unicorn, or is it a tad too much "what-was-I-thinking"?

Next, let's discuss the shape and style of potential statement pieces. Because, darling, fit is everything! Picture this: you've just made an impulse purchase of a stunning oversized beret. In theory, its chic, avant-garde, and screams "fashion-forward," but in reality, you look like a fashionable watermelon trying to balance on a unicycle. The right statement piece should flatter your figure and elevate your sense of self! Look for shapes that accentuate your best attributes while downplaying the parts you may prefer to camouflage. That could mean a dazzling, off-the-shoulder dress that shows off your collarbone or a fabulous long-line coat that oozes sophistication while allowing you to wrangle toddlers like a pro.

Let's not forget about material, because darling, we're living in a world where synthetic fabrics pretend to be satin-and let's just say, we're not buying that drama. Quality matters, especially when you're running after pint-sized tornadoes and trying to maintain a semblance of style.

Aim for materials that not only feel fantastic against your skin but can withstand the rigors of a dynamic lifestyle. If you're envisioning wearing a luxurious wool blend but have toddlers who'll turn it into a Picasso painting by lunch, perhaps opt for a chic cotton blend that's both stylish and machine washable. Balance is key, after all!

Now, imagine this: you find a statement piece that you absolutely adore but it comes with a hefty price tag that can only be described as "let's take out a mortgage." Yes, my dear, we want to indulge in our fashion dreams, but we must also keep our budgets in check. Look for ways to snag quality pieces without sacrificing your kid's college fund. Check out my online store at SAM D'MONES, thrift shops, or the marketplace that carries trendy options at a fraction of the cost. You may find a designer blouse nestled among forgotten treasures at a thrift store— and it only costs the equivalent of a fancy latte! Fashion can be a treasure hunt, darling, and who doesn't love a good find?

In general, let's remember the most crucial thing: emotional connection! You want your statement piece to evoke joy every time you put it on.

Whether it brings back fabulous memories, makes you feel like Taylor Swift at a concert, or simply makes you giggle with delight, follow your instincts.

Fashion should be fun, it should lift your spirit, and it should resonate with your essence. After all, life is like a runway-with your toddlers serving as both cheerleaders and impromptu photographers snapping candid shots at every turn. So, choose wisely, embrace the crazy journey, and most importantly— let your style shine like the superstar you are!

## How to Pair Statement Pieces with Everyday Outfits

Pairing statement pieces with everyday outfits can sometimes feel like trying to convince a toddler that naptime is a fantastic idea-challenging but not impossible! The beauty of statement pieces is their ability to elevate even the most mundane outfit into something that dazzles like a disco ball at a wedding reception. But finding that harmonious balance between boldness and practicality can often feel like walking a tightrope while juggling flaming torches (or in my case, two energetic toddlers screaming "mom" as if it were the latest pop hit!). Fear not, however —I'm here to guide you through this fashionable balancing act like your very own style acrobat!

## STATEMENT PIECES: MAKING A BOLD IMPRESSION

First, let's talk about the foundation of your outfit — the everyday basics. You can't go wrong with reliable classics such as a fitted white tee, a pair of flattering jeans, or a comfortable yet chic jumpsuit. These pieces form the quiet yet sturdy support system of your wardrobe, much like the trusty surrounds of a toddler-proof sofa in your living room (because let's be honest, those spills are real). When you think about pairing them with a statement piece, you want your statement item to take center stage like a dazzling Broadway star — while the basics play the essential backing band, harmonizing perfectly without taking all the limelight. Imagine wearing your favorite distressed jeans and a simple black tank top and then draping a vibrant kimono over your shoulders-it's like fireworks against a clear night sky!

Next, let's delve into the world of contrast. A statement piece doesn't always have to match the rest of your outfit; in fact, mixing styles can yield the most unexpected and delightful results. Consider the delightful juxtaposition of a borrowed-from-the-boys oversized blazer paired with a filly tulle skirt and those killer combat boots you can't stop wondering how you ever lived without. You've created an ensemble that screams "I'm fierce and I know it!" while embracing an ethos of delightful disarray. It's akin to infusing your lovingly chaotic life with a little avant-garde charm, allowing the ways of your fashion sensibility to shine bright-even amidst toddler tantrums and peanut butter-stained shirts.

Then we have the world of layering — oh how I love layering! It's like wrapping yourself in a stylish cocoon! The trick here is to have at least one item in your outfit that stands out, while others can feel like background music. Think of wearing a chic, well-fitted turtleneck layered under a statement-print dress, or perhaps a vibrant scarf wrapped like a superhero cape over a casual chambray shirt. Layering allows you to experiment with textures, patterns, and colors while keeping everything balanced and smoothly integrated. Plus, this addictive tactic allows for practical adjustments; if your twins decide that the local park requires full-on mud wrestling attire, voila! You can remove layers and maintain that chill vibe without losing your edge!

Accessorizing is key, my friend! When it comes to statement pieces, the right accessories can either enhance or detract from your outfit. If you've chosen a bold necklace that captivates everyone's attention, consider steering away from additional statement jewelry that rings louder than a toddler's complaint about vegetables. You want your accessories to be supportive partners, like sidekicks on your fabulous superhero journey, not the players who wrestle for attention. Stack a few delicate bracelets or go for some classic stud earrings while allowing the statement piece to reclaim its throne as the reigning monarch of your outfit. Just remember, in the world of accessories, less can often be more— much like the number of toys you want strewn around your home at any given time!

Let's also not forget about the power of color coordination when it comes to pairing your statement pieces, darling! If you've chosen a vibrant statement piece, say a floral, patterned skirt-consider grounding it with a neutral top. This creates a beautiful canvas, allowing the pattern to tell its story boldly without clashing with other elements. On the other hand, matching complementary hues can also yield jaw-dropping results.

A striking mustard yellow jacket coupled with purple pants (yes, we can be daring here!) will not only showcase your personal style but also cozy friends who reek of questionable color choices. Remember, the right palette has the potential to transform your outfit from drab to fab faster than a toddler devours a cupcake!

With this in mind, channel your inner confidence when wearing a statement piece!

Ultimately, it's not just about what you wear but how you wear it.

Confidence is what transforms a simple ensemble into a powerful sartorial expression. Walk tall, flash that radiant smile, and embrace your unique style like an empowered warrior! As you gracefully tackle the chaos of your day, remember that wearing a stunning statement piece is about capturing that essence of fun, creativity, and self-expression amidst the whirlwind of toddler life. So go forth, my daring fashionista, and boldly rock those outfits like the fabulous queen you are!

# STATEMENT PIECES: MAKING A BOLD IMPRESSION

## Creating Balance: Mixing Statement Pieces with Subtle Items

Creating balance when mixing statement pieces with subtle items is much like attempting to mediate a disagreement between two overzealous toddlers-one believes the crayons belong in the mouth, while the other insists, they belong in the coloring book. It's a delicate dance of persuasion, finesse, and maybe a dash of bribery (I mean, what's a mom to do?).

The goal is to achieve a chic aesthetic that screams style while maintaining a sense of harmony that keeps you from leaving the house looking like a walking art supply store. So, grab your metaphorical dance shoes and let's waltz through the world of balanced fashion together!

To begin, one must understand that statement pieces are like those energetic party guests who burst into the room and suddenly grab everyone's attention— they're large, loud, and undeniably fabulous. They provide that electric burst of style energy that lights up even the dreariest of days. However, just like those guests, they require a supportive environment and an audience that can appreciate their flair without overwhelming anyone in the vicinity. This is where subtle items come in, serving as the calm grounding force to balance the exuberance of your chosen statement piece.

First, let's talk about the magic of neutral colors. When selecting your subtle items, think beige, white, gray, or any earthy tone that gently complements and offsets the vibrancy of your statement pieces. Imagine rocking a dazzling emerald, green blouse as your statement piece, elevated by classic black wide-leg pants. The effect is stunning, and you can practically feel your confidence soaring! Those black pants provide stability and act as the trusted friend who knows to keep the party going without stealing the spotlight. And hey, if you manage to find that pair with room for post-snack belly expansion, then you're practically a fashion deity!

Now, let's discuss fabric choices. Mixing textures is an art form, and knowing how to subtly weave delicate fabrics into your statement piece ensemble can create a standout effect worthy of applause! Picture this: you're wearing a glam metallic sequined top that could blind a raccoon on a mission, but instead of pairing it with something equally blingy, you opt for simple denim jeans that provide an effortless backdrop. Now, we have a transformative moment! The balance between the shiny and the muted not only prevents visual chaos but also places added focus on that glittery garment that deserves all the attention. Just remember, restraint is key — no need for sequined pants because that's like trying to two-step while performing a one-man band act! It's simply too much.

Another secret to achieving that harmonious balance is by playing with proportions. A chunky oversized sweater paired with a form-fitting pencil skirt provides both structure and softness, ensuring your ensemble feels fabulous without becoming a fashion free-for-all. The oversized piece plays coyly with boundaries while leaving tons of room for playfulness while allowing you to combat any potential toddler-snatch-related wardrobe malfunctions. The charm of this combination lies in the intricate interplay between the two styles, making your outfit feel dynamic and layered without losing cohesion.

Don't underestimate the extraordinary power of layering, my fashionable friends! Imagine throwing on a lush trench coat over a whimsical printed dress. The coat, though classic, serves as an understated hero, allowing the dress— a playful riot of colors and patterns- to shine brightly. This artful layering places the focus on your statement piece while giving you the chance to flaunt your amazing sense of style in a way that remains effortlessly cool. Plus, if you happen to spill juice on your dress while attempting to play "clean-up" at a family gathering, fear not! The trench booty covers a multitude of toddler errors.

And you cannot overlook the importance of accessories when it comes to maintaining balance. A dazzling statement necklace demands to make its grand entrance, darling! Pairing it with understated stud earrings or a delicate bracelet allows the necklace to do all the talking without getting lost in the noise. It's akin to introducing your fabulous friend while letting your other friends know they can chill out and just enjoy the festivities—no need to overshadow with too much extra!

# STATEMENT PIECES: MAKING A BOLD IMPRESSION

Lastly, while creating this delicate balance between statement pieces and subtle items, don't forget that confidence is key, my style-savvy queens! Confidence is what truly steals the show! So even when you're layering a bold outfit with subtle pieces, take a deep breath, strut your fabulous self, and own every look with the fierceness of a catwalk model. Because when it comes to fashion, at the end of the day, it's not just about what you wear, it's about how you wear it. With grace, lightness, and maybe a tad bit of chaos, you'll walk into any room and demand attention like the magnificent star you are!

## Confidence is Your Best Accessory: Owning Your Statement Look

Confidence! The elusive elixir that transforms an outfit from "meh" to "wow" in the blink of an eye. In the wild, wonderful world of fashion, confidence reigns supreme as the best accessory you could ever wear-whether you're pairing it with a quirky fedora or strutting your stuff in those jaw-dropping high heels. When you step out into the world adorned in your fabulous statement look, the key to truly rocking it lies not just in the clothing, but in your attitude. Embrace your inner diva and prepare to dazzle, darling, because owning your statement look is all about harnessing that delightful force known as confidence!

Now, let's start by acknowledging the truth: confidence doesn't magically appear overnight like your children's toys after a gigantic tidying-up session (which, let's face it, could take an eternity!). It's more like a garden that you nurture with care— watering it, feeding it with positivity, and occasionally weeding out those pesky thoughts of self-doubt that threaten to crowd your beautiful blooms. You may not have felt confident before, especially during that awkward phase of rearing small children and donning sweatpants like a badge of honor (Lord help us all!), but now is your time to blossom. Embrace the fabulousness that is YOU!

Visualize stepping out in your statement look— the outfit that embodies everything you wish to express. That vibrant, flowing dress that makes you feel like a goddess, those edge-defining ankle boots that push your style boundaries, that killer blazer that shouts, "Watch out, world, I've arrived" When you wear something you love, holding onto that feeling is paramount, It becomes a power suit, allowing you to face whatever chaos the day throws your way — and trust me, after my two boys tackle the breakfast table like it's a demolition derby, I know chaos well! That outfit doesn't just beautify your exterior; it becomes the armor with which you conquer your day.

While putting the effort into curating a statement look is commendable, it's equally vital to embrace your authenticity. Forget about comparing yourself to anyone else or worrying what others might think — because, let's face it, everyone else is likely too busy worrying about what YOU think of them! Your statement look is YOURS. It's an extension of who you are, reflecting your unique personality in all its vibrant glory. So, when you wear that flamboyant statement necklace or those outrageous patterned pants, remind yourself that quirky is the new black! Wear it with pride and sprinkle a little sass while you're at it; after all, confidence is all about embracing your individuality, quirks and all!

And then there's the magical aura that permeates when you own your look. When confidence radiates from you like the sun shining down on a park full of playing children, people can't help but be drawn to your energy. It's a magnetic pull that captivates and invites genuine compliments, allowing those around you to celebrate your fabulousness! Have you ever noticed how a confident person walks a little taller, makes eye contact, and carries an air of possibility? Guess what? That's me! (And no, this isn't a punchline!) That's what owning your look is all about-it's about stepping into your power and giving yourself permission to shine.

It's that feeling of belonging, as if you've plopped yourself smack-dab in the middle of the cosmic spotlight, twirling with glee.

But let's keep it real for a second — there may be days when insecurity sneaks in like an unwanted guest at the door of your

## STATEMENT PIECES: MAKING A BOLD IMPRESSION

heart, whispering that you don't look good enough or that nothing fits the way you want it to.

And though those thoughts may come a call, here's the kicker: you have the ability to shoo them away! Try looking in the mirror and give yourself a little pep talk. Remind yourself of that fierce energy that came alive the first time you put on that statement piece. Love those curves, embrace imperfections, and acknowledge the captivating journey of motherhood you've journeyed through. Because, let's be honest, if you can successfully navigate tantrums, sticky messes, and endless pile of laundry, you possess a superpower that deserves to shine.

Overall, remember that confidence flourishes with practice. It's not about being perfect; it's about showing up. Own your statement look day after day, strutting into the world like the fabulous icon you are, and soon enough, you'll build a style confidence workout equivalent to deadlifts and power poses. Embrace each moment as it comes, revel in the uniqueness that is you, and above all, spread love and light to those around you. Because when you confidently wear your statement pieces, you're not just dressing up, you're reminding the world that fashion is not just about clothes; it's about self-expression, empowerment, and conquering the everyday chaos with a smile on your face. So come on, strut your stuff and make the world your runway — you've got this, gorgeous!

## CHAPTER 6
# EVERYDAY CHIC: EFFORTLESS STYLE TIPS

**The Art of Effortless Chic: Defining Everyday Style**

The elusive concept of "effortless chic." It's that magical phrase that futters around fashion circles like one of those over-saturated Instagram filters, luring us in with a false sense of security: you too can dress as if you just strolled off a Paris runway while juggling a toddler and a carton of milk! It conjures images of the eternally composed woman-cool, calm, and collected-sipping her organic chai latte in a perfectly pressed blazer and designer jeans that cost more than my whole closet combined. But fear not! I'm here to demystify the art of effortless chic, all while embracing your inner drama queen and the many lovable absurdities of everyday life.

First, let's clarify something right out of the gate: "effortless" does not mean "lazy." I mean, I adore a good pair of yoga pants as much as the next mom, especially when they double as pajama bottoms after a long day of parenting my mini tornadoes. But let's be honest: unless you're planning an exclusive event for pajama- clad mothers (which could totally become a thing—no judgment), it's okay to brush yourself off and put in a smidge of effort. The key to nailing that chic look is choosing versatile pieces that can transition seamlessly from one chaotic moment to the next, because who has time for multiple outfit changes? Not this mom, thanks to my two rambunctious little sidekicks!

Essentially, effortless chic revolves around a wardrobe foundation composed of timeless classics that whisper "I rolled out of bed like

# EVERYDAY CHIC: EFFORTLESS STYLE TIPS

this, but in reality, it probably took me a solid two hours with a toddler glued to my leg." These classic pieces include tailored blazers, crisp white shirts, a well-fitted pair of jeans (that don't mind an occasional ketchup stain), loafers that whisper of comfort but strut with confidence, and an oversized tote bag that can handle everything from sippy cups to unexpected toddler souvenirs. Don't forget the accessories - scarves, bold earrings, and dainty necklaces that draw the eye, all while hiding the last remnants of last night's dinner on your shirt. Voila! You've mastered the quintessential effortless chic look! Of course, let's not forget the power of a curated color palette. Seriously, it's like creating the soundtrack to your fashion symphony. When colors harmonize beautifully, they layer on that effortless vibe, making you look stylish while running errands, trying to find your other shoe, and dodging flying LEGO bricks. You don't need to wear flashy colors to be truly chic; soft neutrals can create a canvas that radiates calmness— perfect for your 'me time' amidst all the maternal chaos! And if you're feeling zesty one day? Rock those flamingo-pink shoes or try a citrus-colored skirt that sings "Where's the beach?' while you're in the grocery store aisle.

Now, let's talk about layers. Layering is your trustworthy sidekick in the quest for everyday chic. It's like building a style burrito: you start with a base (your well-fitted tee), add some tasty toppings (the layering piece, be it a stylish cardigan or a structured jacket), and finish it off with delicious garnishes (accessories and shoes). This technique allows you to be prepared for unexpected temperature changes —like that time I found myself sweating in a chunky sweater during a playdate, only to be hit with goosebumps the moment the toddler brigade decided to open a window. I mean, who knew that toddlers were also mini weather reporters?

Confidence, my friends, is the cherry on top of our chic sundae. Picture this: you're wearing your carefully curated outfit, and you stroll into the room (or grocery store-same vibe, right?). And as you walk in, you hold your head high because you championed the art of effortless chic. Nothing sends the message of style quite like strutting your stuff with assurance-even if the chaos of everyday life swirls around you like a tempest in a teacup. Own it! If you believe it, the world will see it too. So, as you embark on your quest for effortless chic, remember that style isn't about perfection. It's about truly embracing the delightful, chaotic, messy, yet beautiful life you lead while looking fabulous doing it. The next time you find yourself struggling to figure out what to wear amidst the clutter of parenthood, just think of how you can make it all work without losing your marvelous sense of self (and sanity). Effortless chic isn't a destination; it's a journey filled with laughter, style accidents, and perhaps a few too many outfit changes. Happy styling!

## Fabric Matters: How to Choose Comfortable Yet Stylish Materials

Fabric! That delightful element of fashion that can elevate your look from "I rolled out of bed" to "I'm ready to conquer the world (or at least the toddler tantrums of the day)." Choosing the right materials is paramount—especially when you're sprightly dodging crumbs from last night's pizza party while also aiming for a look that somehow says, "I have it all together." As a busy mom—it sometimes feels like we spend more time wrestling with our fabric choices than our kids. But fear not, dear fashionista! Let me unravel the mysteries of selecting comfortable yet stylish materials with humor and a sprinkle of chaos that only parenthood can provide.

First, let's talk about the all-knowing miracle fabric: cotton. Oh, sweet cotton! It's like that reliable friend who always shows up with a coffee when you need one (and occasionally the pizza). Cotton is breathable and soft —perfect for those days when you want to feel cozy while you tackle the grocery store with a wild gang of toddlers in tow. Think about it: you'll endure sticky fingers and surprise spills, and the last thing you need is a fabric that's clinging to your body like a regime of clingy exes. Give cotton a try, be it in the form of a relaxed tee or chic dress. Because you never know when a random game of tag will break out in the produce aisle, and you'll need to sprint after a wily four-year-old!

# EVERYDAY CHIC: EFFORTLESS STYLE TIPS

And then there's linen—the stylish choice that shares the same set of priorities as you do: comfort and coolness with a touch of elegance. Picture yourself in a flowy linen dress, feeling the gentle breeze as if you were frolicking through an open field, instead of just trying to wrangle your toddler who decided that today was the day to practice their metal detector impression in the sand! Linen's lightweight nature ensures you won't melt into a puddle of frustration during a sunny park outing. Just a tiny reminder: embrace the wrinkles! Beneath the messy exterior of a mom, this fabric whispers elegance, giving off that effortlessly chic vibe as you strut your stuff on the playground carpet.

Next up in our merry fabric journey is the glorious realm of blends. Trying to achieve comfort without sacrificing style? Enter the world of cotton-spandex blends—a match made in stretchy heaven! These fabrics hug your curves in just the right places, without the constrictive feeling of layers of cellophane wrapped around you (ladies, you know what I'm talking about). Whether you're donning a fitted athletic tee or a soft pair of leggings, these blends take you seamlessly through a day filled with running errands, dodging tantrums, and finally collapsing into couch oblivion by 9 PM. Plus, they stand up against the inevitable toddler finger-painting escapades. Now, that's what I call multitasking!

Oh, and let's not forget the wonders of rayon! This light-as-a-feather fabric can swoosh beautifully around your body as you elegantly navigate the aisles of your local supermarket, desperately trying to remember your shopping list and praying you don't bump into anyone you know while wearing a shirt with a stubborn spaghetti sauce stain. Rayon drapes nicely, and it always has that remarkable ability to make you look put-together —even if your hair resembles a bird's nest. When styled correctly, it can easily take you from school pick-up to your best friend's "please-help-me-figure-out-this-baby-sleep-situation" coffee crisis.

Now, let's address the elephant in the room: polyester. Sigh. Polyester, while it may have its place in this fashion universe, is a tricky beast. It can look fabulous while swishing gracefully around on a clothing rack, but wear it in the rush of your daily life, and you might feel like you're trapped in a sticky, gasping inference of fashion torture. Because who needs the sweat-soddy of polyester clinging to you while you're trying to tackle family life? Save it for your "never-wear-but-love-to-laugh-at-in-the-back-of-the-closet" items, my friends.

In conclusion, as you embark on your quest to find the perfect fabrics for your wardrobe, remember comfort is key, but so too is style. You can—and should—have both. Opt for materials that allow flexibility and breathability, while ensuring your outfits don't scream "three-week-old leftovers." When your fabric choices leave you looking stylish and feeling comfortable, you're already winning the game of life (especially when it's a game where extra snacks, superheroes, and spontaneous dance parties abound!). So, embrace cotton, linen, charming blends, and the occasional rayon number, while lightly avoiding the polyester pitfall. After all, life deserves a fabric that gives both a little flair and a sense of cozy freedom! Happy fabric hunting!

## Mastering the Essential Basics: Building the Perfect Wardrobe Foundation

The "perfect wardrobe foundation" — the holy grail of fashion! You know, the kind that can make you feel fabulous whether you're running late to a playdate or attempting to make small talk in the check-out line while your child dramatically performs "The Scream" in full force. Building a stellar wardrobe foundation is a bit like assembling a puzzle— you've got to find those essential pieces that fit just right, and sometimes, despite your best efforts, you're left with an odd piece that doesn't seem to belong anywhere.

Fear not, my fellow wardrobe warriors! Let's embark on the delightful quest to master the essential basics, turning chaos into chic as we navigate the cluttered world of motherhood.

First things first: let's talk about the cornerstone of any fabulous wardrobe-those fabulous staples that quietly hum "fashion" while doing the heavy lifting of style responsibility. Think classic white tees that can seamlessly transition from playground shenanigans to

## EVERYDAY CHIC: EFFORTLESS STYLE TIPS

brunch with the girls, and a chic pair of jeans that fit you like a glove, not like a sausage casing.

These staples are your foundation; they can be dressed up or down, layered under and over, and they provide the solace of knowing you have something to wear with the proverbial brain fog of parenting (which, if we're honest, can hit like a freight train at 6 AM).

Now let's sprinkle in some versatile cardigans or lightweight jackets to your ensemble. These nifty pieces are like a comforting hug when life becomes a whirlwind of unexpected chaos. Imagine strutting into a child's birthday party with a cute denim jacket-one that says, "I'm fun and approachable," while also camouflaging the remnants of Cheerios that seem to want to attach themselves everywhere. They add a layer of intrigue to your outfit, while simultaneously shielding you from the bold, crumb-filled world of toddlerhood. Plus, who knows when the temperature may drop? Nothing keeps the chill at bay quite like your trusted cardigan.

Next, let's not forget the power of a great pair of shoes. Walking in your trusty sneakers is one thing, but what about those wonderfully chic flats that allow you to keep up with your little ones while simultaneously ensuring you don't look like you just emerged from an exercise class? They strike that perfect balance of style and function, transforming even the most casual of outfits into something that says, "I mean business, while also having a blast chasing after my spawn!" A versatile collection of shoes is essential-flats, loafers, and sandals all have their rightful place in the magical wardrobe structure that sustains your everyday chic.

And, oh, ladies, let's not forget about accessories! Think of them as the icing on the wardrobe cake, and boy, do we love cake! Little statement pieces-like vibrant scarves, stunning necklaces, and eye-catching handbags-bring your basics to life. They're charming cheerleaders that shout, "Look at me!" while you're still desperately trying to remember where you left your keys. A well-selected accessory can brighten your entire outfit, turning your 'too-comfy-to-have-a-sanity-attack' look into a delightful expression of your individuality. I mean, if you're going to break an intense toddler scuffle at the playground, let's do it in style, right?

As you curate these essentials, remember to focus on fit. You could be wearing the most fabulous outfits, but if they don't fit properly, you could unintentionally be announcing to the world, "I chose this from the discount rack while under the influence of half-caf coffee!" Which let's be real, sometimes it can happen! So, rule number one is to consider tailoring. A little nip and tuck can transform the most unassuming basic into a dazzling fashion statement. It's the secret power you have, so use it wisely, like knowing how to calm a toddler mid-meltdown with a surprise snack.

Finally, let's talk about color, my friends. While your basics should be versatile, they can still have a touch of flair! A mix of neutral hues interspersed with a splash of vibrancy can create the ultimate wardrobe magic. Picture this: a staple black top feeling fresh with a bold, patterned statement skirt or colorful trousers. This joy can elevate your basics from mundane to magnificent, ensuring you feel fabulous even when the demands of motherhood threaten to drag you down.

In conclusion, building the perfect wardrobe foundation is about embracing the delightful chaos of life while expressing your personal style by selecting classic, versatile pieces that fit beautifully and incorporating playful accessories, you'll be one step closer to mastering the art of everyday elegance. So, arm yourself with essentials, get creative with your layering, and strut your stuff with that fabulous head held high! You've got this!

## Versatile Outfits: Transitioning from Playdates to Dinner Dates

The enigmatic art of transitioning your outfits from playdates to dinner dates-like morphing from an artful Picasso toddler masterpiece to a serene Monet at twilight! As a mother, you juggle an inexhaustible array of responsibilities. One moment, you're knee-deep in crayons and fruit snacks during a playdate, and the next, you're expected to dazzle over candlelit conversations amid

## EVERYDAY CHIC: EFFORTLESS STYLE TIPS

the aroma of delectable cuisine. But fear not! I'm here to guide you in crafting versatile outfits that effortlessly transition between the worlds of sticky fingers and suave dinner jackets— without losing your mind (or your sense of style) in the process.

Let's start by embracing the power of layering, my fellow fashionistas! Layers are your style besties and, much like your amazing parenting instincts, they can adapt to any situation. Whether it's a cozy cardigan that camouflages all those daggers of leftover toddler mess or a light blazer that screams "I mean business!", this is your toolkit for versatility. Picture this: your base layer is a comfortable yet chic jumpsuit (because who said moms can't rock a jumpsuit?). It's the perfect pick to handle playground shenanigans while exuding an effortless vibe. Add a fitted blazer, and voilà!

You've elevated your outfit to dinner-ready status without the hassle of a full wardrobe change. Just remember; if you accidentally get a swing-set splatter on it, you can still totally pull off that "I'm-so-quirky" vibe that Picasso would envy.

Now, let's talk about essential accessories— the ultimate allies in the quest for stylish versatility! Accessories have the magical power to change your entire look, and they're like your personal cheerleaders shouting from the sidelines, "Yay! You can do this!" A simple change in earrings or swapping your daytime tote for a sleek clutch can effortlessly elevate your outfit for a dinner date. Choose statement pieces that pop and catch the eye— maybe that beautiful necklace you wore just last week during a chaotic art project! When you layer these playful flourishes onto your well-planned base outfits, it creates delightful surprises that will leave you feeling fierce and fabulous when it's time to step out into the world.

Footwear is another crucial element in your mission to transition from playdates to dinner dates. Comfort is essential-especially when you're on the battlefield of managing energetic toddlers— but it doesn't mean sacrificing style! Opt for chic ankle boots that offer comfort and versatility while adding a swanky edge to your ensemble. You could go with cute ballet flats that whisper elegance, accompanied by some bright-patterned tights to channel the "mom-who-has-it-together" aesthetic that us busy gal strive for-never mind the remote-control toys masking themselves into luring décor pieces on the living room floor!

As you craft your outfits, think about prints and colors that travel well through both worlds. Earthy tones and soft patterns can feel playful for a day out but transition smoothly into evening chic with the right drama added in. Your charming, printed top can work wonders! During the day, it's the delightful partner to some relaxed trousers for playtime antics, but once evening rolls around, you can pair it with a sleek skirt that twirls just right to make you feel like a queen dispensing snacks rather than merely surviving snack time.

Now, let's not forget about makeup — a handy ally for transitioning your look into dinner mode from daytime mama mode. If your routine typically involves little more than a pop of lip balm and a glance in the mirror after a long day, try keeping some travel-sized essentials in your diaper bag. You know, for those unexpected unplanned dinner dates?

A dash of mascara and a touch of highlighter can truly transform you from "just-got-off-the-playground" to "ready-to-sip-cocktails-like-a-boss" in mere moments. Just remember, if the kids smeared food on your top, you can always blame it on the enriching experience of parenting!

Finally, keep your ever-optimistic mindset engaged as you redefine your notion of versatility! Embrace the beauty of your journey — those glorious moments when everything goes wrong, and perhaps your date night ensemble transforms into a "sublime mess" due to a surprise ketchup explosion. Laughter is the best accessory, and at the end of the day, confidence and joy in your choices will shine brighter than any outfit ever could!

So, regarding transitioning from playdates to dinner dates, remember that versatility is your friend! Equip yourself with layers, fabulous accessories, and adaptable pieces, and lock in a mindset that allows for joyful spontaneity. With the right outfit, you'll seamlessly transition from a magnificent huddle of caring mom to an enchanting dinner date —all while earning that standing ovation from your little ones who still think you're a style icon. Channel your inner superstar and let your versatile outfits tell your unique story!

## The Power of Confidence: Wearing Your Style with Assurance

Confidence-the elusive elixir that can elevate your style game from mediocre to show-stopping with just a sprinkle of self-assurance! It's the secret sauce that transforms the nervous mom in the playground into a chic runway model strutting with purpose (while trying to dodge a rogue soccer ball). Let's face it: in the grand fashion circus of life, confidence is your ticket to the front row, where the lights shine a little brighter, and the compliments flow freely. Today, we'll explore how you can harness this power and wear your unique style with the assurance of a thousand trendy influencers-all while navigating the delightful mayhem of motherhood.

First and foremost, understand that confidence doesn't come pre-packaged with fabulous fashion pieces-it's something you cultivate from within. Think of it as a seed you plant in the fertile ground of self-acceptance and self-love. That doesn't mean you need to strut around thinking you're the next supermodel (unless that's your vibe, then go for it!). It's all about embracing who you are and wearing your outfits like they were tailored just for you —because ultimately, they are! Remember, your style should reflect your personality, quirks, and all the glorious chaos that comes with parenting. So, when you slip into that cute dress or those fabulous boots, own it! You are not just wearing clothes; you are showcasing your story and creativity.

One of the delightful side effects of confidence is the way it can completely transform the way clothes fit you. When you wear something with assurance, it doesn't matter if the dress was on sale, or if the shoes were borrowed from your teenage daughter's closet (no shame in snagging a killer pair!). You instantly elevate the ensemble simply by strolling in with your head held high and a cheeky grin on your face like you just conquered the world— or at least the cereal aisle at the supermarket. It's all about that "I own this" mentality that makes onlookers stop and think, "Wow! She's rocking that look!" Your positive energy radiates, making the outfit pop and leaving everyone (even the toddler throwing a tantrum in the snack aisle) in awe.

Self-expression through fashion also plays a significant role in building your confidence. What you choose to wear is like painting your unique fashion canvas, where you can combine colors, patterns, and styles that resonate with you. If you love flamboyant prints, go for that rainbow-colored top! If you feel chic in tailored pieces, wear it like you mean it! No one can rock your personal style like you can! As the founder of SAM D'MONES, I can attest to the importance of freedom in expression.

Creating and showcasing beautiful clothing that encourages women to embrace their authentic selves has been an absolute joy. So daringly express yourself with your fashion choices— let your outfits reflect who you are!

Let's also address the power of positive affirmations! I know it sounds a little "woo-woo," but hear me out. Each morning, as you get ready, twist those parenting uncertainties into self-affirming mantras. Stand in front of your mirror and tell yourself you're fabulous—not just because of your fashion (though, let's be honest), but because you are you, unique and irreplaceable! Repeat phrases like "I am worthy of feeling beautiful" or "I am unstoppable" until you truly believe them. They'll help you husk away the self-doubt that tries to sneak in as you navigate motherhood's never-ending demands— because you deserve to look and feel your best, even when you've just pulled a crayon from your hair.

Another crucial aspect of confidence is surrounding yourself with supportive people. Seek out those uplifting friends who empower you and embrace your individuality. Don't be shy about sharing your style goals and passions with them. When you have a solid circle of fabulous cheerleaders, there's no stopping your style potential! Empowering friendships help you weather the storms of insecurity, and they encourage and inspire you to be bold with

## EVERYDAY CHIC: EFFORTLESS STYLE TIPS

your clothing choices. It's like a mini fashion army ready to fight for your right to shine— without the need for a superhero cape (though that could be a great outfit addition too).

In the end, let's remember that confidence is an ongoing journey— it's adding more richness to life with each step you take. There will be days of uncertainty, days when you glance at your reflection and think, "Who am I wearing and why?" But that's part of being human! So when those days come, be gentle with yourself. After all, fashion isn't just about perfection; it's about embracing the glorious ebb and flow of life while wearing what feels best to you.

In conclusion, confidence is a powerful force that impacts your style and daily experiences. It's not just about the clothes you wear —it's about loving yourself and sharing that love with the world. As you take on motherhood and life each day, wear your style with assurance, knowing you are beautiful just the way you are. Embrace your inner fashionista and let self-confidence become your ultimate accessory! After all, nothing screams style quite like walking confidently through life, exuding the vibrant spirit of a fabulous woman! Cheers to expressing your glorious self!

# CHAPTER 7
# SUSTAINABLE STYLE: FASHION THAT CARES

## Understanding Sustainable Fashion

Let's kick off our sustainable fashion journey not with drab statistics or convoluted jargon, but with a clear and vibrant picture of what sustainable fashion truly entails. Picture this: you're standing in front of your wardrobe, and instead of head-to-toe fast fashion, you gaze upon an ensemble that sings the sweet melody of sustainability-fashion that doesn't just look good but feels good in a way that even your fraction-of-a-cent-per-wear t-shirt could only dream about! Sustainable fashion is like that supportive friend who always knows the right outfit for the occasion but also makes sure the Earth is feeling fabulous too.

Now, let's clarify what I don't mean by sustainable fashion. It's not just about sporting linen fabrics that vaguely resemble the curtains from your grandma's living room. No, my fabulous friends, sustainable fashion means making conscious choices about our clothing- that means considering how our favorite outfits are made, who makes them, and the impact they have on our beloved planet. You know, the planet we occasionally sacrifice our sanity for at the local playground. It's also about reducing waste, embracing eco-friendly materials, and rejecting the notion that you need a hundred wardrobe staples that fall apart after one wash (I mean, who can afford that, right?).

## SUSTAINABLE STYLE: FASHION THAT CARES

One of the biggest misnomers out there is that sustainable fashion has to be equivalent to crunchy granola with a spritz of kombucha. But fear not! Sustainable fashion can be chic, cutting-edge, and, dare I say, downright fabulous. You don't have to trade your stylish wardrobe for beige sack dresses made from hemp to do your part for the Earth. The modern sustainable movement encourages a celebratory approach. It's all about infusing style with consciousness-think of it as adding a zesty lime to your sustainably sourced entangle of sushi rolls instead of serving them plain!

In the glorious world of sustainable fashion, the spotlight shines on eco-friendly materials that don't threaten our precious oceans and air and won't leave you wondering if you accidentally ordered a costume belonging to a 1970s polka dot horror film. There's a plethora of options today, from innovative fabrics like Tencel (made from eucalyptus trees, which, let's be honest, is a much sexier conversation starter than "recycled plastic") to organic cotton and even fabrics utilizing upcycled materials. And let's not forget about the incredible technology that allows us to repurpose just about anything — so yes, toss that regretful high school prom dress, because it could turn into something fabulous!

But wait, there's more! Understanding sustainable fashion also means delving into the world of ethical brands that genuinely care about their impact (no empty promises here, thank you very much). These brands offer transparency in their supply chains, proving that they not only produce gorgeous clothes but also ensure fair working conditions. Wearing chic designs shouldn't come at the price of someone else's happiness-now, that's a fashion faux pas even I can't tolerate by simply accessorizing it away.

With an ever-increasing number of brands jumping onto the sustainability bandwagon (or rather, the design runway), there's so much variety for everyone. Who knew saving the planet could allow me to rock those eco-friendly stilettos?

So, there you have it! Understanding sustainable fashion is more than a buzzword, it's a playful revolution that champions self-expression while caring for our planet. Think of it as true fashion with a conscience, where your outfits become a canvas to showcase not just your incredible style but also your dedication to a better world— for your toddlers and the ones yet to come. Embrace the lively colors of sustainability, be the dramatic queen you are, and let's turn our outfits into a heartwarming ode to the Earth! So, grab that sustainably-sourced dress and run —no, sprint— toward a world that embraces style with intention. Every beautiful clothing choice contributes to something bigger. Who knows? You might just inspire that neighbor with the questionable taste to make a better fashion choice—at least if the toddlers leave the house without a sticky finger-painting disaster on their clothes.

## The Benefits of Eco-Friendly Materials

Let's dive headfirst into the fabulously eco-friendly world of materials! Imagine a wardrobe that not only looks good but gives a warm hug to Mother Earth while you sizzle with style— because those two things should go hand in hand! Eco-friendly materials are the unsung heroes of the sustainable fashion movement, and I'm here to unveil the glorious benefits of wrapping yourself in fabrics that are kinder to our planet and, dare I say, your fabulous self!

First up, let's talk about the delightful realm of organic cotton. Imagine wrapping yourself in that soft, fluffy goodness that feels as if a cloud decided to be your new best friend, all while knowing it was grown without harmful pesticides or toxic chemicals. Seriously, why should we suffer just because we want to wear something that doesn't resemble a potato sack? Organic cotton not only provides comfort, but it also nurtures the Earth. While your non-organic counterparts are out there guzzling up resources like thirsty toddlers after a bubble bath, organic cotton crops require less water and are way less taxing on our precious soil. They're basically the responsible grown-ups in the cotton family, allowing you to frolic about in style without feeling guilty.

But hang on - let's not forget about everyone's favorite textile: Tencel!!

## SUSTAINABLE STYLE: FASHION THAT CARES

Made from the pulp of eucalyptus trees, Tencel is our chic little secret.

First, can we just appreciate that we're literally wearing a tree? The green goals of Tencel are downright impressive. Not only is this miracle material biodegradable (so no more worrying about your outfit becoming a permanent resident in a landfill), but it's also a joy to wear. If soft had a fashion ambassador, it would be Tencel — definitely don't take my word for it put it on and have a flamboyant dance party, because life is too short to wear scratchy fabric! By choosing Tencel, you're not just elevating your style game; you're making a fashion statement that says, "Yes, I love trees and myself." Now, let me introduce you to the magical world of recycled materials!

By using plastic bottles, old textiles, and even fishing nets, we've turned waste into the stylish pieces of clothing you're now drooling over. Seriously, when I first donned a fabulous jacket made from recycled materials, I felt like a superhero. Forget the spandex, I was ready to save the world, one stylish outfit at a time! Using recycled materials means we aren't tapping into new resources but instead saying a triumphant and sassy "thank you" to the old stuff that was hanging out in landfills. It's a win-win for your wardrobe and our Earth. Plus, if anyone questions your outfit choice, you can dramatically declare, "This? Oh, it's made from recycled plastic! I'm basically a tree-hugging fashionista!"

And what about bamboo? This miracle plant grows like a teenager raiding the fridge during a growth spurt - fast and furious! Bamboo fabric is naturally moisture-wicking, antibacterial, and oh-so-soft. Imagine wearing pajamas made from bamboo fabric that felt like clouds swirling around you while also being eco-friendly. Talk about a win-win situation! And it's hard to feel guilty about your late-night snacking when your pajamas are practically shouting, "I'm saving the planet!" Plus, if anyone tries to criticize you for what you wear to bed, just toss on a cute pair of slippers and tell them you're doing it for the owls. Who wouldn't want to save the world in comfort and style?

The beauty of eco-friendly materials goes beyond just being gentle on the environment; it allows us to express our fabulous selves without compromising our values. You can strut down the street in a killer outfit made from sustainable materials and announce to the world, "I'm not just here for the likes; my clothes are saving the planet too!" It's a conversation starter, a statement of style, and a tribute to a future free from fashion guilt.

By transitioning to eco-friendly materials, we not only become partners in style but also leaders in responsibility, paving the way for a more vibrant, sustainable planet for our little ones.

So, my fabulous friends, let's not just embrace eco-friendly materials-let's throw caution to the wind and wear our eco-conscious choices like a sash of honor! Let's make the world our runway as we frolic in the soft embrace of organic cotton, the splendor of Tencel, the recycled wonders, and the luxurious comfort of bamboo. Because when you shine in eco-friendly style, there's no telling just how radiant— and sassy — you can be!

## Building a Sustainable Wardrobe

Welcome, wardrobe warriors, to the grand adventure of building a sustainable wardrobe! If you assume that sartorial sustainability requires some kind of magic trick (a la Disney-style fairy godmother), then think again! While I can't promise a "bib bidi, bob bidi, boo" moment, I can definitely guide you on crafting a closet that's not just fashionable but also friends with the planet. Buckle up because we're about to embark on a stylish journey that even your toddler would pause their chaotic playtime to admire (or at least demand to be dressed in the same outfit).

To kick off this ambitious yet fabulously stylish mission, we need to embrace the philosophy of "quality over quantity." Hear me roar, my fashionista darlings! We're not just collecting clothes here-oh no, that would be the fashion equivalent of trying to herd a bunch of ferrets.

Instead, we want to curate a selection of high-quality pieces that scream sophistication and eco-friendliness. Skip the fast fashion

## SUSTAINABLE STYLE: FASHION THAT CARES

that falls apart after one wash (yes, I'm looking at you, 3-for-$10 T-shirt clearance). Invest in timeless garments made from sustainable materials, think of carefully crafted dresses, snag-proof pants, or even that sassy jacket that speaks to your inner-style queen. Remember, your wardrobe should reflect your fabulous personality, not your desire to fill every nook and cranny of your closet with items resembling a suspicious clearance sale at a discount store.

Next, let's make a promise to ourselves: we'll prioritize versatile pieces that can be styled in a multitude of ways. Step into the realm of the proverbial "capsule wardrobe." This doesn't mean you have to go full minimalist (unless that screams your name); it simply suggests that each carefully chosen item can be mixed and matched for maximum flair. Picture this: a single pair of tailored trousers could go from a smart casual work meeting to a spontaneous dinner date with your partner (or a "you've dropped the ice cream at the park" tantrum with your kids). When you can pull off being chic while shielding yogurt sauce, you know you're doing something right.

As we brave the depths of sustainable fashion, don't overlook the charm of secondhand shopping. Thrift stores are hidden treasure troves just waiting for you to dig through fashionable pieces that have stood the test of time —kind of like that random toy you found under the couch last week that your toddler won't stop playing with. Vintage stores can yield fabulous finds that have a story to tell, all while saving the planet— who knew a previously loved dress could come with backstories of other fabulous nights out? And let's be honest, nothing gets your fashion-loving heart pumping like stumbling upon a designer piece at a thrift store. It's like winning a mini lottery, but instead of cash, you're richer with style!

And while we're talking about finding gems in unexpected places, let's have a moment for the world of clothing swaps! Organizing a clothing swap with your fellow fabulous friends is like hosting a fabulous fashion party —who needs a book club when you could be swapping snazzy outfits? It's a chance to refresh your wardrobe without breaking the bank or guilt-tripping your conscience. Plus, just think of the fun you'll have watching everyone try to convince each other that disasters like the neon 80's jumpsuits aren't as horrible as they seem. You'll leave the event with stylish goodies, a sense of community, and a fabulous new reputation as the modern-day fashion matchmaker!

But hold up! As if that wasn't enough, we need to talk about maintenance and care. Your sustainable wardrobe isn't a set-it-and-forget-it deal; it needs love and attention! Extending the life of your beloved garments is paramount. Learn the art of washing clothes properly, follow care labels, use eco-friendly detergents, and avoid over-washing. And when you're ironing? That's right—be gentle! Treat your clothes like the precious little treasures they are, not like a bag of chips crunching after a rough day. When we care for our clothes properly, we reduce waste and extend their life, making us eco-warriors in our own right!

Now that we're on this beautiful journey of building a sustainable wardrobe, remember that every choice matters. Each lovingly selected piece highlights your commitment to style and the planet. You're not just dressing for the day; you're making a statement. With every pair of trousers of flowy top, you're revolutionizing the way the world perceives fashion, trading guilt for glory one outfit at a time. So, let's strut your stuff, flex your sustainable vibes, and proudly wear your fabulous creations, knowing that each ensemble is not only a reflection of your unique style but also a celebration of our beautiful Earth! Who knew saving the world could be done in such chic fashion? Now, let's hit those stores (or online boutiques such as, SAM D'MONES) and get to work—you've got a sustainable wardrobe to build!

## Ethical Brands to Support

Buckle up, my style-savvy friends, because today we're diving headfirst into the fabulous world of ethical brands! As we journey through this realm, we'll unveil the artisans, innovators, and change-makers who are winning the sustainable fashion game, all while leaving a trail of sparkle and eco-friendly glam. Yep, you

## SUSTAINABLE STYLE: FASHION THAT CARES

heard that right-because who said being kind to the planet could never be stylish? In fact, ethical brands are the true fashion superheroes we didn't know we needed! So, grab your cherry-flavored organic snack (because we're classy like that) and let's celebrate these fabulous individuals and companies that are as fashionable as they are responsible.

First up, let's raise a toast (with our eco-friendly bamboo straws, darling) to "SAM D'MONES"! If ever there were a brand that encapsulates the chicness of sustainability, it's this gem. SAM D'MONES creates stylish and trendy clothing while being committed to reducing waste and water consumption. We proudly flaunt transparent practices, giving you all the juicy behind-the-scenes characters you never knew you needed. Each piece combines playful designs with their mission to maintain eco-friendliness.

I don't know about you, but putting on that iconic dress with a side of sustainability feels like the ultimate power move. Plus, you can strut around knowing that your clothes were made with love, not with toxic fumes that make Mother Nature cry— so that's a double win for everyone involved!

Imagine wearing outdoor gear that doesn't just keep you warm on the slopes but also helps protect our beloved planet! It's as if every time you zip up that jacket, you're also giving a high-five to a glacier hanging out in your favorite mountain range. I mean, how could you not want to be the cool cat wearing threads that are fighting for the greater good?

So, as you strut your sustainable style, remember that every choice matters. Supporting these fabulous ethical brands only amplifies our mission to create a more stylish and responsible world. Grab your chic pieces powered by compassion and wear them with pride— because being fashionable and eco-friendly is the new black, and we're leading the charge!

So, join me in this fabulous movement, because together, we can not only dress like queens and kings but also give a royal hug to our planet in the process! Let's show the world that kindness, charisma, and a fabulous wardrobe go hand-in-hand; can I get a 'yes'?!

## Sustainable Fashion Hacks for Busy Moms

The life of a busy mom-a whirlwind of chaos, tantrums, and sticky hands, along with the overwhelming desire to look fabulous while navigating through it all! Let's be real: between juggling toddlers, packing lunches, and conducting daily negotiations with your little ones (who knew a single vegetable could come with such high stakes?), finding time to curate a sustainable wardrobe can feel like a game of hide-and-seek, with the wardrobe always winning. But fear not, my stylish mamas, because I've crafted a dazzling array of sustainable fashion hacks that will allow you to shine like the star you are, all while being kind to our beloved planet!

First on the list is the art of multitasking and let me tell you, it's a skill every mom needs to master. When shopping for clothes, think of "multi-wear" pieces. You know, the kind of clothing that feels stylish enough to wear to a brunch but also casual enough to smother in the remnants of last week's spaghetti. Look for dresses that can be easily dressed up with a statement necklace for a night out or dressed down with comfy sneakers for a fun adventure with the kiddos. Versatility is no longer just a buzzword; it's your secret weapon! And if anyone dares to question your fashion flair while you're racing around with a juice box in hand, you can smirk and say, "Darling, this is sustainable elegance at its finest!" Truly, with the right outfit, you can juggle life, motherhood, and style all at once— equally as impressive as holding two toddlers in each arm!

Next, let's talk about the miraculous world of secondhand shopping. You'd think it was a sport —navigating thrift stores like a fashion ninja with the agility of a toddler on a sugar rush! Secondhand shopping not only allows you to save a boatload of cash but also contributes to sustainable fashion by giving pre-loved items the age-defying glow they truly deserve.

And let's face it, between dirt art projects and juice spill disasters from the kiddos, anything with a little history is bound to fit right in with your ever-expanding collection of spaghetti sauce stains. Who needs the latest trends when you can own a unique vintage jacket that transforms grandma's style into a fashion sensation no one else can match? Plus, I dare you to try and concisely explain

## SUSTAINABLE STYLE: FASHION THAT CARES

the gorgeous tapestry of that jacket to your friends at playdates. It's a conversation starter, a style statement, and an eco-friendly choice catapulted into one fabulously quirky ensemble!

Now, we all know that time is of the essence when you're a busy mom, and nothing eats into your precious minutes faster than ironing (were not trying to win the "Smoothest Pants Award" here!). But don't toss your chic outfits into the dryer and pray for the best! Instead, master the art of steaming. A handheld steamer can work magic on those wrinkles, allowing you to look effortlessly polished in the time it takes your little one to decide which superhero costume to put on. Plus, steam is way gentler on fabrics and can extend the life of your clothes— because let's be honest, nothing feels more fabulous than fitting into a well-preserved ensemble while juggling crayons with one hand and snacks with the other!

Ah, let's not forget accessorizing, my darlings! Here's a little secret: a great bag can make any outfit scream "fashion icon" rather than "I've been living in yoga pants for the last three days." Invest in a solid, stylish bag that can carry your essentials (snacks, toddler toys, and perhaps a little wine tucked away for emergencies). You'll be able to tackle the day while looking polished, proving that being a mom doesn't mean losing your style-savvy identity. A fabulous bag can instantly elevate that "I-poured-my-coffee-on-my-shirt" vibe right into chic territory —no one will ever suspect that you once had a run-in with an energetic toddler! Sustainable fashion hacks also extend beyond clothing and accessories-let's reduce our fashion footprint by adopting clever care practices. Gentle washing techniques, cold water cycles, and air-drying your clothes can keep your items sparkling clean without devouring energy and resources. And think of the thrill when you see your favorite sweater retain its shape longer than that elusive balance between motherhood and sanity!

You'll be saving the planet and your dollars all at once— win-win, if you ask me. As we embrace this whirlwind of busy motherhood, let's channel that chaos into some fabulous choices. Incorporating sustainable fashion into our lives doesn't have to be daunting; it can be stylish, fun, and a reflection of our unique personality as mothers, as women, and as eco-friendly queens!

Every day is an opportunity to explore creativity while being kind to our planet. We can wear our newfound sustainable styles with pride, knowing that we're not just fashion icons in our little worlds, but also warriors for a healthier Earth. So, dear mamas, let's conquer motherhood and sustainable fashion one fabulous outfit at a time! Now go out there and show the world how it's done-you've got this.

## CHAPTER 8
# ACCESSORIZE LIKE A PRO: THE FINISHING TOUCH

**The Essential Role of Accessories in Outfits**

Accessories! The unsung heroes of the wardrobe world. They are the delightful cherry on top of your style sundae, the secret sauce that elevates your outfit from "blah" to "whoa, girl, where did you get that?" It's a magical realm where a simple outfit can explode into a full-on fashion tornado just by adding the right jewels, bags, belts, or scarves. But let's be real; sometimes, we treat accessories as if they're the last-minute additions we make on Halloween when we peer into the mirror and realize, "Oh wait, I'm still just a basic cat without a tail or a whisker in sight!" So, let's dive deep into the essential role that accessories play in our lives... and how to rock them like the drama queens we are!

First, let's talk about the pivotal role accessories play in self-expression. Clothes are amazing, right? But they can't scream your personality the way a fabulous statement necklace or a sassy handbag can. An outfit can be as straightforward as a plain pair of jeans and a white tee but throw on a neon green pair of oversized sunglasses, and you're instantly channeling "I am here to slay!" instead of "I've just emerged from my cave." Accessories take your personality and amplify it. They're an extension of who you are — each piece telling the world one part of your story. You could be on the run for the mom of the year award, but a fabulous fedora over a messy bun? Suddenly, you're on a high-fashioned runway, armed with children and snacks!

Now, let's not forget the practicality of accessories. I mean, who needs pockets when you have a giant tote stuffed with 48 different items that might one day serve as a life-saving tool? They say necessity is the mother of invention, and oh boy, is my tote a testament to that! Accessories provide that ultimate functional flair that makes managing toddlers and life feel a tad more stylish. A chic crossbody bag lets you wrangle little hands while looking fabulous. A stylish scarf can double as a baby blanket in emergencies (or let's be real, a bib). You simply can't underestimate how these gorgeous add-ons can keep your life from descending into complete chaos... or at least make it look good while you're doing it!

Furthermore, let's discuss the versatility of accessories. Oh, the endless possibilities! You can take an LBD (little black dress!) from day to nighttime glam simply by switching out your daytime fanny pack-yes, I said it-and replacing it with a glitzy clutch and a statement earring. Accessories are essentially the Swiss Army knife of fashion. They allow you to express your mood, the season, or even your inner diva! Maybe it's 2 PM, and you're about to step into the carpool line, but with that bold piece of arm candy wrapped around your wrist, you're ready to own that school run like a runway-it's all about bringing your A-game!

Now, a word of caution, my dear fashionistas: accessories can be like the hot sauce of a fashionable meal -too much can set off alarms and fire alarms! Yes, we've all been there, layering on every piece that sparked joy, only for our family and friends to tilt their heads and ask if we've been blessed by the Fashion Police. The key lies in balance, like juggling two toddlers while tiptoeing through a minefield of toy cars — pick a few statement pieces and let them shine. Be mindful; let those lovely accessories play harmoniously together rather than staging a full-on accessory riot.

Lastly, let's talk about confidence, the ultimate accessory! No matter how fabulous your earrings are or how dazzling your purse, The Number One Rule is that you HAVE to wear them with attitude. Clothes can be fabulous, but without confidence, you'll resemble a deer caught in the headlights. When you strut into a room outfitted with your well-curated accessories, it's like a

## ACCESSORIZE LIKE A PRO: THE FINISHING TOUCH

confetti cannon of "I own this!" If you feel fabulous in your style, those accessories will uplift you even more. Remember, darling, no matter how great the accessories are, it's how fiercely you own your outfit that leaves a lasting impression.

So go ahead, unleash your inner couture sorceress! Dive into the delightful realm of accessories and transform not just your outfits, but your entire approach to fashion. Scrutinize your accessories like a true queen with a discerning eye and embrace this whimsical ride that allows you to shout, whisper, and express every bit of your splendidly multifaceted self.

### Choosing the Right Accessories for Your Style

When it comes to accessories, let's face it: choosing the right ones can feel like stepping into an ancient temple filled with glittering treasures that could either elevate your outfit or lead you into a mysterious fashion void, where you end up wearing a traffic cone as a hat. Yes, darling, a fine line separates "fashionista" from "fashion disaster"! With my years of experience juggling toddlers, chaos, and fabulousness, I'm here to guide you through the maze of accessories like a chic Indiana Jones in search of the world's best handbag!

First and foremost, you need to understand your personal style. Are you an "elegant minimalist" or more of a "whimsical bohemian wizard"?

Maybe you're an "edgy rockstar" or a "colorful preschool art project" kind of gal. Identifying your style enables you to navigate the accessory wonderland with confidence. Take a good look in the mirror and have a little heart-to-heart with yourself. You're not just a mom; you're also a powerhouse of creativity, and your accessories should reflect that amazing identity! So, whether it's vintage pearls that sing sweet melodies of sophistication or funky geometric earrings that shout, "I'll have the kale smoothie," make sure what you adorn yourself with matches your fabulous vibe.

Next, consider your wardrobe. You wouldn't take a poodle to a dog show designed for hunting hounds, right? Similarly, your accessories must align with your existing ensemble. Ask yourself, "Do my accessories harmonize with my outfits or sound like a cat fight?" If you have a closet brimming with neutral tones, a neon yellow statement necklace might look like it crashed a funeral. On the contrary, if you're someone who thrives in color, then more muted accessories could have you blending in with the background like a poorly dressed wallflower. Think about colors, textures, and patterns that your wardrobe embraces and choose accessories that complement rather than compete.

While you're pondering your wardrobe, don't forget the fabulous role that proportions play in accessory selection. Channel your inner architect and consider the architectural elements of outfit proportions. If you're wearing a billowy maxi dress reminiscent of a bohemian fairy, pair it with delicate jewelry that doesn't fly in the face of your flowy fabric. Heavy chunky pieces would clash like a toddler's tantrum at the Lego store!

Similarly, if you're feeling fierce in a tailored suit, jazz it up with striking statement pieces that demand attention-like a necklace so bold it could have its own fanbase! Remember, balance is key and achieving that perfect equilibrium between statement and subtlety will keep your look on point.

Now, let's chat about occasion and functionality-because boring can happen unexpectedly. You might find yourself needing to sprint after a rogue toddler while striving for runway-ready status. It's like a game of Frogger, but with more glitter! So, ask yourself: "Are my accessories practical?" If you choose large earrings that resemble flying saucers, are they going to interfere with your ability to comfort a crying child or snag on the swing set? Opt for versatile pieces that can transition seamlessly from playdate to brunch with your friends, ensuring that while you're throwing cheerios around in a park, you're still dripping with chicness.

Also, let's be real, life is too short to wear accessories that don't spark joy—or at least snickers! No matter how fabulous that chunky bracelet or embellished headband looks on someone else, if it doesn't resonate with you, it's not worth your precious wardrobe space. Find pieces that make you beam like a neon sign,

## ACCESSORIZE LIKE A PRO: THE FINISHING TOUCH

ones that have stories, emotions, and maybe even a touch of drama woven into them —because darling, who doesn't love a splash of fair? When your accessories resonate with your style, they morph into a reflection of your personality and become the armor you wear in your own fashion battlefield. And finally, don't overlook experimentation!

Embrace your inner child and play with accessories without fear of judgment- even that traffic cone hat! Try unconventional combinations, mix metals, textures, and colors. If you feel silly, great — turn that silliness into your secret weapon! Break the rules of traditional styling. You might stumble upon your new signature look unexpectedly, like finding a hidden treasure buried beneath your toddler's mountain of toys!

Choosing the right accessories for your style can truly be a whimsical journey-remember to have fun, stay true to yourself, and embrace all your glorious quirks along the way. After all, the world is your runway!

### How to Layer Accessories Without Overdoing It

The fine art of layering accessories —a skill akin to mastering the craft of building a delicious sundae without sliding the entire concoction into a hot mess on your mom jeans. The secret lies in finding that magical balance where your look exudes "I woke up like this" chic without resembling a walking thrift store explosion. As a self-proclaimed accessory aficionado, I've navigated the treacherous waters of layering and emerged victorious (minus a few battle scars from my kids' snack spills). So, let's talk about how to layer those fabulous goodies without crossing into the chaos realm!

First things first, start with a solid foundation-LITERALLY! Before we even think about glitzing up your outfit, ensure that your clothes fit like a glove (or maybe even like those stretchy pants that fit too well after too many snacks).

Build the perfect canvas for your accessories, so they can shine like stars rather than casting shadows on a poorly designed outfit.

Consider layering textures and hemlines that establish a foundation for accessories to build upon. If you're rocking a collared shirt, try stacking some dainty necklaces just beneath the collar, letting them peek through like a playful secret. If you're layered with a shawl or cardigan, wrap yourself in a beautiful brooch of two to create an impact without overwhelming your frame.

Next, let's talk variety— oh, darling, this is where the fun begins! When layering accessories, it's essential to mix and match types, sizes, and lengths to create an eye-catching balance. Think of it as assembling your own fashion army; the key is to unite unique pieces that complement each other rather than engage in a full-on fashion warfare. Pair chunky bangles with slender rings, mix metals like gold and silver, or combine leather with delicate pearls. Don't shy away from tension, my darling! It can be a delightful embrace of opposites that keeps your ensemble engaging without devolving into an accessory mutiny. Remember, a little bit of chaos can create the best kind of order!

But wait—there's a secret ingredient here! Restraint! Yes, I said it; it was hard for me too! Layering is all about restraint, which can feel like trying to convince a toddler that broccoli is as exciting as candy. Focus on no more than three key accessory groups that speak to you that day. Perhaps one fabulous statement necklace, layered with a couple of delicate bracelets, and a chic pair of earrings to complete the story. Resist the urge to channel your inner holiday tree! Too many pieces can confuse the eye, causing your fabulousness to suffer instead of shining. Like seasoning your favorite dish, remember—less is often more when it comes to layering.

As you continue your accessory adventure, pay attention to the neckline of your outfit. Whether plunging or crew, your neckline is like the stage, and your accessories are the star performers. If you're donning a turtleneck (where, let's be honest, we feel like a human burrito), there's no need to go wild with long necklaces-stick with shorter ones that gracefully nestle just above the jacket collar. If your top has an open neckline; this is a golden opportunity to experiment with layering longer chains or statement pendants.

The goal is to create visual interest, and your neckline will always be the first act that draws attention.

Now let's address color harmony — because we must avoid looking like we crossed the rainbow bridge only to land in the land of mismatched accessories! As you layer, consider how your color palette interacts. Opt for complementary colors, of play with shades within the same family for a flawless blend. For example, if you've chosen a warm-toned outfit, layer accessories in gold and bronze hues, which can tie everything together like a well-crafted fashion bow. Don't forget — it's okay to inject a pop of color! A bright pair of statement earrings can create just enough zing, drawing the eye without overwhelming your ensemble.

Lastly, don't forget to channel your innate confidence when rocking those layered accessories! Consider them an extension of your dazzling personality rather than something you have to wear. Embrace how those pieces come together to tell the tale of your fabulous self! Whether you're walking into a boardroom or managing the playground — own your layers like a main character on a dramatic runway — and without failing, you will feel empowered, radiant, and, most importantly, striking!

So, my fabulous fashionista, remember that layering accessories should feel like a dance rather than a wrestling match. Embrace variety, maintain restraint, play with styles, honor your neckline, harmonize colors, and own your look! After all, life is too short to shy away from a little pizzazz, especially when confidence is the ultimate accessory! Happy layering!

## Seasonal Accessories: What to Add or Remove

The joy of seasonal accessories and the sweet, sweet chaos they bring into our lives! Each change of season opens a whole new world of chic opportunities-like an enchanting wardrobe door that beckons you to step inside and experiment! One moment you're happily bundled up in oversized scarves, and the next, you're doing a sun salutation while tossing statement sunglasses onto your face like a glamorous goddess. So, let's dive into the magical seasonal transformation of accessories, because trust me, darlings, this is where the real fun begins!

As we transition into the crisp embrace of autumn, prepare yourself for layers of texture and charm! This is the time for that essential oversized scarf-you know, the one you can practically wrap around yourself like a cozy burrito. Perfect for snuggling up as the leaves begin to change color!

Add luxurious statement earrings made of rich, warm materials-think golds and deep jewel tones that echo the colors of fall foliage. Transitioning into autumn is all about letting your accessories play together, so don't be afraid to mix materials! Pair a chunky knit sweater with a sleek leather bag that whispers sophistication while you stomp predictably through the pile of leaves your toddler made. Fun times ahead!

But then, in a blink, winter arrives like an uninvited relative searching for leftovers! Ah, winter — the time when your scarf becomes your best friend, and your gloves transform into your occasional nightmare of searching for one of the pair (if only they came with a GPS tracking device!). Embrace warmth with snuggly hats, fluffy earmuffs, and kitschy holiday-themed accessories that scream "festive!" Layering becomes key here; a delightful statement necklace can peek out over a turtleneck or be replaced with a sassy brooch on your coat. Remember, winter is the time to brighten up those dreary days! A pop of color in your accessories can battle those gray hues outside while doubling as a rescue signal for any lost mittens you might encounter along the way.

Now, as we gracefully tango into spring, prepare to shed the layers like a butterfly emerging from its cocoon! Out go the heavy scarves as lightweight wraps and airy chiffon scarves become your new essentials.

Fling on a pair of colorful sunglasses that say, "I am ready for brunch and adventures!" — because who doesn't want to be that fabulous? Add floral prints and pastel hues to your accessories lineup, bringing that cheerful energy to life! Spring is also the

## ACCESSORIZE LIKE A PRO: THE FINISHING TOUCH

perfect time to reintroduce fun hats- think Hoppy, stylish fedoras or charming straw hats that would make even the most skeptical garden gnome nod in appreciation. This is your time to dance with color, darling!

Oh, and don't get me started on summer accessories! If there's ever a season that begs for flamboyance and fun, it's summer. This is your moment to shine brighter than the midday sun! Break out the oversized sun hats that double as makeshift umbrellas, and don't forget the ridiculously fun statement earrings that dangle like intricate chandeliers from your lobes.

Flip-flops or chic espadrilles? May I suggest both, dear? The versatility of summer accessories allows you to exude a care-free vibe while still looking like a goddess as you navigate the chaos of family vacations or fun beach outings. And those beach bags? Choose one that can hold enough snacks and sunscreen to conquer a whole day!

But with seasonal accessories comes the inevitable question: what do you REMOVE? Oh, sweetie, let's spare ourselves from the sins of clashing seasons! As we transition from one season to another, it's time to clear the detritus of past accessories. I mean, summer visors have no business lurking around as the leaves fall, and that chunky knit scarf. You won't need it when the sun is beating down on you! When summer vacay ends, toss those Hawaiian-print accessories into the back of your closet with gleeful abandon. Trust me; they'll thank you later.

Equally important is responding to the whims of climate change. Who's to say your accessories can't reflect your running through puddles on a rainy day or you're gliding elegantly past sunbathers on hot sands? Stay attuned to the seasons, observe the palettes and moods they bestow upon us! Your accessory choices set the tone, allowing you to dance through life's changing rhythms with joy and flair.

So, my fashion-forward darlings, remember that seasonal accessories are not just items to pile on; they're your seasonal companions as you navigate the harmonious chaos of life! Celebrate those transitions, embrace the different moods of each season, and have fun with layering and removing accessories to create that stunning masterpiece every time you step out.

Whether wrapped in a cozy blanket scarf or strutting boldly with a sun hat-your accessories are the captivating tales waiting to unfold. Happy accessorizing!

## Budget-Friendly Accessories That Make a Statement

Budget friendly accessories - the delightful gems of style that allow you to look like a million bucks without emptying your wallet or selling a kidney on the black market. In a world full of extravagant price tags and fashion that often requires a second mortgage, it brings me pure joy to tell you that you can absolutely snag fabulous accessories that say, "Oh, darling, I'm fancy!" without sacrificing all your precious pennies. So, let's embark on this whimsical journey together to uncover the treasure trove of budget-friendly wonders— your wardrobe will thank you!

First, let's talk about the magic of thrift stores and vintage shops! These places are like candy stores for fashion lovers, teeming with one-of-a-kind finds just waiting to sprout life back into your wardrobe. You can stumble upon quirky statement pieces that have stories woven into their seams —pieces that ensure you'll never bump into someone else wearing the same thing at a crowded brunch! Perhaps you'll find an adorably oversized brooch that instantly transforms your plain cardigan into a collector's piece worthy of a gallery showing. The best part? You might find these treasures for just a few bucks, allowing you to channel inner Audrey Hepburn while staying true to your budget! So, grab a friend, put on those funky thrift store shoes, and go hunting for your next fabulous statement accessory.

Next on our whimsical wish list are local artisan markets and craft fairs. These dazzling gatherings are where creativity and budget-friendly fashion collide! You'll find jewelry handcrafted with love (and maybe too much caffeine) by talented artisans who offer their creations at prices that won't send your wallet into existential crisis. Seek out those unique pieces-like delicate resin earrings or funky clay necklaces— that capture your artistry-loving heart. It's

## ACCESSORIZE LIKE A PRO: THE FINISHING TOUCH

like giving your wardrobe a spark of creativity while supporting local talent, turning you into a style-savvy superhero! So, embrace the market, fill your arms with glorious goodies, and prepare to have your friends drooling over your standout style.

Now let's give a nod to the DIY world, where the limit is truly your imagination! You don't need a degree from an Ivy League school of fashion to create stunning accessories; sometimes, all you need is a bit of glue, some glitter, and ten inspirational You Tube videos showing how to make earrings from pasta. Yes, I really went there! There's a whole universe of possibilities waiting at the end of every craft aisle. Grab some vintage buttons and get those creative juices flowing by converting them into quirky hair chips. Or take that long forgotten chain necklace you inherited from your great aunt and turn it into a glorious mala bracelet. With a sprinkle of creativity, you can transform the mundane into extraordinary — talk about making a statement without breaking the bank!

Let's not overlook the grandeur of scarves, my friends! Scarves are the chameleons of accessories; they can change their form and elevate any outfit from drab to fab in just a matter of minutes. You can find chic scarves at unbelievably low prices; these beauties add pops of color and texture without requiring multi-generational savings. Wear them as hair accessories in a bohemian chic style, twist them around your bag's handle for that effortlessly put-together vibe, or even rock them as a belt for a 90's throwback scream! With just one budget-friendly scarf, you have a world of fashionable options waiting to be explored — so go forth and collect a rainbow of these fabulous fabrics!

And finally—let's not forget about online shopping! I know, I know, you've heard of it, but have you immersed yourself in the world of budget-friendly accessories? It's a trove of trendiness where flash sales and discount codes reign supreme! Websites and apps that specialize in affordable, fabulous fashion allow you to find statement pieces without losing your mind over designer prices. Search specifically for online stores that cater to budget-conscious fashionistas-it's like a candy store but minus the sticky fingers! From chunky earrings to adorable bracelets, you'll uncover hidden treasures while sipping your coffee from the comfort of your couch. Who knew lazy afternoons could be so rewarding? Go on! Try www.samdmones.com and discover what awaits you!

So, my fabulous friends, remember that style doesn't have to come with a scary price tag. Budget-friendly accessories hold the power to elevate your look, transform your outfits, and make you feel like the fierce fashion queen you are! Whether it's thrifting, supporting local artisans, indulging in crafty DIY projects, embracing the versatility of scarves, or getting lost in the wonder of online shopping— there's no shortage of options for dressing elegantly without financial shame! Put on your fierce face and go forth with confidence, knowing that your style speaks volumes without whispering about your budget.

## CHAPTER 9
# HOW TO SHOP LIKE A SUPERHERO

**Understanding Your Shopping Superpower: Knowing When and Where to Shop**

When it comes to shopping, it may seem as though you need a crystal ball, a magic wand, or perhaps a very patient saint to guide you through the land of towering racks and never-ending aisles. But fear not, fellow fashionistas. I'm here to reveal your shopping superpower: knowing when and where to shop, and why it can save your sanity while elevating your style game to heroic levels!

Get ready for a humorous expedition through the chaotic world of retail, and trust me, you'll walk away wielding your shopping prowess like a true superhero. First up, let's have a little chat about timing. Picture it: you wake up, sip your coffee (or five cups if you're a mom of twins like me trying to survive the day), and suddenly you have an epiphany - it's time to tackle that fabulous wardrobe transformation you've been craving! But wait! Is Saturday the best day? Spoiler alert: Unless you enjoy elbowing fellow Shoppers and pretending your cart doesn't knock down half a display while doing a charming pirouette, Saturday was NOT designed for shopping.

The best days for shopping are often weekdays. Mondays through Wednesdays are sacred if you want to roam the aisles like a majestic gazelle instead of a frantic bumblebee jostling with the swarm. On those peaceful days, stores are less crowded, staff is more attentive (they might even remember your name!) and finding that perfect outfit becomes an attainable goal. Don't get me wrong - weekends have a certain appeal to them. They offer endless possibilities for social events filled with sparkle (we are talking post-pandemic-style sparkle here). Just be prepared for the escalators and cash register lines that remind you of a high school gym class obstacle course.

Now, let's dive into the where of your shopping journey. Our world is bursting with stores and boutiques just waiting to be explored - much like an oversized birthday cake at a toddler's party! Depending on your fashion mission, you'll want to scope out different types of shopping locations that fit your needs and desires. Looking for something special and unique?

Trends 101: Local boutiques scream individuality, while chain stores are perfect for those times when you want to blend in with the brunch crowd (the shopping equivalent of a cute-but-friendly beige). Don't make the colossal mistake of thinking that the big-name retailers just have the latest trendy items. If you're hunting for specific pieces, consider mall sales that might lure unsuspecting shoppers with promises of discounts! Those designer pieces are the filet mignon of clothing, but they can taste better when you snag them at half the price. Forget about that kale diet, you'll want to throw your financial restraint out the window once you see that fabulous pair of shoes marked down 70%. They practically jump into your cart; after all, who can resist such foodie-fashion deals?

But oh, let's not forget about online shopping! In this digital age, spending hours browsing from your couch is almost a rite of passage. The secret is to know WHEN to embark on your online shopping escapades.

Pro shopping tip: Avoid shopping during your kids nap time if they seem set on waking up every 5 minutes to beg for juice! The key is timing and a little clever planning, which, if you're like me, means completing other household chores all while pretending that the pile of laundry isn't giving you the evil eye. And as you plunge into this exhilarating world of shopping, always keep your eyes peeled for those elusive "shopping events." They come around like a shooting star and can feature incredible deals. Fashion weeks, sample sales, and clearance events are like treasure hunts that make you think you've hit the jackpot! Just remember to don an outfit with stretchy pants and comfy shoes, or you might find yourself regretting that cute ensemble in line while constantly scanning the clock, hoping it's now socially acceptable to buy a pair of joggers instead.

So, there you have it, my fabulous friends! Armed with the knowledge of when and where to shop, you will soon master the art of shopping like the superhero you are. Now grab your cape (or T-shirt), get your shopping list intact, and prepare to take on the world of retail! With a little savvy planning you can conquer the fashion battlefield that awaits. Just remember to use your powers wisely; you wouldn't want to acquire a shopping hangover, after all!

## The Hunt for Style: Creating a Game Plan for Shopping Trips The thrill of the hunt!

Shopping is not just a transaction; it's an exhilarating adventure, akin to searching for buried treasure, except instead of pirates and maps, you have your closet's crying for help, and perhaps a list scribbled on the back of a grocery receipt (not the most glamorous start, but we work with what we've got!). Every shopping trip needs a game plan, and I'm here to help you strategize like a seasoned general, because let's face it: in the jungle of retail, it's survival of the stylish.

First things first, you need to assess your mission objectives. Think of it as reconnaissance for your wardrobe. What are you shopping for? Are we talking mission-critical essentials like a pair of trusty jeans or the pièce de résistance for a wedding you just got invited to (thanks, Aunt Rita!)? Knowing what you need makes all the difference. If your goal is to spice up your look, it's a good idea to start with items that compliment things you already own. No one wants to bring home that adorable blouse only to find out that it doesn't match anything in your closet - trust me, it will void all feelings of joy faster than your toddler can swipe crackers off the counter.

Next, create a shopping list. Sure, it sounds mundane but think of your list like the GPS tracking system of your adventure. It'll guide you through the potentially overwhelming deluge of choices. Wearily wandering through endless racks, sweating from your self-inflicted cardio, without a clear direction can lead to purchasing items that are not only unflattering but also completely useless. So, write it down! If you're feeling fancy, color-code those must-haves versus nice-to-haves. I personally recommend pastel for the essentials and bold neon for the "Well, it's cute, and I'm in a bought-something-just-to-satisfy-my-inner-shopaholic mood!"

As you prepare for the day of magic and mayhem, gather your battle gear. Comfortable shoes are a requirement! Let's face it: we're not here to impress anyone with the latest runway strut; we're here to collect steals.

Trust me, the environment inside a busy mall gets chaotic, and you'll want to make sure that your feet don't cry louder than your kids when they realize you've locked them in the shopping cart (hey, it's just for a moment, right?).

Sneakers or those fab flats from last season can be your best allies on this retail battlefield!

When you arrive at your chosen retail destination, you might feel that rush of excitement, the retail adrenaline coursing through your veins. But wait! Before you rush into the sea of shiny baubles, take a moment for a strategic overview. Scan the store like you're a hawk surveying its territory from a high perch. Is there a clearance section waiting for you? Is the sale rack trying to lure you with its seductive markdowns? Warm your inner bargain hunter up - it's about to go down!

Once you've surveyed your surroundings, it's time to dive in like a graceful swan — err, maybe more of an exuberant duck since we're talking about shopping here. You'll want to be a proactive hunter, and if you spot something unique or stylish, grab it! Don't wait for a second opinion from your friends or the mirrored maze in the

## HOW TO SHOP LIKE A SUPERHERO

fitting room that always makes you question your existence. If it feels like it could deliver happiness, bring it to the fitting room, where that pile of fabrics will either make you shriek with joy or induce a crisis that could rival the latest episode of your favorite reality show.

Now, let's address the elephant in the room: the fitting room struggle!

You know what I'm talking about. There's nothing quite like the exhilarating high of finding an incredible item, only to discover that it transforms you into a lumpy marshmallow once you step inside that tiny box of torment. The lighting in fitting rooms is the stuff of legend; it's particularly unforgiving. Carry a full-length mirror in your back pocket if you must! It's always wise to add a bit of personal flair to the trial process; twirl, jump, and throw a celebratory dance for each victory.

As you find your shopping gems, remember to stay aware of your budget and use it wisely. Like a superhero sidekick, your bank account is there to support you, but it should not be your main character! Keeping track of your expenses is crucial if you don't want your shopping trips to transform into a heck of a comedy show when your husband checks the credit card statement and looks at you as if you've committed a fashion felony. Allocate your funds according to your priorities - after all, paying rent and feeding your toddlers should come first.

Having your game plan set can transform shopping trips into joyous escapades rather than chaotic obstacles. Think of it as your personal treasure map; with every successful shopping encounter, you'll be one step closer to a wardrobe filled with outfits reflective of your fabulous self. Now, gear up and get ready to hunt for style in style! You've got this, and I'll be right here cheering you on from the sidelines with a shopping bag in one hand and a fabulous latte in the other. Happy hunting!

## Online vs. In-Store: Finding Your Shopping Zen

The age-old debate: online shopping versus in-store shopping. It's like choosing between chocolate and vanilla, cats and dogs, or yoga and Cross Fit!

Both options have their merits, yet they also come with their own unique tangles that can complicate your quest for fashion nirvana. So, grab a cup of coffee, and let's dive into the pros and cons of each mode of shopping like we're diving into the chicest pool at a summer resort!

First, let's talk about the undeniable magic of online shopping. Ah, the joys of scrolling through endless pages of fabulous clothing, all from the comfort of your living room — where the only distraction is your toddler demanding a juice refill every five minutes or the recognizable, yet daunting noise of that laundry pile begging for your attention. Online shopping provides this beautiful escape; you can do it wearing sweatpants and a face mask while looking slightly disheveled, and nobody will bat an eye! I mean, who wouldn't want to sport duck slippers while searching for the latest must-have maxi dress? It's basically fashion freedom, with a side of pajamas!

Now, let's address the elephant in the virtual storefront-sizes and returns. With online shopping, the thrill of surprise often turns to a gasp of horror when that dress you ordered arrives, and it looks like it was designed to fit a very enthusiastic toddler, or worse, a superhero in their off-season.

So, you're left with that sinking realization that those size "faux-mignons" (faux-plus sizes, as I like to call them) are not quite the haute couture you were expecting. The truth is, understanding size charts can feel like deciphering ancient hieroglyphics — what does "petite" even mean? And as for that infamous "easy return" policy? Let's just say it sometimes operates with the same reliability as a toddler's promise to keep their toys in one place!

On the flip side, we have the glorious in-store shopping experience. Picture it: you walk into a store and are bombarded by beautiful displays beckoning to you, promising joy, style, and just a hint of drama. There's nothing quite like physically feeling that fabric

## HOW TO SHOP LIKE A SUPERHERO

between your fingers or inhaling the beautiful, lingering scent of new clothes— it truly is fashion therapy! You can twirl in front of mirrors, channel your inner model (sashay, sashay!), and experience that glorious moment when you discover something that makes your heart sing. Plus, you can experience immediate satisfaction— you find it, try it, buy it, and wear it, all in the same day! Talk about the instant gratification that our busy lives so desperately crave, However, let's be real — there's an unfortunate downside to in-store shopping. The semi-awkward interaction with sales associates can take a life of its own. Picture yourself fighting a battle with two screaming toddlers while simultaneously trying to avoid the overly enthusiastic saleswoman who won't stop suggesting "the latest must-have items." Spoiler alert: they probably won't be anywhere near your style, but you nod with feigned enthusiasm as you desperately try to wrestle your kids into a more manageable state.

Now, the true genius of shopping lies in a harmonious blend of both worlds. Yes, that's right! The shopping yin and yang! You can absolutely scour the internet for the best styles, fill up your cart, then make a strategic list based on how each item fits your fabulous plan for seasonal bliss. Afterward, just waltz into the store, brandishing your shopping list like a high-powered fashionista! This way, you maximize your time, minimize hasty decisions, and preserve your sanity while engaging in a delightful retail experience.

But no matter which route you choose-online or in-store— finding your shopping Zen ultimately comes down to your own preferences and lifestyle. So, trust your instincts! Are you an online ninja who can calculate the exact moment when free shipping is just on the horizon? Fantastic! Lean into that. Or are you the in-store aficionado, who loves the whole experience of rummaging through racks and engaging in delightful chitchat with fellow shoppers? Embrace that!

And if you're feeling particularly brave, make a day of it! Host an "online versus in-store" showdown with your besties. Right in your living room, decorate it like a fab little fashion lab with snacks, drinks, and perhaps even a few outfits to try on during the in-store excursion that follows!

With this magical blend of both online and in-store shopping, you'll master the art of retail, keeping your style vibrant while preserving your shopping Zen! After all, whether you're clicking away at home or galloping around the mall in style, fashion is meant to empower us, enhance our confidence, and remind us that we are all regal queens navigating the beautiful world of fabric and flair! Now go forth and shop like the fabulous beings you are!

## The Secret to Avoiding Impulse Buys: Know Your Triggers

Impulse buys! Those sneaky little temptations that often feel like having your hand caught in the cookie jar - except the cookies are actually a trendy blouse you don't really need, and the cravings can bring on a hefty dose of buyer's remorse. Let's face it, fighting against impulse purchases can be as challenging as herding cats — particularly when a 75% off sign sparkles at you like a shiny disco ball on a Saturday night. But fear not, my fabulous fashionistas! Knowing your triggers and how to outsmart them is like having your very own secret weapon in the world of retail.

To kick things off, let's dive into the realm of emotions! Yes, you guessed it: emotions play a massive role in our shopping decisions. You walk into a store feeling like a smoky-eyed goddess, and suddenly you spot a stunning pair of shoes that whisper sweet nothings to your inner shoe addict. "Buy me! You need me!" they seem to say. Next thing you know, you're trying them on and floating around the store like Cinderella. But keep in mind that excess emotional shopping can resemble a rollercoaster ride-thrill-filled at first, but you might end up nauseous and regretting that entire whirlwind experience.

So, sit down with a warm beverage (preferably something caffeinated to turbo-charge those neurons) and take a moment to reflect on what triggers your inner shopaholic. Is it boredom? Stress? Or perhaps that momentous day when all of your Zoom calls could easily disguise the fact you were wearing pajama pants below the waist? Recognizing your emotional triggers will empower you to make more mindful decisions. The next time you

## HOW TO SHOP LIKE A SUPERHERO

feel the impulse rising, like a volcano ready to erupt, grab a cozy blanket, a good book, or even some yoga pants — anything that provides an emotional buffer before you dive headfirst into the retail world.

Let's venture into the realm of social influence, my friends. Ever found yourself shopping with your besties, and suddenly the "need" for that peacock-patterned dress that's two sizes too small seems totally justified because your friend said it "looks fabulous?" Bam! You've just succumbed to the potent force of peer pressure - the kind that can make Pyrex look like a fashion statement. Stand strong amidst the sirens of temptation! When you're out and about with your pals, channel your inner fashion guru; think of what you have in your closet that you love. Ask yourself: "Would this item genuinely add value to my wardrobe, or am I simply trying to keep up with the frenzy of my friends?"

Now, let's dive into the dreaded habit of scrolling through social media (cue the dramatic music!). There are influencers out there with killer styles and teeth that seem way too perfect— thanks to the miracle of filters- and trust me, their curated content can ignite that shopping spark in our minds faster than you can say "I'll take three of those!" Know this: if your thumbs are going rogue while scrolling through your feed, it might lead to that just one more click' that ultimately spirals into a full-blown shopping spree. Set up healthy boundaries: limit your screen time, avoid shopping sites after a tough day (unless you want a closet full of sweater vests you'll never wear, and unfollow brands that like to poke and prod your wallet.

Oh, and let's not forget the irresistible allure of sales and discounts! Markdowns make us feel like savvy shoppers-as if we're somehow defeating the retail system with our keen strategic skills. But here's a fashion fact: just because something is on sale doesn't mean it's a steal. The secret to not being swept away in the tide of discounts is to remind yourself that taking advantage of sales only makes sense if you're genuinely in the market for that item. Save the celebratory dance for items you've put thought into, rather than for products that are simply marked down.

And finally, create a 'cooling-off period' for large purchases (yes, you can actually build space between your impulses and your wallet). That means giving yourself a solid 48 hours to mull it over. If after two days you're still dreaming about that blouse as if you were plotting its royal reign in your closet, maybe it's time to retrieve it from its blurry space in the "ringing in Your head without any practical use" category and proceed to the checkout. After all fit brings you genuine joy or happiness, it deserves a spot alongside your favorite comfy pants and signature sweatshirts.

Navigating impulse buys might sometimes feel like a game of dodgeball - dodge the temptations, dodge the regrets — but with a little awareness of your triggers, you can absolutely emerge victorious from the retail battlefield. The next time you feel your willpower slipping, remember the power you hold, you are the supreme ruler of your shopping kingdom, and only you can decide what truly deserves a place in your fabulous life! Now go forth, armed with your newfound wisdom, and conquer that shopping jungle with confidence and flair!

## Building a Fashion Wish List: Prioritizing Your Closet Needs

The fashion wish list! The magical scroll that every sartorial queen and king should wield like a powerful wand! Picture this: a well-organized catalog of dreamy items that will elevate your closet from drab to fab. Building a fashion wish list is not just about wanting things; it's about prioritizing your needs in a world overflowing with temptation and choice, like a kid at a candy store trying to make sense of a sugar high!

First off, let's chat about "why" you need a fashion wish list, my fellow style maven. It's simple, really: without it, you might find yourself glancing longingly at that eye-popping sequined jumpsuit -totally impractical for a day filled with toddler-related chaos— and thinking it would be a great addition to your closet. Cue the epic internal battle: practicality versus whimsy! Having a wish list keeps you focused and ensures you invest in pieces that truly matter. It helps keep your wardrobe aligned with your lifestyle, avoiding that impulse to snag pieces that will leave you questioning your life choices when they inevitably sit unworn in the back of your closet, like forgotten relics of a fashion disaster.

Head over to your favorite digital notepad or good ol' fashioned paper; now it's time to start mapping out your fashion visions! Begin by assessing your current wardrobe. Grab a glass of wine (or, if you're on toddler duty, a soothing cup of chamomile tea and take a close look at what you own. What pieces do you wear on repeat? Be honest with yourself-haven't worn that funky, oversized sweater since your college days, perhaps it's time to exclude it from your "must-have" list!

Next, think about the gaps in your closet that are crying out for attention. Do you find yourself constantly rummaging through your drawer full of mismatched socks while hunting for that perfect work outfit? A reliable pair of tailored trousers may just be the answer! Note down those wardrobe holes; these are genuine needs that will enrich your style journey and boost your confidence while navigating the everyday chaos. Remember, your wish list is akin to your own personal shopping genie-it grants you the perfect items to transform your outfits while making sure you're never left with that "I have nothing to wear!" panic.

Now that you've identified your closet needs, let's sprinkle a bit of pizzazz on it. Cap it off with a few "want" items— pieces that might not be essential but are too fabulous to ignore! Maybe it's that outrageously chic, fringed handbag or the glimmering sequin top that would make your heart sing.

It's essential to allow yourself a few of those delightful non-essentials to keep your fashion-spirit alive. After all, doesn't life deserve a dash of glam? Just make sure those wants don't overshadow the practical necessities. That way, when you're swirling around the mall, channeling serene shopping vibes, you'll make well-informed decisions while still leaving room for sprinkle-induced joy.

Let's not forget about the wonders of planned shopping! Treat your wish list like a sacred text, referring to it before every shopping spree. I'll function like a trusty compass guiding you through the torrential sea of retail choices.

Your wish list will save you from spending money on that impulse buy of a whimsical unicorn sweater that honestly doesn't fit your lifestyle (not unless all your meetings are themed, of course!). With your focus homed in on the items that matter, you'll cut back on frivolous spending, thus nurturing a wardrobe that not only makes your heart skip but also sends your savings account waving in delight.

A note of caution: as you embark on your shopping adventures with your shiny wish list in hand, practice the art of waiting. It's surprisingly powerful when you spot that turquoise jumpsuit that calls you like a siren, pause and sleep on it figuratively, of course). Two days later, you might realize that it fits into the fleeting "nice to have" category rather than the tear jerking "need to have" one. This simple trick helps provide clarity and strengthen your determination as you build a fashionable closet filled only with pieces that not only suit your style but also tell your story.

So there you have it, my fabulous fashion warriors! Your adventure in building a fashion wish list starts today. Prioritizing your closet needs while sprinkling in a bit of your fabulous flair will make the shopping process not just strategic but downright thrilling! Armed with this envy-inducing wish list, you'll journey through the retail world like the fashion unicorn you are— gracefully conquering those racks one expertly curated outfit at a time. And remember, style isn't just about what you wear; it's about how you express yourself while feeling fabulous in every moment of life.

## CHAPTER 10
# ZODIAC STYLES: FASHION BASED ON YOUR STAR SIGN

### Understanding Your Zodiac Sign's Influence on Personal Style

As a self-proclaimed fashionista, I'm often asked about the hidden secrets behind finding one's unique style. And voila! I found the answer in the stars literally! Each zodiac sign has a set of personality traits, quirks, and preferences that influence not just how you tackle your day, but also what you wear while doing it. That's right, darling— your horoscope isn't merely a guideline for dodging existential crises, it's also an oh-so-chic map to your personal style!

Let's start with fiery **Aries**. Known for their boldness and fierce energy, Aries typically gravitate toward vibrant colors and daring styles that say, "Look at me!" The signature red hue isn't just for bulls; it's the beacon of Aries passion! If you're an Aries, embrace statement pieces, those show-stopping outfits that could practically take on the world. But let's be honest, they might also need a sturdy bar stool nearby for all the high-energy swaying. Just remember, dear Aries, that while your outfits can radiate "powerhouse," they shouldn't come equipped with the potential to incite world domination— unless you plan on ruling the fashion empire!

Next up, we've got the quiet yet elegant **Taurus**. These earth signs are known for their love of luxury and comfort. Soft fabrics, rich textures, and soothing colors are what make a Taurus thrive. Think cashmere, silk, and a color palette reminiscent of a tranquil afternoon spa. Dressing for you, oh celestial bull, should feel indulgent-like a warm hug from a stylish cloud.

Of course, we all know that leisurely strolls in the park can quickly turn into a sprint for your favorite boxed wine, so blend seamless comfort with functional attire. No one wants a wardrobe malfunction while frolicking with vintage bottles!

The chatty **Gemini** is known for their dualistic nature. One minute you're a bohemian goddess, and the next, you're channeling your inner corporate rock star! Celebrate your multifaceted self by incorporating eclectic styles and statement accessories that cater to your ever-changing whims. Colorful patterns, mismatched prints, and layers are your best friends. Just don't get caught in a wardrobe malfunction when attempting to showcase both styles at once, or you may end up sparking a neighborhood fashion trend only the boldest dare to follow!

When it comes to our nurturing **Cancer** friends, we know they just want the world to feel cozy and loved, right? Soft hues and flowing fabrics are the keys to their hearts —but with a touch of whimsy, of course! Think of floaty dresses or oversized cardigans that you could curl up in while sipping chamomile tea. After all, what's a Cancer without an outfit that screams, "I'm comfortable, but I'll also reminisce about my childhood teddy bear as we share feelings!" Every outfit for a Cancer should be an invitation to pastel colors! Generational hugs — just be on the lookout for accidental spills on those soft pastel colors!

Moving on to our glamorous **Leo**, roar with confidence, my dazzling lion! When you dress like you belong on the red carpet, you'll inevitably attract attention like a moth to a flame. Golds, rich reds, and dramatic silhouettes are all essential elements in your royal wardrobe.

Unapologetically bold, Leos should never shy away from dazzling embellishments or daring cuts! Yes, we see you working it- just remember that you want to engage the audience rather than blind them. Finding that fine line is vital; you want to shine like the sun, not temporarily redesign an entire neighborhood with your reflective wardrobe choices!

## ZODIAC STYLES: FASHION BASED ON YOUR STAR SIGN

**Virgos** are practical, which often translates into their style. You're not just dressing; you're executing a mission: looking polished while successfully dodging toddler tantrums and laundry disasters. Clean lines and classic cuts are your armor in this fashion battlefield. Aim for timeless pieces that can withstand the epic superhero story of your life— potential cape optional! Don't forget to accessorize. After all, even the most classic ensemble can use a little pizzazz.

**Libra** zodiac styles focus on elegance, balance, and harmony. Libras gravitate towards soft pastel colors and classic neutrals. Their wardrobe includes tailored blazers, flowing dresses, and chic blouses, with luxurious fabrics like silk and satin. They prefer subtle patterns and classic prints, accessorized with elegant jewelry and stylish handbags. Footwear choices often include ballet flats and elegant heels. Overall, Libras aim for a timeless and refined aesthetic.

**Scorpio** zodiac styles are an enigmatic blend of intensity and mystery, captivating all who dare to gaze upon them. Scorpios have an innate attraction to deep, mesmerizing hues like rich reds, midnight blacks, and regal purples, mirroring their fiercely passionate souls. Their wardrobe is an artful curation, featuring iconic pieces like sleek leather jackets and striking accessories that infuse an edgy flair into their ensemble. The essence of Scorpio style is irresistibly alluring and powerfully magnetic, weaving a spell that leaves a lasting impression and commands attention.

**Sagittarius** are like a fashion passport to fun and freedom! These adventurous souls gravitate towards a rainbow of vibrant blues and purples, as if they're dressing for a perpetual festival of wanderlust. Their closets are a delightful chaos of casual jeans that have seen every corner of the globe, bohemian dresses perfect for a spontaneous beach party, and footwear that says, "I can climb a mountain and dance all night, watch me!" The Sagittarius style is an effortlessly eclectic mix that blends comfort with a sprinkle of "where-to-next" magic, capturing their unstoppable adventurous spirit in the most fashionable way possible.

**Capricorn** are defined by a classic and sophisticated elegance. Capricorns gravitate towards neutral tones like grays, blacks, and earth tones, which reflect their practical and disciplined nature. Their wardrobe often includes tailored suits, structured blazers, and high-quality fabrics that exude professionalism and timeless style. The overall aesthetic is polished and refined, with an emphasis on quality over quantity, perfectly embodying their ambitious and grounded spirit.

**Aquarius** are all about individuality and innovation. Aquarians are attracted to unconventional and eclectic looks, often incorporating futuristic or unique elements into their fashion choices. They love experimenting with bold colors, quirky patterns, and unexpected combinations that make a statement. Their wardrobe might include avant-garde pieces, vintage finds, and accessories that are distinctly one-of-a-kind. The overall aesthetic is creative and forward-thinking, reflecting their progressive and independent nature.

And last but certainly not least, our friend **Pisces**, Pisces zodiac styles are a dreamy blend of romantic and whimsical elements. Pisceans are drawn to soft, flowing fabrics and gentle colors like sea greens, pastel blues, and lilacs, reflecting their deep connection to the water element and their imaginative nature. Their wardrobe often includes ethereal dresses, bohemian tops, and delicate accessories that add a touch of magic to their look. The overall aesthetic is effortlessly enchanting, capturing their artistic and compassionate spirit with a touch of fantasy. If the stars have conspired in your favor, then you know-your zodiac sign is not just a trivial part of your life; it's a sartorial gem! Whether you're channeling a fierce Aries or a calm Taurus, your style is uniquely you, shaped by the cosmos and your own fabulous flair. So embrace your star-signed self, sway through life with infectious confidence, and let the universe guide your closet choices! After all, shopping is cheaper than therapy — especially when you're decoding the cosmic clues of your fabulous fate!

# ZODIAC STYLES: FASHION BASED ON YOUR STAR SIGN

## Identifying Key Colors for Each Zodiac Sign

Welcome back, fashionistas! If your wardrobe feels more confused than a cat in a swimming pool, let's whip it into shape by tapping into the dazzling world of colors — specifically, the colors that resonate with each zodiac sign. The ancient astrologers may not have had a say in today's voguish trends, but they certainly understood the enchanting relationship between color and personality. It turns out that your star sign not only reveals your character traits but also the shades that can transform your closet from drab to fab! So, grab your favorite iced coffee, or perhaps a glass of agitated toddler tears (just kidding), and let's dive into the color palette fit for the stars!

Scaring with the fiery **Aries**, color is your battle cry! Bold reds and fiery oranges epitomize the Aries spirit - passionate and courageous, with a hint of "I am the queen of the world, bow down!" Whether you're rocking a dramatic red dress or parading about in an orange power suit that screams "notice me", these colors ignite the flares of your vibrant personality. Red is the color of statements, not just on runways but in life! So pair that audacious red lipstick with your best "I-just-conquered-the-playground" strut and let the universe know that the world is your stage!

Now, let's traipse along to lovely **Taurus**, the earth sign that delights in comfort and luxury. Think lush greens, soft pastels, and rich earthy tones, pulling you toward color choices that resonate with the tranquility of nature. These aren't just any greens — we're talking about the sultry, rich greens of a forest after a refreshing rain, mixed with hints of rosy pinks to reflect your innate love for lush textures. After all, what's a Taurus without a wardrobe that can multitask as a relaxing retreat? Imagine accessorizing with a jade necklace while wearing a soft moss-green top. You'll feel so cozy you could practically nap standing up-some would argue it's a Taurus superpower.

As we zigzag through the astrological spectrum, we arrive at our whimsical **Gemini**. Colorful, playful, and still utterly sophisticated, you Geminis thrive in shades of yellows, vibrant purples, and multi-color patterns that mirror your vivacious nature. Your wardrobe should function like the stock market— diversified, bold, and constantly fluctuating! Think statement pieces that scream, "I'm here to have fun, so why are you still wearing beige?" Drape yourself in a colorful scarf or slip into clashing prints that make you a walking, talking art installation. Just remember— only a Gemini can pull that off while still managing a fierce conversation at the same time!

Next up is the nurturing **Cancer**, whose colors complement your tender and soulful nature. Soft whites, gentle pastels, and calming blues align beautifully with your warmth. Picture yourself in a seafoam green dress that floats like gentle waves, paired with soft pastel pinks that resemble a rosy sunset-it's the perfect poetic tribute to your inner mermaid (or merman, if you're feeling adventurous). Allow these delicate hues to cradle your spirit while embodying the soothing essence that makes you a nurturing presence in everyone's lives. But, for heaven's sake, keep a stain-removing pen close by; those kiddie snack accidents are the only tidal waves you want to tackle!

As we venture to the heart of the zodiac, there's the regal **Leo**, whose presence commands access to the most dazzling shades! Golds, sunny yellows, and hot reds reflect your vibrant charm, and the world— my dear Leo— is your stage! Think luxurious fabrics adorned in golden hues fit for a queen (or king— your royal status is indisputable!). Whenever you walk into a room, it should feel like the grand finale of a fireworks show—sparkling confident, and just a tad glorious! Wear those brilliant hues with pride, and trust me, you'll have everyone cheering for an encore!

As we round out our colorful journey, our stylish **Virgo** friends will appreciate clean, muted tones-think soft browns, earthy greens, and delicate neutrals that cater to your structured personality. Virgos thrive on organization, and so should your wardrobe! Custom-tailored clothes in soothing colors will complement your practicality while still making you look impeccably stylish. Let subtle shades elevate your polished persona, making "I woke up like this" your ultimate fashion mantra!

## ZODIAC STYLES: FASHION BASED ON YOUR STAR SIGN

**Libra** colors emphasize harmony and balance, reflecting their love for beauty. Drawn to soft pastels like pinks, blues, and greens, Libras appreciate hues that showcase their diplomatic nature. This soothing palette highlights their elegance and aligns with their desire for grace and aesthetics.

**Scorpio** captivate a blend of mystery and intensity, reflecting their passionate spirit. Drawn to deep reds, purples, and blacks, these hues embody their powerful, enigmatic aura. This magnetic palette is rich with intrigue, perfectly capturing Scorpio's bold and transformative nature.

**Sagittarius** are vibrant and adventurous, mirroring their optimistic and free-spirited nature. Sagittarians are often drawn to bold and energetic hues like royal blue, purple, and turquoise, which reflect their love for exploration and knowledge. These lively colors highlight their enthusiasm and zest for life, creating a palette that is both dynamic and inspiring. The overall color scheme for Sagittarius exudes a sense of adventure and curiosity, perfectly aligning with their expansive and philosophical character.

**Capricorn** are sophisticated and grounded, reflecting their ambitious and disciplined nature. Capricorns are drawn to earthy and classic hues like deep brown, gray, and forest green, which mirror their practical and reliable character. These colors emphasize their elegance and stability, creating a palette that is both timeless and refined. The overall color scheme for Capricorn exudes a sense of maturity and determination, aligning perfectly with their strong and focused personality.

**Aquarius** zodiac colors are unique and eclectic, much like their innovative and forward-thinking nature. Aquarians are attracted to unconventional and vibrant hues such as electric blue, silver, and violet, which reflect their love for originality and progress. These colors highlight their inventive spirit and desire for change, creating a palette that is both futuristic and inspiring. The overall color scheme for Aquarius exudes a sense of individuality and creativity, perfectly aligning with their visionary and independent character.

And lastly, enchanting realm of the ocean's dreamers, the **Pisces**. For Pisces, colors typically include shades of sea green, lavender, and soft blues. These hues reflect the intuitive and gentle nature of this water sign, symbolizing their deep connection to emotions and the mystical sea. Pisces individuals are often drawn to these calming and spiritual colors, which resonate with their imaginative and compassionate personalities.

Identifying key colors that energize and resonate with your zodiac sign isn't just a recipe for fashion success; it's a brilliant way to harmonize your personal style with the universe. Play, experiment, and express yourself through color! Embrace those astrological hues with the passion of a crochet-loving Capricorn or the playful curiosity of a curious Scorpio.

Remember, when your wardrobe speaks the language of your stars, it's not just fashion— it's cosmic couture! So go ahead, let your zodiac shine, and dress boldly, because those stars are waiting to twinkle in your fabulous getup!

## How to Incorporate Zodiac Trends Into Your Wardrobe

Alright, my stylish stargazers, it's time to unleash that inner fashionista and let your zodiac sign take over your closet! You've spent long enough at the end of the horoscope reading, wondering why your chosen brunch outfit isn't giving you the same cosmic energy as your astrological counterpart. Well, fret not, for I'm here to guide you through the whimsical galaxy of integrating zodiac trends into your wardrobe! So buckle up, because fashion is about to align perfectly with the stars.

First things first: tap into your zodiac sign's archetype and let it inform your personal style choices. Take sassy **Aries**, for example. They're all about bold statements and being unapologetically fierce. Picture rocking a rich red leather jacket paired with fiery boots, throwing in a touch of "I'm the boss of everything!" at your local coffee shop. As an Aries, think outside the box and don't hesitate to indulge in loud accessories or graphic t-shirts that scream confidence. The goal is to embrace those Aries vibes in colors and fabrics that elevate your fiery mood. Pair those killer

## ZODIAC STYLES: FASHION BASED ON YOUR STAR SIGN

heels with a leather mini skirt, and voilà! Your zodiac aura is radiating.

Now, let's stroll over to the delightful **Taurus**, the sign known for its love of comfort and luxury. If you're a Taurus, your wardrobe can be a tactile explosion of soft textures and elegant silhouettes. Imagine draping yourself in silky fabrics and cozy cashmere, all while looking as chic as a high-end café manager who's just served a molecular gastronomy coffee. The key is to choose quality over quantity. Invest in those stunning pieces that make you feel like you're pampering yourself, whether it's a plush robe that you somehow convince yourself is perfect for running errands or an eye-catching emerald, green flowy dress, complete with a pair of fashionable flats! Let your zodiac sign guide your pursuit of elegance and quality.

Onward we go to our charming **Gemini**, who thrives on duality and trends that change faster than your mood when the Wi-Fi goes down. For my lovely Geminis, mixing prints and colors is the name of the game! Feel free to channel those eclectic vibes by adopting layering techniques that keep you versatile. Maybe you're feeling bohemian today with a crochet top paired with a bright plaid skirt- why not, right? Experimentation is your strong suit! Combine casual with classy and let your clothing choices reflect your myriad moods. Incorporate vibrant accessories that can shift with your outfits, like a playful scarf that can double as a headband— great for those times you spill your matcha latte and need to hide the evidence. Trust me, those fashion risks lead to the most interesting conversations at brunch!

As we sashay to our tender-hearted **Cancer**, it's time to embrace soft, romantic styles that will transport you to cloud nine. Think of flowing maxi dresses and cozy oversized sweaters topped with artisanal prints- sweaters that just scream "I bake cookies for everyone!" When incorporating zodiac trends, don't shy away from introducing sentimental elements to your ensemble, even if it's just a pearl necklace your mother passed down.

Your outfits can showcase your nurturing spirit while exuding warmth and comfort. Layering is still your friend; combine those delicate pastels with comfy rubber-soled shoes, and you'll be the epitome of sophisticated coziness!

Now, let's not forget the glorious **Leo**! If your mane is gorgeous and you're ready to unleash your royal flair, why not incorporate dazzling statement pieces into your wardrobe? Always opt for outfits that demand attention! Wear that eye-catching sequined top and pair it with tailored high-waisted trousers that make your legs look like they should be gracing the covers of fashion magazines. For accessories, think large, ornate necklaces that simultaneously establish you as a style icon and human disco ball! Incorporate trends by linking back to your regal nature; lavish textures with pops of gold and bold reds will bring out that confident roar.

Moving on to our industrious **Virgo** friends, you'll want to channel those organizational skills into creating staple outfits that are nothing short of timeless. Simplicity is chic! You can upgrade your classic white collared shirt with tailored pants while layering a stunning beige trench coat-because who doesn't love a good trench?

**Libra**, ruled by Venus, is known for elegant and balanced fashion. They favor classic, sophisticated styles with a modern twist, often in neutral tones with soft pastels or jewel accents. Libra accessories include delicate jewelry and stylish handbags or scarves, enhancing their charm and love for beauty.

**Sagittarius**, known for its adventurous and free-spirited nature, often embraces bold and eclectic fashion choices. They are drawn to vibrant colors and patterns that reflect their love for exploration and travel. Sagittarius enjoys mixing styles, often blending casual with exotic elements. Accessories for Sagittarius might include bohemian jewelry, wide-brimmed hats, or unique travel-inspired pieces. They appreciate items that express their individuality and wanderlust, capturing their energetic and optimistic spirit. **Capricorn**, are practical and sophisticated, favors timeless, structured styles in neutral tones like black, gray, navy, and brown. Their wardrobe includes tailored pieces and elegant silhouettes. Accessories are understated yet refined, such as quality watches,

## ZODIAC STYLES: FASHION BASED ON YOUR STAR SIGN

leather bags, and minimalist jewelry, reflecting their disciplined and ambitious nature.

**Aquarius**, with their original and forward-thinking nature, often gravitates towards unique and unconventional fashion choices. They love experimenting with bold colors, futuristic designs, and eclectic patterns. Aquarius enjoys expressing individuality through innovative and quirky styles. Accessories for Aquarius might include avant-garde jewelry, statement sunglasses, or tech-inspired gadgets. They appreciate items that highlight their creativity and progressive mindset, embodying their visionary and independent spirit. Ahhh... my fellow **Pisces**, known for their dreamy and artistic nature, favors romantic and ethereal styles with soft, flowing fabrics and pastel colors. They incorporate fantasy and creativity into their looks. Accessories may include delicate jewelry, scarves, or pieces with sparkle or mystical symbolism, reflecting their imaginative and compassionate spirit. Your zodiac trend can be as straightforward as finding impeccable, well-made pieces that never go out of style. Think of key investments like quality denim, sophisticated blazers, and well-tailored trousers that make you feel like an all-star at every meeting. And let's be real, these essential pieces are perfect for concealing toddler-related messes and still having you strut out looking like a fashionista ready for a runway!

Incorporating zodiac trends into your wardrobe doesn't have to feel like an astronomical task— it can be a whimsical journey of self-expression!

Embrace the colors, fabrics, and personal styles that align with your unique star sign. From becoming the fiery force of nature, that is Aries, to the gentle embrace of nurturing Cancer, every zodiac sign has its aesthetic flair and fabulous possibilities. So, shake your celestial tail feathers and let the stars guide your style, because when your wardrobe resonates with your cosmic essence, YOU become the universe's most fashionable exhibit!

## Pieces of Clothing and Accessories for Each Sign

Fabulous fashion enthusiasts, here we are again, ready to merge the celestial with the sartorial! As we continue to unlock the secrets of the zodiac, I present to you the ultimate guide to wardrobe essentials that align with each sign. You see, dear readers, each zodiac sign has a distinct personality, and with personality comes an accompanying ensemble just waiting to be unveiled. So, grab your astrological chart and perhaps some inexpensive wine— in case your wardrobe needs an emergency makeover as we take a hilarious yet enlightening journey through the celestial fashion landscape!

Let's kick things off with our impulsive and fabulous Aries. **Aries**, you fierce fireball! You thrive on adrenaline and excitement, so it's only fitting that your wardrobe consists of striking statement pieces. Think of bold leather jackets to make you feel like the ultimate badass; add some edgy graphic tees to let your rebellious spirit live out loud! Accessories? Oh honey, stack up those chunky rings and mix and match some big earrings that scream, "I'm here for a fashion fight, so stand back!" And don't forget those sultry ankle boots— because there's no turning back once you step into a room wearing those. A stylish but functional fanny pack— or "fashion waist bag," as I like to call it, will keep your essentials secured while you lead the charge into coffee shops and art openings, head held high!

As **Taurus** saunters in with earthy grace, let's craft a wardrobe that speaks to comfort, luxury, and the finer things in life. The ideal pieces for you, dear Taurus, are sumptuous fabrics that beg for a cozy hug. Think oversized cashmere sweaters in lush colors like sage green, paired with sofa high-waisted trousers that make you feel like you've just walked off a golden sunset. Your accessories should exude effortless elegance, like a pair of delicate hoop earrings or a classic leather tote that screams "I do yoga and sip green smoothies." And don't forget the ultimate indulgence: a luxurious robe that doubles as an outfit when ordering takeout at home. Because comfort is style! Now, let's dance into the world of **Gemini**, the ever-changing chameleon of the zodiac. For you, dear Gemini, the wardrobe is a delightful hodgepodge of eclectic pieces that reflect your vivacious spirit. Stock up on coats with vibrant

## ZODIAC STYLES: FASHION BASED ON YOUR STAR SIGN

colors and geometric patterns that will leave others guessing your outfit choice for the day. Layering is your secret weapon — think of flowy floral blouses beneath textured vests, all topped of with a sassy pair of photo-worthy combat boots. You know accessorizing is key and let your choice of playful jewelry come from carousels of option-layered necklaces, cheerful mismatched earrings, and even rings that sparkle like the stars. Honestly, avoiding style boredom is your superpower!

As we greet our sensitive **Cancer**, we must craft outfits that embrace warmth and comfort. Flowing maxi dresses in soft pastel shades are essential; they make you feel like you're in a perpetual hug while simultaneously channeling your inner mermaid. Don't forget to stock up on oversized cardigans that can act as blankets while twirling around your home. Silky blouses adorned with moon patterns or seashell prints can channel your nurturing vibes. Accessorize with delicate and sentimental jewelry, like a charm bracelet filled with treasured memories — the same way you collect invisible emotional baggage! Let's also give a nod to homey touches like comfy slip-on shoes that allow you to manage snack duties and fashionably greet guests alike.

Next, we arrive majestically at the dazzling **Leo**. Your wardrobe should be filled with show-stopping pieces that radiate confidence! Think along the lines of glittery tops, tailored blazers adorned with animal prints, and stylish statement pants that demand attention — and yes, they should be as dramatic as you! Accessorizing is paramount — why not crown your outfit with a head-turning statement necklace, perhaps even an oversized sun hat? Don't skimp on the bold colors, bright yellows and radiant reds are essential! And let's face it — with an outfit as striking as yours, a matching cocktail that matches your neon high heels is a non-negotiable.

As we transition to our perfectionist **Virgo**, let's celebrate the beauty of timeless simplicity. The key pieces in your wardrobe should be classic, structured, and oh-so-chic: think a crisp white shirt, tailored trousers, and a navy blazer that would prompt compliments at a business meeting or brunch. Your accessories should be minimalist but sophisticated -gold studs, a chic structured bag, and perhaps a silk scarf to channel your inner Audrey Hepburn. For shoes, think classic loafers or sleek ankle boots that resonate with your organized spirit. After all, you want to look put-together while ensuring your ensemble remains practical enough to chase after chaotic toddlers! **Libra**, the zodiac's fashionista, adores a wardrobe that screams "I woke up like this" elegance. They're all about those sophisticated styles with just a hint of romance, like a rom-com hero on a catwalk. Colors? Think soft pinks and blues—pastels as chill as a cat in a sunbeam. Libras accessorize like pros, flaunting chic handbags, elegant scarves, and jewelry that whispers sophistication. They love anything that keeps them balanced and looking like the charming diplomats they truly are!

**Scorpio** is a mysterious enigma. They dress like they're about to star in a noir film or solve a crime in style. Their fashion sense is all about intensity and drama, with a wardrobe full of dark, moody colors like deep reds and blacks that say, "I mean business." Scorpios accessorize with pieces that have a hint of mystery—think statement jewelry that looks like it could hold a secret, or sunglasses that say, "I'm watching, but you'll never know." They have a magnetic charm and a style that's as intriguing as a plot twist in a thriller!

**Sagittarius**, the zodiac's adventurous spirit and world traveler, dresses like they're ready to hop on a plane at a moment's notice. Their style is a fun mix of comfort and flair, with a love for bold colors like purples and royal blues that scream "vacation vibes." Sagittarians accessorize with items that are both practical and playful, like a hat that doubles as a sun shield, or a backpack filled with stories from their latest escapade. They're the friend who show up in the coolest patterned scarf that could double as a map, ready to take you on a spontaneous adventure!

**Capricorn**, the CEO, dresses like they're about to close a major business deal at all times. Their style is all about classic elegance and sophistication, with a wardrobe full of power suits and timeless pieces that say, "I'm in charge." They favor colors like sleek blacks, grays, and navy blues—anything that pairs well with success.

## ZODIAC STYLES: FASHION BASED ON YOUR STAR SIGN

Capricorns accessorize with functional yet stylish items, like a high-end watch that could double as a time machine, or a leather briefcase that holds their secrets to world domination. They have a knack for making professionalism look effortlessly chic!

**Aquarius**, the quirky visionary, dresses like they're a trendsetter from the future. Their style is a unique blend of eclectic and avant-garde, with a penchant for vibrant colors like electric blues and silvers that say, "I'm ahead of my time." Aquarians love accessories that are as original as their ideas, think tech-savvy gadgets, funky jewelry that looks like it came from another dimension, or eyewear that doubles as a conversation starter. They're the ones who show up in an outfit that seems a little out there, but somehow, by next week, everyone else is trying to copy it!

**Pisces**, the dreamer and resident mermaid, dresses like they're floating through a whimsical fairy tale. Their style is all about soft, flowy fabrics and ethereal vibes, with colors like seafoam green and pastel blues that whisper, "I just emerged from a mystical lagoon." Pisceans accessorize with items that seem to have a story, like delicate seashell earrings or a scarf that looks like it belongs in a fantasy novel. They're the ones who can pull off wearing glitter as a fashion statement, and their outfits always have a touch of magic and mystery, making you wonder if they're about to sprout wings or swim away!

In this cosmic style adventure, we've carefully curated the must-have pieces and accessories for each zodiac sign, ensuring they truly resonate with their astrological essence. Fashion isn't just about fabrics and cuts; it's a vibrant expression of who we are— touched by the stars and uniquely our own, no matter how wild our planetary alignments may seem. So go forth and fill your closets with zesty Aries energy, luxurious Taurus comforts, dynamic Gemini twists, cozy Cancer vibes, glorious Leo statements, Virgo sophistication! And so on.... The universe is waiting for you to dazzle, so it's time to dress like the celestial being you are!

## Celebrating Your Unique Style Journey Through Astrology

My dazzling trendsetters! Today, let's embark on a fabulous expedition to celebrate your unique style journey through the intriguing lens of astrology. This isn't just any run-of-the-mill journey — no, no! We're talking about a cosmic fashion odyssey where the stars and your personal flair collide in a whimsical explosion of fabulousness! So, slap on your most outrageous statement necklace, grab a cup of herbal tea, and let's dive into this astra adventure together.

First things first: your style is as unique as the celestial bodies that influence your being. Each zodiac sign comes with its own flair, quits, and — dare I say — fabulous fashion faux pas that we must avoid at all costs!

Take **Aries**, for instance, with their fiery temper and adventurous spirit. Your style journey is all about embracing bold fashion choices that reflect your fearlessness. Celebrate your daring outfits and those moments when you slipped into a garish color and boldly proclaimed, "I can pull this off!" because nothing says "ignite change" quite like an oversized neon dress. So, wear that outfit with pride! It's your style journey, and it should be vibrant, audacious, and unapologetically YOU!

Moving on to steady **Taurus**, your journey is rooted in the joy of comfort and luxury, and let's face it, who doesn't need a little pampering along the way? Each piece of clothing you accumulate should be a reflection of your desire for quality and softness — the perfect sum of style and comfort.

Remember those fashion moments when you splurged on that snuggly cashmere sweater that felt so divine you nearly considered sleeping in it? Cherish those memories! Embrace the notion that your unique style should be an exquisite tapestry of comfort, elegance, and understated luxury, reminding everyone that a snug ensemble can be just as chic as a high-end ball gown.

## ZODIAC STYLES: FASHION BASED ON YOUR STAR SIGN

As we journey deeper into our astrological realm, let's twirl into the airiness of **Gemini**. Your style journey is a celebration of diversity! May I remind you of the sheer delight of mismatched patterns and swirling colors? Each outfit is practically a testament to your ever-evolving personality. Wear that mixed-print dress with a fierce confidence, and should anyone raise an eyebrow, just throw in a casual wink and say, "Fashion is a dialogue, darling!" Embrace the chaos of layering! Revel in those wardrobe choices where one moment you're a boho queen, and the next, you're channeling your inner corporate diva. Each metamorphosis is part of your glorious Gemini journey, capturing the essence of variability as you flit between vibrant personalities like a butterfly!

Now, let's not forget our emotionally intuitive **Cancer**! Your style journey sweeps through heartfelt sentiments and memories synonymous with cozy aesthetics. You don't just buy clothing; you collect pieces that narrate stories of love, family, and warmth-like that summer dress you've worn every family gathering for the past five years! It's these touches that truly celebrate your journey. Embrace styles that express your nurturing side-flowing maxi skirts adorned with floral prints that remind you of flower-crowned picnics. And those sentimental pieces passed down through generations?

Don't ever underestimate the sartorial power of a cherished heirloom necklace. Your style story is written in the stitches and fabrics of love!

As we roll into summer sparks, dear Leo, your journey is all about being larger than life! Your wardrobe should uplift and celebrate your radiant persona with dazzling colors, bold patterns, and the kind of oracle-like jewelry that leaves others starstruck! Revel in those moments when you strut down the street like you're on your own personal runway-after all, your style journey is poised for accolades! Wear those outrageous outfits and unique accessories with pride and remember that your journey is one of expression and power. Share those fabulous outfits on social media and remind the world to embrace their own uniqueness while channeling their inner lion or lioness!

As we welcome **Virgo's** practicality into our astrological stew, your style journey is a celebration of timeless elegance and meticulous fit. You have an eye for detail, and every outfit should resonate with sophistication. Whether it's a tailored suit perfectly crafted or a minimalist shift dress with matching accessories, your journey captures the beauty of simplicity. Embrace the fact that you thrive on organization - each color palette carefully curated to evoke both refinement and comfort. And let's not forget those moments of indulgence when you splurge on that designer piece you've been eyeing for eons! A well-timed investment is a testament to your style journey and dedication to self-expression. **Libra**, the style guru, blends elegance and charm with effortless grace. With impeccable taste, Libras favor sophisticated, romantic outfits in soft pastels and luxurious fabrics. They skillfully accessorize with delicate jewelry and chic handbags, creating a curated wardrobe of timeless pieces. Always ready for any occasion, Libras' fashion journey is a pursuit of beauty and balance, making them ultimate trendsetters. **Scorpio**, the mysterious figure, embarks on a fashion journey of boldness and allure. Favoring dramatic styles, Scorpios choose deep colors like black and burgundy, exuding intrigue. Their wardrobe features daring pieces with leather, lace, and statement accessories. Scorpios masterfully blend sensuality with sophistication, creating captivating ensembles. Their fashion journey focuses on making a powerful impression and embracing their enigmatic charm.

**Sagittarius**, the adventurous and free-spirited zodiac sign, embarks on a fashion journey full of exploration and eclectic style. Known for their love of travel and discovery, Sagittarians favor comfortable yet stylish clothing that allows freedom of movement. They gravitate towards vibrant colors, bold patterns, and global-inspired pieces, reflecting their wanderlust and cultural curiosity. Accessories often include bohemian touches like hats, scarves, and layered jewelry. Sagittarius' fashion journey is all about expressing their adventurous spirit and embracing a carefree, eclectic style that stands out.

**Capricorn**, the ambitious and disciplined zodiac sign, embarks on a fashion journey marked by sophistication and practicality. Known

## ZODIAC STYLES: FASHION BASED ON YOUR STAR SIGN

for their preference for classic and timeless styles, Capricorns gravitate towards tailored pieces and neutral colors like black, navy, and gray. Their wardrobe is filled with high-quality, versatile items that reflect their professional and polished demeanor. Capricorns often accessorize with understated elegance, choosing minimalistic and refined jewelry. Their fashion journey focuses on creating a strong, reliable impression, balancing tradition with a touch of modern flair.

**Aquarius**, the innovative and unconventional zodiac sign, embarks on a fashion journey defined by originality and individuality. Known for their love of unique and avant-garde styles, Aquarians embrace vibrant colors, quirky patterns, and unexpected combinations. They enjoy experimenting with futuristic and eclectic looks, often incorporating bold accessories and statement pieces. Aquarius' fashion sense is all about breaking norms and expressing their creative personality. Their journey is a celebration of individuality, making choices that stand out and reflect their forward-thinking nature.

**Pisces**, the imaginative and intuitive zodiac sign, embarks on a fashion journey filled with romantic and dreamy elements. Known for their love of ethereal and whimsical styles, Pisceans gravitate towards soft colors like pastels and oceanic hues. Their wardrobe often includes flowing fabrics, delicate textures, and bohemian influences that reflect their artistic nature. Accessories might feature mystical motifs or vintage touches. Pisces' fashion journey is about expressing their inner dream, creating looks that evoke a sense of fantasy and gentle elegance.

So, my cosmic companions, celebrate your unique style journey through astrology! Each sign brings its own fabulous flair and delightful quirks, allowing you to craft a wardrobe that captures your essence with glee. Your journey is not merely about putting on clothes; it's a vibrant celebration of self-discovery and expression. As you embrace the celestial influence of your zodiac sign, remember that style is fluid, personal, and always evolving- just like the stars themselves! So, strut your unique journey with flair and let the universe shine its light on your fabulous fashion adventures!

## CHAPTER II
# CREATING OUTFITS FOR EVERY OCCASION

**Understanding Different Occasions: The Fashion Spectrum**

The age-old question: "What do I wear?" This is a conundrum that all of us, especially those juggling toddlers and the demands of daily life, face on a regular basis. Fashion is like a buffet of attitudes, colors, and styles, and just like you wouldn't put spaghetti on a burger (unless you're at one of those experimental restaurants), you also shouldn't pick your outfit without considering the occasion. Let's dive into the fashion spectrum and unwrap this delightful parcel of misunderstandings and revelations.

First, we must accept that different occasions call for different styles. The notion that one can simply throw on a sundress for a work meeting, or slip into pajamas for a date night, is a fallacy that needs to be eradicated.

The fashion gurus have bestowed upon us the sacred motherhood of attire, but alas, in the chaotic world of parenting, it's all too easy to forget which attire goes with which occasion! Fear not, my friends, for I, your fashion superhero, am here to guide you through the maze of life events one outfit at a time.

Let's start with the playdate! Picture this: you're in a park, children running wild with energy that defies the laws of physics, and you, my dear, are standing there looking like a Pinterest board exploded onto your persona.

## CREATING OUTFITS FOR EVERY OCCASION

Playdates demand comfort, yet they shouldn't scream, "I just rolled out of bed and forgot I have a social life!" Opt for stretchy fabrics that could handle unexpected swings and slides, but avoid looking too casual- unless you want other moms to think you're trying to audition for the role of "The Hot Mess Mom." A stylish tee, comfy yet chic leggings and a pair of cute sneakers can elevate your look while ensuring you can chase down that runaway toddler who suddenly thinks he's a gazelle.

Now, moving on to the office. Many of us are required to make that dreadful commute at some point in our lives. But office chic isn't about wearing the same staid black pants and white blouse ensemble every day—the horror! Have some fun with it! You can channel your inner businesswoman while still letting your creativity shine through. Blazers are your best friends here; they take a simple blouse and jeans combo and transform you into a confident working goddess. And don't forget to accessorize! A statement necklace can whisper sweet nothings to your coworkers that "I mean business" while allowing you to express your zest for fashion at the same time.

Then comes date night, the equivalent of a superhero's transformation scene, minus the glittering cape (unless that's your thing). This is where you can really let loose! Go from drab to fab with a quick outfit change that will leave your partner questioning how they scored such a stellar catch. A little black dress is always a classic but give it some flair with funky shoes or bold colors. And if you're a mom who hasn't showered in days or is sporting the classic "I-stopped-the-kids-from-screaming-outside-the-school" hairdo, fear not! A good pair of statement earrings or a bold lip can draw attention away from the shambles of daily life you're juggling. Voilà! Suddenly, you're the glamazon of your evening!

Weekends, ah yes, the time for family adventures! Make sure to keep it stylish yet functional. Remember, we are not in the Olympics, and we certainly don't need to dress like we're ready for a marathon unless, of course, that's your family outing of choice. Comfortable yet chic outfits, like denim shorts paired with a stylish tank top or a cute summer dress, are perfect for those spontaneous outings at the zoo or the local ice cream parlor.

The goal is to look effortlessly stylish while keeping in mind that you might need to wrangle a child away from petting zoo goats at any moment.

Finally, we have special events- those delightful occasions that are often filled with joy, cake, and the inevitable horror of trying to navigate through a crowd in a formal outfit while spilling something on yourself. Whether you're dressing for a wedding or an anniversary party, always remember that comfort should never be sacrificed for style. If you can't dance the night away without worrying about ingrown seams, then it's time to rethink your outfit. A flowy, beautiful dress allows for movement while providing the charm that will have others asking you where you got it.

Understanding different occasions means opening alliances with your wardrobe, strategizing with intention, and of course, embracing your inner drama queen —because who said fashion can't be entertaining? So, the next time you're stumped by the endless possibilities, laugh it off, throw on something fabulous, and step out with confidence and a dash of irreverent humor. After all, life is too short to wear boring clothes, especially when you have toddlers to outrun!

## Play date Perfection: Balancing Comfort and Style

The playdate! A beautifully chaotic ritual where coffee-fueled parents gather to watch their little ones engage in a sophisticated dance of shared toys and the ever-looming threat of snack negotiations. It's in these playground arenas that comfort and style must harmoniously exist—no easy feat, I assure you. The mission, should you choose to accept it, is to look put-together while wielding the finesse of a ninja to tackle the imminent ketchup spills and inevitable tantrums!

You might be thinking, "Who has time to dress stylishly while keeping an eye on a toddler who thinks he's auditioning for the role of the next parkour champion?" I get it. You want to be the

## CREATING OUTFITS FOR EVERY OCCASION

mom who emanates effortless chic, not the one who looks like she's just finished a marathon in yesterday's pajamas. So, here's the magic ingredient: layers. Yes, consider your clothing as the supportive friend who always has your back. A layered outfit allows you to feel comfortable as you chase your tiny tornado yet still allows for sartorial splendor.

Let's talk about fabrics. Coming from someone who can appreciate the sheer resilience of a good spandex blend, stretchy fabrics are key! Leggings have made a glorious comeback in recent years. They're no longer just for lounging in front of the TV and eating ice cream (though they still excel at that too). With fun patterns and styles now available, you can channel the playful spirit of your kiddos while still feeling fabulous. Pair a pair of boldly-patterned leggings with a simple tunic—add a funky jacket, and voilà! You're the trendsetting queen of the playground.

Footwear, my fellow fashionistas, is another battlefield. Remember, you're likely going to be galloping across sandboxes, dodging unexpected rain puddles, and potentially navigating a chicken nugget minefield! Opt for chic, comfortable sneakers-yes, I said chic! There are delightful options out there that don't look like you just walked out of a gym locker room. Think stylish slip-ons or snazzy trainers that can elevate a simple ensemble while also allowing you to make a quick getaway when a rogue soccer ball aims for your head.

Now, let's discuss accessories - the often-underrated heroes of any outfit.

A distinctive statement necklace can distract onlookers from the fact that your kid just painted himself with mud from head to toe. Or perhaps a bright scarf can serve not just as a pop of color, but also as a makeshift bib or emergency blanket when requested during an impromptu snack when your little one insists on sharing half-eaten cheese puffs with their new best friend! You see, these accessories are more than just decoration; they're superheroes in disguise that come to your rescue at playdates!

Dressing for a playdate also means utilizing your magical powers of color.

Trust me, wearing bright colors doesn't just ward off the fashion cops; it makes you feel lively! When you wear a colorful top, it provides an instant mood boost. If the idea of a raucous group of 4-year-olds gives you anxiety, channel that energy with vibrant hues that say, "I got this!" Even if on the inside, you're screaming, "Please, just let little Timmy keep his snack to himself for five seconds!"

Remember, my stylish mentee, that confidence is your best accessory. So, embrace the glorious unpredictability of playdates! If you end up with a crayon scribble on your new blouse or grass stains on your new leggings, wear it with pride. Each stain is a battle scar showing that you've braved the tumultuous world of miniature chaos warriors. Your ability to balance comfort with style is proof that you're truly slaying the art of parenting.

Lastly, playdate perfection lies in finding that harmonizing balance between comfort and style. As you venture out to nurture friendships and support little ones, just remember to own your vibe, throw on that cute outfit that makes you feel like your best self, and prepare for the whimsical ride that is parenthood. And if you somehow lose a shoe in the process, it just means you're ready for a fun spontaneous dance party! So, go forth, fearless moms and stylish warriors, and conquer those playdates with flair, a little paint, a sprinkle of mud, and a whole lot of fabulousness!

**Office Chic: Dressing for Success Without Losing Your Personality**

The office! That wondrous realm where daily decisions require coffee stronger than your last three parenting-related escapades and where your wardrobe can sometimes feel like an extension of that boring corporate culture. But fear not, my fellow fashionistas, because dressing for success in the office doesn't mean you have to tuck away your personality into a dull suit that whispers, "I'm just here to clock in and collect my paycheck." Instead, it's all about finding that sweet spot between professionalism and a reflection of your unique self!

## CREATING OUTFITS FOR EVERY OCCASION

Let's kick things off with the foundation of every great office outfit: the good ol' blouse. Gone are the days when your only option was a standard-issue white button-down that makes you feel like an extra in a corporate training video. Oh no! Long live the flowing blouses adorned with whimsical patterns, vibrant colors, or even that quirky print of kittens wearing tiny bowties, because why should your wardrobe be as dull as the last meeting you sat through? Pair a chic blouse with sharp trousers- trust me, black slim-fit pants are your allies here. They're comfortable enough to maintain your mobility when you realize you've left your important document on your kitchen counter, yet still chic enough to assert that you have things under control. (Or at least pretend convincingly!)

And let's talk about blazers— the mighty armor of the office warrior. A well-tailored blazer can transform any basic ensemble from "I woke up late" to "I'm here to save the day!" And who said you have to stick to boring greys and blacks? Nah, sprinkle a little spice in your office life! Go for jewel tones— think emerald greens or cobalt blues that scream ambition while still feeling cordial. You could even make a case for florals, just avoid any patterns that would camouflage you with the office décor —not a good look when you're trying to stand out during presentations.

Footwear is another battlefield. You want options that declare, "I'm smart, savvy, and still know how to hustle" but that won't condemn your feet to a realm of agony as you traverse the office like you're walking through an obstacle course. Strappy heels may look fabulous, but unless you're accustomed to wearing them daily, you might find yourself marching back to the car with blisters and regrets. Enter stylish loafers or chic block heels! They're the happy medium between fashion and function, and you won't be fighting those "damn I-should-have-worn-flats" horror at the end of a long day. Remember, friends, a confident walk can sway meetings and allow you to conquer the corporate terrain while keeping your elegant fair intact.

Now, let's not forget the magic duo of accessories! They are like the cherry on top of that fabulous sundae we call our ensemble.

Statement necklaces, bold earrings, and fun scarves are an essential part of the outfit arsenal. Imagine strutting into the office with a dazzling necklace adorning your neckline, instantaneously moving from being just plain ol' the person who works in the corner' to 'the fashion-forward maven everyone wants to emulate!' Just be careful you don't end up channeling Picasso and have your accessories become more colorful than the office decoration, unless that's the goal you're going for.

Speaking of personality, the goal here is to communicate who you are through your clothing choices. Sure, you want to fit into the office culture (the last thing you want is HR calling you in because your blouse is too flamboyant), but there's no reason to mute the fabulousness that is YOU! If you have a penchant for funky prints or an eye for detail in accessories, lean into it! You can be professional while showcasing your playful side. A quirky pair of socks peeking out from your ankle-length trousers may be quite the conversational piece. Or how about wearing bright red lipstick that says, "I mean business!" while also demanding attention for your bold fashion choices?

Now, navigating office chic doesn't come without its quirks and pitfalls. The journey is peppered with office politics, unexpected spills, and passive-aggressive colleagues who don't appreciate your sparkle. Embrace the fact that confidence is your best accessory, and don't fret over the small stuff. Did someone sneak a sticky note onto your back while you weren't looking? Laugh it off, and strut like it was the latest trend. Have a wardrobe malfunction that leaves you frantically adjusting your clothes during an important presentation? Own it like a boss-ask if the meeting can be rescheduled for fashion reasons; it adds an air of mystery.

In short, dressing for success at the office should never mean chaining yourself to a dull wardrobe. Office chic is your chance to showcase your personality while conquering the professional world. So, throw on your confidence like a cape, add a pop of color, and conquer that cubicle jungle with flair! Celebrate the multifaceted masterpiece that is YOU; because the boardroom deserves your vibrant, bubbles-of-personality self just as much as

CREATING OUTFITS FOR EVERY OCCASION

the playdate. So go forth and conquer, my chic warriors— your office awaits!

## Date Night Dare: From Casual to Glamorous in No Time

Date night! That magical realm where parents emerge from the trenches of toddler land to frolic once more as sophisticated, somewhat-coherent adults. It's when you finally swap your warrior mom gear for something that says, "I still have it" while also reassuring your significant other that you remember how to dress like a human being. But let's be real: transforming from "mom who just survived another meltdown in the toy isle" to "goddess of glam" can feel like preparing for an Olympic event.

If you're anything like me, the pre-date struggle is real! You start with the question, "What do I wear?" It's often accompanied by your best friend-good ol' fashioned panic! From the closet, you pull out everything that fancy dress you haven't worn since your last bachelorette party (ah, the abs I used to have), the trendy jumpsuit that silently mocks you for your inability to locate a fitting room, and that cute top you just bought still waiting for its moment in the limelight. The goal is to strike this sacred balance between glamorous and practical. After all, no one wants to have to un-jeté their way back into the car after realizing they can't bend without bursting a seam.

Now, let's discuss the foundation of your date night appearance: the outfit! Every magical transformation starts with a solid base, and in this case, an adorable dress or chic combo is your best bet. For starters, consider the occasion. Are you heading to an upscale restaurant, or are you planning to take the scenic tour of your local burger joint? Knowing where you're going will elevate your sartorial choices significantly. If it's fancy, go for a flowy, stellar number that twirls just right when you walk. But if it's more on the casual side, a cute top paired with stylish high-waisted jeans could do the trick while allowing your gorgeousness to shine through.

As you work out these outfit dilemmas, keep in mind the importance of fabric. Nothing says "I'm free and wild" like a well-structured dress crafted from breathable materials. Seriously, choose something that won't have you sweating like you're running a marathon right after you walk through the door, because I can't tell you how many times I've improvised ways to lift my shirt higher to allow proper airflow to my pits. We've all been there, and trust me, it's not cute. So, pick fabrics that are comfortable and wrinkle-resistant, and you'll slay the night without the added stress factor of being an unintentional hot mess.

Accessories, my fashionistas, are the secret sauce! Statement pieces can elevate your ensemble from "I just got off a playdate" to "Look at me, I'm sophisticated!" A bold clutch —whether sequin-encrusted or minimalistic, adds a final touch that says you mean business while allowing you to hold your essentials (rumor has it, snacks fit quite well). And of course, those fabulous earrings that swing ever so lightly as you venture from one delicious cocktail to another. Just remember, if they're longer than your toddler's bedtime routine, you might want to reconsider how practical they are when the dancing starts!

Let's not forget about hair and makeup, my dear glamazons! A quick date night makeover doesn't have to be an elaborate regalia resembling a full-on runway show. A pop of lipstick can go a long way—because who doesn't feel instantly empowered with a punchy red? It enhances your confidence like magic. And if you want to go all out, a light brush of shimmer on your cheekbones can turn you into the glowing goddess your partner fell in love with before daily life set in. If all else fails, just toss your hair into a bun, and embody that effortlessly chic vibe we've all dreamed of. Call it the "I'm too fabulous for a hairdryer" look.

Ah, date night! It's all about the cozy dinner followed by the potential for a romantic stroll, or as I like to call it, the brave 'please-don't-let-me-wipe-my-face-on-my-clothes' adventure. Through it all, remember to enjoy the night and embrace the spontaneity that life has to offer! Wear that outfit that made you feel alive the moment you slipped it on and take the time to be present with your partner.

# CREATING OUTFITS FOR EVERY OCCASION

Date night is your chance to shine without the pressure of playdates or board meetings looming over your head. Revel in the transformation, relish in the confidence, and dare to flirt with outside-of-the-box style choices. At the end of the day, whether you show up in a dress that makes you feel fabulous or in those fun jeans that hug you just right, it's the sparkle in your eyes and the laughter you share that truly makes the night magical!

So, grab your favorite date night shoes, a sprinkle of glitter, and the joy of rediscovery — and remember, you're still the fabulous you behind that mom title!

## Celebration Ready: Dressing Up for Special Events

Special events! Those delightful occasions when we put aside the chaos of toddler tantrums and messy kitchens and don our fabulous outfits to celebrate life's milestones —birthdays, weddings, graduations, or even that spontaneous "let's have a party because we survived another week" gathering. But let's be real, my friends- the challenge of dressing for such occasions can feel like trying to navigate a minefield while balancing a stack of designer shoes on your head. Fear not, for I am here to guide you on how to channel your inner fashionista while still being the prepared supermom you always are!

The first thing to consider, naturally, is the event itself. Knowing what type of gathering you're attending is key! Imagine trying to wear a ball gown to a backyard barbecue— seriously, you might as well put on a sign saying, "I guarantee I won't fit in!" In fact, I once made that epic blunder, stepping out in heels ready for a gala, only to find myself dunking heartily into a kiddie pool full of brightly colored beach balls. Cue the eye rolls and snickers, am I right? So, read the invite carefully and decipher what level of glam suits the occasion you're about to crash.

Now, let's chat about the magical world of fabrics! Nothing screams I just completed a marathon" like an outfit that makes you feel like you're wrestling a sleeping bag with a belt attached. Choose garments that evoke a sense of elegance and comfort. Look for dresses that hug you in all the right places without feeling like a Victorian corset. Midi dresses make for a fabulous option — sassy yet sophisticated, they tumble down your legs like a gentle waterfall, perfect for any occasion. Pairing them with chic flats or block heels ensures you can dance the night away without worrying about twisted ankles or toe-crushing moments.

Let's not forget that special color palette! We all have our go-to shades that enhance our natural beauty. This is the moment to trade in your every-day neutrals for something that pops — a little vibrance, a little sparkle! Think jewel tones or pastel hues that hint at your cheerful disposition without screaming, "Look at me, I'm here to steal the spotlight!" If you're feeling sassy, ross in a foral pattern that captivates while also ensuring you smell mildly of "garden party," which is much better than "last week's leftovers" any day of the week.

Speaking of captivating— accessories, my darling, are your best friends! A statement necklace can turn an ordinary outfit into something explosive. You heard me, the "kaboom" your look so desperately needs! Opt for eye-catching jewelry pieces that complement your outfit while adding an extra layer of pizzazz. However, be cautious of a necklace that could potentially be used as a weapon if your toddler decides that it's their next target during the "let's play with mom's shiny things" game. The last thing you need during cake-cutting is to be ensnared by your own fabulousness!

And let's talk about makeup. Because when you're ready to step into the limelight, you want to feel like the glamorous fairy godmother you are! A splash of foundation, a dab of blush, and a few strokes of mascara can work wonders- turning you from "someone who wrestled cereal and crayons that morning" to "the dazzling diva." And let's not forget lipstick, the magical wand of confidence! You can rock a bold red that says, "I mean business" or a slick-nude that'll make you feel approachable yet sophisticated, like the dazzling goddess you are.

## CREATING OUTFITS FOR EVERY OCCASION

Finally, as you prepare for these celebratory events, don't forget to embrace your inner confidence! Know that you are more than just a beautifully dressed mom, you are a brilliantly bold force ready to take on whatever challenges dance into your life! Position yourself in the celebrations that inspire joy and laughter. Don't forget to soak in every "Congrats!" and "You look amazing!" because you know you do, inside and out!

In closing, being celebration-ready is all about striking a fabulous balance between elegance and authenticity while embracing the joyful chaos of life. Whether you're swirling on the dance floor, indulging in cake, or capturing snapshots of laughter-filled moments with family and friends, the outfit you've chosen is an extension of the love and warmth that defines you. So, go ahead and celebrate like there's no tomorrow! Put on that splendid outfit, strut your stuff like the fabulous supermom you are, and remember: every celebratory moment is another fabulous chapter in your vibrant story. Cheers to you, gorgeous!

## CHAPTER 12
# THE ART OF LAYERING: STYLE AND FUNCTION

**Understanding the Basics of Layering**

When it comes to fashion, sometimes it feels like you need a degree in physics just to figure out how to wear a simple outfit without looking like a walking pile of laundry. Enter the art of layering— a technique that can take you from frumpy to fabulous, all while keeping you one step ahead of the weather. Think of layering as your stylish best friend who always knows just what to say to make you feel warm and cozy while ensuring you look like you just walked off the runway.

First things first, let's get the basics out of the way. Layering is essentially the process of wearing multiple articles of clothing on top of each other, and trust me, it's not just about avoiding an awkward goose chase to the thermostat every five minutes when the temperature dips or spikes. To layer effectively, you need to consider the three key layers: the base layer, the middle layer, and the outer layer. Now, don't roll your eyes yet; I promise it isn't as boring as it sounds! Picture your outfit like a delicious cake—only this cake won't give you a sugar rush followed by a regrettable crash. Each layer contributes to the overall flavor of your look, and when done right, the results are nothing short of mouthwatering!

The base layer is your foundation; the superhero of your outfit is about comfort and fit. Let's face it, nobody wants to be tugging and pulling at a tight turtleneck while chasing after toddlers (trust me, I

## THE ART OF LAYERING: STYLE AND FUNCTION

know.). Think breathable tank tops, sleek bodysuits, or lightweight long sleeves that skim your silhouette without constraining it.

The goal here is to give you that "I woke up like this" vibe without actually looking like you did after a sleepless night dealing with diaper explosions. Let's face it, who needs sleep when you can master the art of looking fabulous while juggling life's hilarious circus acts?

Next comes your middle layer, also known as the MVP (Most Valuable Piece). This is where the fun begins! This layer allows you to add texture, color, and perhaps even a hint of drama to your outfit. Think cardigan, blazers, or floaty capes that effortlessly transition you from playdates to coffee dates (because you totally deserve that caffeine fix!). Remember, this is your chance to let your inner drama queen out to play without needing a grand applause. Want plaid? Go for it! Floral patterns? Yes, please!

Remember: if you're channeling your inner fashionista, every layer is an opportunity to express yourself. Just be careful not to look like you raided your grandma's closet unless that's the vibe you're going for — vintage is a strong aesthetic, but also very specific!

Now we come to the pièce de résistance: the outer layer, the mighty fortress against the elements. This is your superhero cape, the one that seals the deal on your whole look while protecting you from the universe's weather whims. Choose a statement coat, a chic denim jacket, or even that funky oversized puffer (because let's face it, they're great for hiding two-week-old leftovers in your pockets, creative snacks when on-the-go!).

The outer layer should not only provide coverage but also weave the magic between the previous two layers, pulling everything together in a confection so chic that even fashion critics will be left speechless.

Now, layering isn't without its pitfalls. I mean, we all have that one friend who looks like they're auditioning for a role as a walking closet after they've decided to pile on too many layers— at least, I hope you aren't that friend! Finding the perfect balance is essential, so avoid looking like someone dropped an entire thrift store on you. When in doubt, do the "Oh wow!" test: if you catch a glimpse of yourself and think "Oh wow, I look like I'm about to climb a mountain" instead of "Oh wow, I look fabulous," it's time to reassess your layers.

So, there you have it-layering, demystified! Whether you're cozying up indoors or braving the chilly outdoors, the art lies in enjoying the process and letting your personality shine through. As you embrace this beautiful technique, let the world witness your stylish feats of architectural fashion genius, all while managing life's delightful chaos. Now go ahead, layer up my fabulous friends, and conquer the world one cozy outfit at a time!

## Choosing the Right Fabrics for Layering

Oh, the joy of fabric selection! Choosing the right materials for layering is like setting the mood for a fabulous dinner party: it can make the difference between an elegant evening or a chaotic scene with spaghetti flung across the room. The task may seem daunting, but don't worry, I'm here to help you navigate this textile treasure trove. Let's dive into a world where fabric choices are as essential as coffee on a Monday morning.

First things first, you need to consider the weight of the fabric, which is the backbone of any successful layering strategy. Light fabrics like cotton, jersey, and silk are your new besties for those base layers. Think about it- when you're running after your toddlers or dodging conversations with that one relative at family gatherings, you don't want to feel like you're encased in a heavy woolen blanket that someone's conveniently draped over you. Lightweight materials are breathable, keep you comfy, and ensure that you don't end up resembling a Michelin Man impersonator. You want layers that move with you, after all, not layers that require their own personal space!

But then, there's the enchanting world of medium-weight fabrics. This is where layering dreams start to come alive! Fabrics like denim, poplin, and light knits offer that delightful balance between warmth and breathability.

## THE ART OF LAYERING: STYLE AND FUNCTION

Opt for these in your middle layer, allowing you to express your unique style without heading straight into the fashion hall of shame. Is it just me, or do we all have a friend who rocks that middle layer just a little too hard, and suddenly looks like a lost 90s boy band member? Not that there's anything wrong with it, just make sure that your layers say "effortlessly chic and not "my closet threw up on me"!

Of course, one cannot forget the outer layer— the crowning glory of any outfit—where heavier fabrics reign supreme! This is where wool, leather, and massive puffer jackets come into play! Yes, my fabulous fashionistas, embrace those bold materials that instantly transform you into a stylish shield against winter's icy wrath. In these pieces, you'll not only look like a fashionista, but you'll also be prepared for anything life- or the weather — throws your way. The outer layer gives you the freedom to layer up without being concerned about looking like a potato running from the cold, because let's face it, nobody wants to look like they belong in a vegetable patch.

Speaking of looking stylish, let's talk about fabric texture options. Some may think a plain cotton shirt is the ticket to style town, but I beg to differ. Short of belting steaming piles of fabric together, a touch of texture- think linen, corduroy, or chunky knits- will take your layering game to the next level. Mixing textures helps create visual interest. Just imagine: a smooth silk top underneath a fluffy cardigan paired with a rugged denim jacket. The fashion gurus would weep tears of joy at this magical trio! If you're going to layer, why not layer with style, darling?

Now, let's not forget the importance of fabric care! Can I get an "Amen!" for machine-washable layers? Because as fabulous as that delicate silk blouse may be, who's got time for handwashing and ironing in a world where toddlers are actively testing gravity at every turn? You want fabrics that will withstand the inevitable chocolate stains, spilled juice boxes, and who knows what else life throws at you. This isn't merely an expedition into the closet; it's a full-fledged battlefield! So, choose wisely and maintain your sanity with easy-care options.

Lastly, it's essential to listen to your body. Yes, ladies and gents, your skin has feelings too! Fabrics that irritate your skin are the emotional equivalent of a bad breakup-just plain unnecessary. Natural fibers like cotton, modal, and bamboo are generally your best bets. They'll make you feel good while keeping you stylish enough to turn heads. (Cue the dramatic music) the last thing you want is a sneaky itchy layer ruining your day, making you feel like you just tried on that vintage wool sweater that has a mysterious connection to your grandma's cat.

In conclusion, friends, fabric selection is an art, a science, and a delightful adventure all rolled into one. Choose wisely, mix textures, and embrace comfort as your fabric mantra. With the right materials, layering becomes a seamless dance of style, allowing you to strut your stuff with confidence, no matter where life takes you! Now, go forth and weave your fabric dreams into a stunning reality!

## Layering Techniques for Different Body Types

The wonderful world of body types— where no two are exactly the same, just like our children's snack preferences! But fear not, fabulous friends, because when it comes to layering techniques, understanding your body shape can be the secret weapon you never knew you needed. Just as no snowflake is identical, every woman has her own unique silhouette, and that's something to be celebrated! Today, we'll explore how to make layering work for your particular body type so that you can strut with confidence, flip your hair like you're in a shampoo commercial, and ideally avoid looking like a stuffed turkey during Thanksgiving.

First up, let's chat about our beautiful apple-shaped ladies. If you're curvier on the top and a little more delicate around the waist (the quintessential "tummy area" as I like to call it), don't you fret! The fabulous trick here is to add layers that cascade elegantly down your body instead of clinging to it. Opt for longer cardigans or vests that create a beautiful vertical line. Pair these with a lighter base layer to give your silhouette that lovely flow without feeling constricted. And do yourself a favor: skip heavy patterns on your

## THE ART OF LAYERING: STYLE AND FUNCTION

top layers! Instead, channel those chic colors and textures that enhance your natural shape without adding bulk. Who says you can't feel fabulous while waltzing over to the toddler play area?

Next, let's give a nod to our hourglass figures, the envy of stylist everywhere! You lucky ladies have a defined waist and luscious curves that even the mannequins in stores drool over. The key for you? Accessorize that waist to glory with belts or fitted-outer layers that both highlight your lovely curves and give you structure. Layering tops with a peplum cut can create even more drama and look fabulously chic. Feel free to experiment with wraps or fitted jackets to emphasize your shape— trust me, you'll want to say goodbye to that oversized sweater that's taking up room in your closet. Remember, with great curves comes great responsibility, so layer accordingly!

For our pear-shaped beauties, the way to layer is all about balancing proportions and accentuating those gorgeous curves while maintaining an overall harmonious look. Focus on your upper body by opting for eye-catching jackets, statement robes, or structured blazers that draw attention to your shoulders. Lightweight tops are also fantastic for creating that lovely line, making your outfit flow harmoniously. On the bottom, opt for tailored trousers or dark-hued skirts that elongate your legs while keeping the attention upwards. The golden rule of layering? Remember that it's okay to have a little fun! Don't shy away from those vibrant patterns and colors that elevate your entire outfit, showcasing your playful side while keeping things elegant. Let your personality shine through!

Now, let's not forget our beloved rectangle-shaped ladies — those who are straight up and down without defined curves. You fabulous rulers can strategically layer up in ways that add some shape and femininity!

Play with layers that add volume to your upper body, such as ruffled tops, oversized scarves, or open cardigans. A-line dresses or flowy skirts are your friends— embrace their powers! Experiment with waist-defining belts above your layers to create that enviable hourglass figure. It's all about creating the illusion of curves while layering, so don't hold back on adding those fun textures and mixing fabrics!

For the apple shapes who are also blessed with a little more height, you want to add dimension and structure through your layering. Go for fitted underlayers that hug your form but leave room for a signature statement piece on top. Think of long tunics or oversized cardigans that make you feel "walk-the-runway" glamorous. Mixing prints can also add visual interest, so if you feel like channeling your inner fashion guru by pairing stripes with polka dots — go for it! Just remember to check for any potential dizzying effects before stepping outside; we don't want some poor parents at the playground to get a headache!

And finally, let's give a shout-out to the stunning inverted triangle body type, characterized by broad shoulders and a slenderer waist and hips. To create a balanced appearance, focus on adding volume to the lower body and accentuating the waist. Here are some suggestions: select V-neck or scoop neck tops to direct attention downward and opt for wide-leg pants or flared jeans to add fullness. Empire waist dresses can emphasize the waist and provide a balanced look. Additionally, choose jackets that accentuate the waist or include hip details for an hourglass effect.

With the right choices, you'll be turning heads faster than a toddler can throw a tantrum!

In the end, my glorious style warriors, remember this: layering is about embracing and celebrating the beauty of your unique body shape. Layering should feel like a fun fashion escapade, not a confusing puzzle you can't seem to solve. So, get out there, strut your stuff, and show the world that layering resplendence can be achieved by anyone-one fabulous layer at a time! Because whether you're a pear, hourglass, rectangle apple, inverted triangle or a tall drink of water, your style journey is a unique masterpiece waiting to unfold!

# THE ART OF LAYERING: STYLE AND FUNCTION

## Layering for Seasonal Changes

The glorious dance of seasons! Mother Nature's way of keeping us on our toes and our closet contents forever jumbled-it's like she just loves to challenge our fashion prowess! One minute, we're basking in the golden rays of summer sunshine, and the next, we're bundled up like a yeti because we inadvertently chose to wear our beach attire during a polar vortex. But fear not, my stylish comrades! Let's explore the art of layering for seasonal changes so you can keep looking fabulous while your outfits sing "Do You Hear the People Sing" —because one moment you're singing for joy, and the next, you're just trying to stay warm without resembling a marshmallow.

First, let's take a moment to celebrate summer! Oh, summer layering is like the elegant ballet of fashion, where you twirl from tank tops to breezy cover-ups, concocting a look that can handle those unexpected temperature swings. Start your base with lighter fabrics like cotton or linen that breathe as easily as you do when your offspring have decided that naptime is simply a concept for old people. Your best friends in summer layering are lightweight cardigans or chic kimonos that can be thrown over your outfit with one swift motion— all while dodging the kids toy tornado in your house. Just resist the temptation to layer with heavy fabrics that'll raise your internal temperature to the level of a cute little sauna!

Next up is autumn, my personal favorite! It's that magical season when leaves turn crunchy and nature decides to throw a fabulous color palette party! So how can you make the most of it while layering, you ask? First, grab your trusty crew neck sweater; it's the foundation for your fall look. On chilly mornings, start with a fitted long-sleeve shirt as your base layer yes, fight the urge to pull out that cozy oversized hoodie just yet!). Add the crew neck sweater and top it off with a stylish trench coat or an irresistible leather jacket. Trust me, nothing screams fall fabulousness like walking into a coffee shop sporting a carefree yet put-together look while holding a pumpkin spice latte like it's a trophy of your effortless style mastery!

As temperatures begin to dip further, winter comes strutting in like that friend who thinks they can order five different appetizers and share them all with you. It's a significant challenge for layering, but you're up to the task! First, embrace the magic of thermal tops (yes, those might make you feel like a walking space heater, but your warmth will thank you!).

Opt for lightweight fabrics that can trap the heat, such as merino wool or breathable thermal items. Layer your long-sleeved thermal as your base, a cozy sweater as your mid-layer, and let's get adventurous with that fabulous winter coat that makes you feel like you're walking on sunshine even in subzero temperatures! It's all about adding warmth without sacrificing style—you don't want to be mistaken for an extra in a snow globe scene either!

Now let's not forget to accessorize, because darling, even the coziest snowstorm doesn't excuse a lack of style! Scarves are your best friend during winter and can be layered with finesse to elevate even the simplest outfits.

Choose chunky knits that could double as a blanket or silk scarves that can play dress-up while doing battle against wind chill. And don't even get me started on hats and gloves — one should always be prepared for the onslaught of flurries while still looking as chic as possible!

And then, before we know it, spring tiptoes in like that one friend who's perpetually late — but I digress! The beauty of spring layering lies in the ability to mix and match all those lovely layers as the weather dances between chilly and sunny. Start with a comfortable base layer, such as a fitted tee or a stylish tank (preferably in a pastel to match the blooming flowers!). Add a lightweight cardigan or a trendy denim jacket to keep you cozy during those crisp mornings. As the temperature rises, you can shed off layers without compromising your fabulousness. Just remember, layering in spring is like playing "will they, won't they?" with the weather-so keep your options open and embrace that versatile spirit!

In conclusion, mastering layering for seasonal changes is an art form that requires a mélange of creativity, fashion sense, and the wisdom of Mother Nature herself. By understanding the unique

# THE ART OF LAYERING: STYLE AND FUNCTION

challenges each season presents, you'll undoubtedly nail that stylish layered look that translates beautifully from summer sun to winter wonderland. So, get ready to enjoy the seasonal show, because as you layer up, you'll not only keep warm or cool; you'll be turning heads and snatching compliments like a pro on your fashion runway! Now go forth, fabulous ones, and layer with confidence through the ever-changing mother nature strut!

## Practical Tips for Layering in Everyday Life

The beauty of layering in everyday life! It's like navigating a beautiful maze, where each turn can lead you to boundless opportunities for style while dodging muffin tops and wrestling with toddlers. As a mom who's experienced the hustle and bustle of daily life, I've cultivated a treasure trove of practical tips to make layering a seamless dance rather than an awkward shuffle. Because let's face it: if I must wrestle a moving toddler while bundled up like a burrito in the frigid air, I want to do it in style!

First and foremost, let's talk about the universal rule of thumb: start with a solid foundation! When it comes to layering, your base layer is the unsung hero of your outfit— think of it as the dependable sidekick to your fashion superhero. Opt for attire that fits well and feels comfortable. A great fitted tank top or a long-sleeve shirt in breathable fabric can act as a no-fail canvas for layering. Nothing ruins a look faster than base layers that pinch or ride up, leaving you feeling like the unwieldy dinosaur in a business suit. Avoid becoming a fashion disaster by assuring that whatever you layer next will effortlessly glide over your fitted base.

Once you've got your solid base, let's discuss the art of mixing and matching fabrics. This is where creativity meets practicality. Layering doesn't solely mean putting on ten different layers in an attempt to appear larger-than-life; it's about finding the right balance. Consider light and breathable fabrics underneath while introducing a slightly heavier material on top. For example, pair that soft cotton base layer with a flowy chiffon blouse, then add a cardigan made of cozy wool or cashmere. This not only maintains a functional layering finesse but also adds texture and interest to your look without costing an arm and a leg. Remember, every layer has its purpose— it must work harmoniously with its companions!

Speaking of companions, let's focus on the wonderful world of contrast!

Layering doesn't have to mean always sticking to neutral tones like black and beige. Play with colors and textures to create visual intrigue that pops! Imagine a marvelous explosion of colors and patterns that unfurl as you step outside, leaving every passerby astounded by your flair. Feeling brave? Mix patterns like stripes with florals— the sublime beauty of layering lies in experimentation! Just keep in mind to balance those bold patterns with more subdued colors to prevent looking like a hyperactive circus clown—unless, of course, that is your goal!

As we meander through the layering landscape, let's not forget about the magical power of versatility. Choose pieces that can easily transition through various endeavors in life, like taking the kids to the park or heading into a spontaneous coffee date. A tailored blazer can effortlessly polish up your look while also acting as a cozy layer for those breezy afternoons.

Remember, it's all about finding garments that can serve multiple purposes, so you don't end up looking like a wardrobe tornado exploded in your living room every time you open your closet!

Practicality is key, my fabulous friends, especially when you're managing the circus, that is family life. When selecting layers, ensure they're easy to take off and put back on, especially when you're dodging the chaos of a playground or the hustle and bustle of grocery shopping. Have you ever tried wrestling off a coat only to discover your twin toddlers have decided it's a game of tug of war? Avoid cumbersome garments that might turn you into a fashion hostage during your daily endeavors. Instead, lightweight pieces are your allies in such capers!

When it comes to accessories, opt for pieces that enhance your layered look without overwhelming it. Lightweight scarves can

## THE ART OF LAYERING: STYLE AND FUNCTION

effortlessly elevate your ensemble while remaining practical; just remember, if you land on that toddler's snack corner later, you can stow it easily in your bag rather than leaving it draped over a nearby structure like a decoration from your last party. How about chic hats? They not only serve a style statement but also protect you from those "mom, you have a huge leaf stuck in your hair!" moments when roaming about with the little ones.

Finally, embrace the magic of confidence! Layering can feel intimidating, especially when it requires a dash of creativity and an eye for detail. However, when equipped with these practical tips, you're not just dressing; you're crafting your personal narrative. So, wear those layers with pride. Strut down that street like a runway model, knowing that every layer you put on communicates who you are: a dazzling, multi-faceted individual capable of conquering the worlds of fashion and motherhood all at once!

As you embark on your layered journey in everyday life, remember practicality and style can and should coexist blissfully together. With a pinch of creativity, a splash of confidence, and the right layering tactics, you'll look like you just stepped out of a style magazine—albeit maybe with a trail of cookie crumbs following you! And let me assure you, whether you're navigating a playground or a boardroom, the right layers will keep you feeling fabulous and ready for any adventure that life decides to throw your way!

## CHAPTER 13
# FUN FASHION FOR MOMS ON THE GO

**Finding Your Fashion Formula: Comfort Meets Chic**

The eternal fashion conundrum: how does one maintain a stylish appearance while simultaneously keeping the comfort level on par with sinking into a luxurious cloud of marshmallow fluff? For busy moms like me who juggle toddlers, tantrums, and the occasional existential crisis finding that elusive fashion formula can feel like searching for unicorns in a haystack. But fret not, my fabulous fellow mamas, because I've unearthed the secret to marrying comfort with chic style. Spoiler alert: it may involve some creative maneuvering and a sprinkle of magic dust!

Let's start with the fabric-yes, the fabric! It's truly the foundational love language of every outfit. You want to be draped in materials that feel like a hug, not a straitjacket. Soft cottons, breathable linens, and stretchy knits are your new "BFFs". If I could, I'd wear pajama material everywhere, what a dream! But alas, we live in a world where showing up in pajamas might lead to some inquiries about our personal life choices. Instead, opt for soft, fitted bottoms that drape effortlessly and flatter those postpartum curves while still feeling like a cozy fleece blanket wrapped around your body. Think of it as the delicate balance between being a runway model and a pillow fort architect. How chic, you ask? Very.

Next on the agenda is the art of layering- my timeless go-to for effortlessly upgrading any casual look. Layering is like building a fashionable lasagna: begin with a comfortable base layer (think that

## FUN FASHION FOR MOMS ON THE GO

perfectly snug tank top), add some zesty seasonings (a colorful cardigan, perhaps) and top it off with the pièce de résistance — an eye-catching statement necklace or a sassy hat that says, "I'm totally in control, even if I just wiped snot off my sleeve." Ah, the enchantment of appearing both casually thrown-together and perfectly polished at the same time!

Accessorizing is where the real magic happens, my stylish mamas. The proper accessories can elevate your look from "I just crawled out of bed" to "I am here to take on the universe, armed with mom juice in one hand and a toddler in the other." Picture this: you're sporting chic high-waisted jeans with a simple top, and you throw on a bold statement belt. Voilà! Instantly, you're now the proud owner of an outfit that even the high-fashion gates of Paris would bow down to. And let me tell you, that belt has effectively transformed you into a goddess. Pair it with statement earrings and suddenly, your four-year-old's snack-stained shirt has become an extravagant expression of joie de vivre. Dare I say, it's practically avant-garde?

But let's also take a moment to discuss shoes, the not-so-quiet protagonists of our comfort-chic story. I'm a firm believer that the right pair can make or break an outfit and protect your soles from the relentless assault of tiny, dubious, sticky fingers. Choose footwear that doesn't come with the price of enduring pain reminiscent of medieval torture. Stylish sneakers or ankle boots blend comfort and flair perfectly, allowing you to tackle playdates without looking like you've just completed a 5K marathon barefoot. Think chic ninja warrior vibes here; you want to blend into your surroundings while still standing out, and sneakers can help you do just that.

Another delightful trick is embracing the oversized trend-loose silhouettes can be utterly freeing, especially when you're attempting to slay and conquer post-toddler chaos. Picture an oversized shirt with three buttons missing, paired with fitted leggings. Listen closely, the secret here is that the bagginess of the top distracts onlookers from the fact that you've possibly been living in mom mode while simultaneously giving an air of effortless style. Who would have guessed your pajama shirt could double as an eye-catching fashion statement? I'd call that a win in the 'fabulous yet functional' category.

Ultimately, finding your fashion formula is about blending what feels good with what looks good, without sacrificing either for the other.

Remember, as you navigate through self-expression, wear your outfits not just with style but with confidence. Trust me, when you feel good in what you're wearing, you'll tackle toddler meltdowns and challenges like the fierce fashionista you are! So go ahead, embrace your inner diva, and strut through life with that effortlessly chic look, marshmallow fluff clouds be damned! Fashion is about embracing who you are— beyond the toddler-hair-pulled-back look you occasionally rock. Have fun with it, laugh at it, and know that we are all in this beautiful mess together.

## Wardrobe Staples: The Perfect Blend of Style and Ease

Wardrobe staples— the unsung heroes of our closets! You know, those trusty pieces that transform between a chic, polished goddess and a disheveled mom scrambling through the wildness of a toddler tornado. These are the garments that hold our lives together, weaving a fabric of style and practicality into the fabric of motherhood, because let's be honest: if you're going to be wiping sticky fingers and dodging Legos, you might as well look fabulous while doing it! Today, we delve into the essence of wardrobe staples that scream, "I am effortlessly stylish! Oh, and I can also take down a toddler in a duel for a snack!"

First up, the classic white button-down shirt. This timeless piece is like the Swiss Army knife of fashion versatile enough to be dressed up or down for any occasion. Picture this: a sudden playdate that turns into an impromptu picnic. One moment you're in your comfy sweatpants, and the next, you're throwing on that white shirt like a magic cape, instantly going from "Mom, I'm not ready!" to "Hello, darling, let's discuss the price of gold!" The beauty lies in its adaptability: tuck it in for a clean, polished look, or leave it loose and flowing like an elegant superhero ready to save the day.

## FUN FASHION FOR MOMS ON THE GO

Bonus points if you manage to spill grape juice on it and still look like you meant to do that. A little Turbulent Tornado Charm, if you will!

Next, we need a solid pair of high-waisted jeans-oh, sweet denim! These magical jeans are the key to feeling put-together while still being able to reach the toy under the couch without wincing from discomfort.

High-waisted jeans embrace your shape, combining style and practicality in a heavenly embrace. They are the armor protecting us from the persistent tug of gravity while giving us that lovely hourglass silhouette that even Botticelli would approve of. Toss on a comfy flowy top and suddenly you're not just a mom; you're an icon. You could be strutting down the street, ready to discuss the profundities of life or, uh, just navigating the options in the snack aisle-it's all in the style, darling!

Now let's give some love to the little black dress. Ah, the LBD, it is the pièce de résistance in any mama's wardrobe! This enchanting piece is the go-to for everything from casual brunch dates to elevated espresso-fueled escapes in the city. Here's the kicker: it's also perfect for layering. You can rock that LBD with a chic blazer and heels for an evening tête-a-tête or throw on a denim jacket and white sneakers for a day out managing the chaos of your wildlings without losing your flair. And the best part? The moment you step into that iconic garment, you transform into the magnetic force of "See, I "do" have my life together!", even if you forgot about snack time and you have broccoli in your hair. So, if anyone asks, just confidently declare it a fashion statement!

Let's not forget the power of the statement accessory, because who says you can't have a bit of fun while navigating the toddler minefield? Think chunky earrings of a bold necklace that could distract anyone from the questionable stain on your shirt or, at the very least, draw attention away from the fact that you might still have breakfast lingering in your hair (don't worry, it happens to the best of us!). Accessories are like the cherry on top of the mom sundae— elevating even the most casual outfit into something fabulous and fierce. They shout, "I've got things going on, and I'm fabulous about it!" They can even be the conversational piece assuring anyone you meet that yes; you did plan this look— not just throw it together in a moment of panic a full two minutes before arriving at school pick-up.

Last but certainly not least, a comfortable pair of stylish sneakers. Believe me, these beauties deserve a spot on their own golden pedestal! When you're chasing toddlers of out-maneuvering rogue shopping carts, you want your feet to be treated like royalty. Choosing a sleek, chic pair can make you feel as though you're strutting the runway, ready to navigate life's many escapades.

Ever thought you could feel that hot? Sneakers will make you look like you're ready for anything, whether it's conquering that toddler Olympic marathon or simply surviving a grocery store trip that feels reminiscent to The Hunger Games.

So, there you have it, fabulous mamas, the essential wardrobe staples chat blend style and ease. These pieces are here to boost your confidence while keeping the comfort levels high enough to gracefully leap into action at a moment's notice. With these staples, you're not just surviving the wild ride of motherhood; you're thriving in style! So, mix, match, and most importantly, dance around your home in those wind-swept wonders, knowing you're ready for whatever adorable chaos your little ones will throw at you next. After all, life's a runway, and you're a star!

**Dressing Up Your Basic Tee: Elevating Everyday Pieces**

The classic basic tee—our reliable daily companion, the unsung MVP of the wardrobe world. It doesn't matter if you're a mom in the trenches of toddler turmoil or a stylish superhero secretly battling against the evil forces of laundry- this simple piece is a canvas ready for your fashion artistry.

Elevating a basic tee isn't just a noble endeavor, it's a quest to transform everyday into the extraordinary. So, gather around, fashion-forward fashionistas, because we're diving deep into the art of taking that plain, unassuming t-shirt and turning it into a show-stopping ensemble that will make everyone wonder if you

## FUN FASHION FOR MOMS ON THE GO

just stepped off a magazine cover-or at least off the page of your favorite IKEA catalog!

First things first, let's explore the magical power of layering. You might think a basic tee is already a declaration of "I have my life together," and it certainly is, but layering can elevate that declaration to a full-on Talk of style! Toss on an oversized denim jacket or a chic leather bomber, transforming your tee into a statement of laid-back coolness. Suddenly, your outfit is declaring, "I handle tantrums like a pro, but I can also combat the chill in the air." The beauty of layers is their ability to accommodate the wild fluctuations of motherhood — temperature-wise and chaotic-wise. You can conquer the local park and simultaneously conceal the snack crumbs adorning your shirt. So yes, my dear warriors, layer to your heart's content; it adds a sense of nonchalance that says, "I dressed up, but I'm absolutely "not" trying too hard."

Now, let's talk about accessorizing like it's an Olympic sport. Your everyday T-shirt is just waiting to be adorned with dazzling additions that can turn heads. Think of bold necklaces and ear cuffs that whisper sweet nothings to your neckline. A chunky statement necklace can be the superhero cape that transforms your basic tee into a Holy Grail of fashion fabulousness.

Why not drape your neck in layers of colorful beads or metal chains, proving that you mean business but can also rock the playful side of everyday life? It's like you're flashing a wink and saying, "Yes, I might have forgotten about last night's leftovers in the fridge, but I can create magic with a simple T-shirt!" A sprinkle of personality and flair is the fairy dust necessary to shift your everyday ensemble into something a little more enchanting.

And have we mentioned the power of printed scarves? Scarves are like the Swiss Army knife of accessories— they spice up any outfit faster than you can say "cuddle monster." Tie one around your neck in a chic knot, and your basic tee goes from "blah" to "brava!" in mere seconds. Feeling flirty? Drape the scarf over one shoulder for a casual, bohemian vibe. The possibilities are endless—wrap it around your wrist, tuck it into your jeans, or even transform it into a headband, because we all know a fabulous look should come with at least a "little" hair of the dramatic. Plus, if your kids try to steal or pull it, you can use it to playfully fend them off — fashion and self-defense at its finest!

Another way to elevate that trusty T-shirt is to play with texture and fabrics. Maybe it's time you explored unusual materials because why not bring out the inner style deity lurking within? A basic cotton tee can easily be swapped for a soft linen alternative, or one made from luxe jersey knit, leaving everyone wondering if you magically charm the fabric fairies for materials. Wearing lightweight, breathable fabrics will make you look effortlessly sophisticated, while still embodying that delightful spirit of comfort. If you find a tee adorned with playful textures-like ruffles, flounces, or cute little eyelets— snatch it up faster than your kiddos can swipe the last apple at snack time.

Let's not forget about your bottoms because pairing a well-chosen piece with the right bottoms is like finding the perfect dance partner. A fitted pair of trousers or culottes can elevate your entire look while allowing you the freedom to twist and turn with your little tornadoes. Sure, jeans might be the classic go-to, but don't be afraid to venture into the realms of patterned joggers or even wide-legged pants. You want something that tells the world, "It's casual, but "I'm sophisticated!" Achieving that effortless combination is an art form within itself teetering on the fine line between practical and luxurious.

So, my fabulous mamas, you see that dressing up your basic tee isn't confined to the realms of magic tricks of fairy dust. It's about confidence, exploration, and having a little fun with fashion. Embrace your basic tee for what it is: an open invitation to create, accessorize, and elaborate your fabulousness while celebrating who you are — the unstoppable, trendsetting mom ready to tackle the world, one stylish outfit at a time! So, throw on that tee, layer on those accessories, and strut your way through the chaos of motherhood because, darling, you've officially turned the mundane into something truly marvelous!

FUN FASHION FOR MOMS ON THE GO

## Embracing Bold Patterns and Textures for Fun

Bold patterns and textures! The daring diva's secret weapon, the vibrant armor that can easily transform an everyday outfit into a work of art Now, some may cower at the thought of sporting a geometric abstract or a cascading floral print, thinking, "Who am I to wear such audacity? What if I become a walking optical illusion?" Fear not, my fashionable coven of motherhood! I'm here to invite you on a journey of embracing bold design and textures that will elevate your style-game while also ensuring you look nothing short of fabulous— even as you're wrestling simultaneously with rogue toddlers and untamed crayons!

Let's start by talking about prints that demand attention— the equivalent of a confident redhead strutting into the room (you know what I mean). Animal prints, paisleys, polka dots, and daring florals are all entries into the style-playground where fun takes center stage. Imagine donning a leopard print skirt that makes you feel like a queen, ready to rule the urban jungle. You'll be turning heads as you confidently collect all the snack pouches from your little minions! Mixing print with practicality is like merging a little sophistication with chaos and trust me; it's an exhilarating ride. But always remember, the rule of thumb with bold patterns is balance, darling! Pair your fierce printed piece with those basic staples; think simple tees or fitted bottoms that make your printed piece sing like it's the headliner at Coachella.

Let's not forget about a fabric that raises the bar— texture! Oh yes, the allure of tactile pieces that beg to be touched. From sumptuous velvets to airy linens, textures can add a rich-layered depth to your outfit while simultaneously making you feel like you stumbled into a tactile wonderland. Seriously, who wouldn't want to feel like a walking cloud of chic? A textured knit sweater paired with sleek, leather-like leggings can send your look over-the-top, epitomizing the essence of "Oh, I just casually woke up like this." Spoiler alert: you didn't just wake up like this, but who needs to let anyone in on that little secret, right?

And let's discuss the joy of mixing prints and textures- as terrifying as that may sound! Think Shakespearean Tragedy meets Game of

Thrones. It sounds risky but hold onto your hats because it can work wonders!

Imagine an elegant floral blouse paired with a striped pair of high-waisted pants, a bold nod to the eclectic yet harmonious vibe of 'who cares, I'm fabulous!' This act of rebellion tells the world you're a woman who embraces combinations that defy conventional wisdom or, as I like to call it, the modern mom manifesto! The key here is to understand that even seemingly clashing patterns can blend harmoniously if you consider color palettes. Stick to a unifying theme, and let your innate creativity thrive—I promise, your outfits will radiate pure joy as you skip through life like a well-dressed gazelle.

Now, let's address an unspoken truth: wearing bold patterns doesn't just unleash your inner diva, it offers a powerful armor against mom-induced chaos. When you swathe yourself in vibrant hues or eccentric prints, you become a beacon of color amidst the frantic whirlwind of picky eaters and toy disasters! Kids often find joy in coloring outside the lines, so why not embody that spirit yourself? It's like your outfit could be a firm "mom-life" statement, one that declares that while you might have encountered a rogue chocolate finger on your sleeve, your outfit still radiates "I'm fabulously fierce". Ahh, and let's not forget the magnetic power of accessorizing with boldness! Statement accessories that reflect your personality can be the cherry on top of your sartorial sundae. You could wear a wildly patterned scarf around your neck, allowing it to dance around your shoulders as you conquer the school drop-off line. Large earrings in contrasting patterns add that "I just invested in popcorn" charm while sending a clear message: "I'm here and fabulous!" Keep in mind that even the boldest patterns deserve the thrill of the spotlight, and your accessories and layering can amplify that. Ultimately, embracing bold patterns and textures is about joy and self-expression -a celebration of your uniqueness as a mother and woman.

You're not just dressing to cover your beautiful self; you're adding layers that echo your vibrant spirit and individuality. So, go boldly into that wild world of patterns, textures, and overall fabulosity!

## FUN FASHION FOR MOMS ON THE GO

Give life to your outfits, infuse them with fun, and unleash your most stylish self as you tackle tantrums, impromptu dance parties, and unexpected messes. Because darling, when you embrace boldness, you're not just wearing an outfit; you're embodying an attitude— a statement—a fabulous way of life! Now, go ahead and let your wardrobe roar!

### Mixing Comfort with Personal Flair: Your Unique Style

The enigmatic dance of comfort and personal flair— a ritual as essential to the modern mom as ensuring you've always got snacks on hand! If you're anything like me, finding that exquisite balance between feeling fabulous and remaining comfortable while navigating the full-scale hurricane that is motherhood can sometimes feel like a high-stakes game of fashion Jenga. But fear not, my fellow warrior queens, because I'm here to guide you through the enchanting labyrinth of mixing comfort with your unique style, allowing you to step out into the world both feeling cozy and looking effortlessly chic.

Let's kick things off with the foundation of any fabulous outfit: "the fit." It begins with knowing your lovely body shape and embracing it like it's an old friend. You see, a great outfit is like a beautiful symphony, and your unique flair becomes the crescendo of that melody. Whether you're curvy, athletic, petite, or towering over the crowd (and likely dodging basketballs during pick-up time), it is vital to choose silhouettes that feel good. When you wear clothes that complement your shape, you're not just fashioning a look; you're telling the universe, "Here I am, confident and ready to slay!" So, unleash that magic fit, my fabulous friends, and wander through your wardrobe as though you're shining under the spotlight.

Color is another powerful tool in your arsenal of unique flair. It's like the secret sauce that turns a mediocre dish into a culinary delight. Think of colors as your style's personality! Do you crave the vibrant energy of reds and yellows, or perhaps the soothing measures of pastels? My advice: wear colors that evoke joy and make you feel like a billion bucks. Because guess what? What you put on your body truly affects how you feel throughout the day! Picture yourself rocking a sunny yellow top while chasing your toddler through the park, transforming you into the radiant sunbeam illuminating the chaos of dozens of playdates. It's all about channeling the vibes that fuel your spirit while simultaneously wrapping yourself in comfort.

Now let's dive into the realm of layering— because, oh honey, layers can do more than just keep you warm! They provide the perfect opportunity to flaunt your unique flair while sustaining comfort. A lightweight tank top can be the base layer for any ensemble, and don't you dare forget to drape it with that fabulous, oversized cardigan you've been hiding in the back of the closet! Not only is it chic, but it also brings warmth that can fend off that sudden gust of chilly air that might unexpectedly materialize while securing your child's wayward kite. Throw a belt around that cardigan to cinch it and create definition, instantly turning casual layering into a fashion moment worthy of catching the eye of the toddler mom brigade! Each added layer becomes another dimension to your style-creating personality, depth, and comfort.

One of the simplest ways to intersperse comfort with flair is through accessories. Imagine giving a classic outfit an instant jolt of zest with a statement piece— whether it's that bold necklace that shouts, "Look at me!" or those striking earrings that remind everyone that you mean business, even if you're still trying to decipher yet another game of "what did Mommy say?" Accessories are the playful, spirited children of your closet, ready to dance in the spotlight and amplify your individuality. Throw on a chic printed scarf or a wide-brimmed hat while leaving the house and bam— you've just transformed that basic jeans-and-tee combo into something that would make the fashion guru grin with delight.

Also, let's chat about the ever-glorious realm of footwear! Swapping out traditional sneakers for a more fashion-forward pair can transcend your look instantaneously. Whether it's loafers that whisper elegance or funky printed sneakers that scream playful spirit, your shoes are like the grand finale of your outfit. I personally adore a good pair of ankle boots— they provide comfort while boasting that extra flair of being "a little too cool for school"! Your feet deserve to carry the load of motherhood while also serving as a fabulous representation of your personal style choices. So, strut your stuff, ladies, and let those shoes do the talking!

Ultimately, my charming mamas, embracing comfort while mixing in your unique flair isn't just about throwing things together — it's an art form. It's the beautiful balancing act of presenting who you are while managing the colorful whirlwind of motherhood. Remember to find joy in your wardrobe, explore what feels good, and incorporate your individuality into everything you wear. Show the world that you're boldly and authentically you, even when life gets crazy! So go ahead, unleash your fabulous self and strut through your day adorned in both comfort and style because you, darling, deserve nothing less than to feel exquisitely chic while embracing your fabulous adventure in motherhood!

## CHAPTER 14
# PAJAMAS TO PARTY: DRESSING UP AND DOWN

**The Magic of Versatility: Day to Night Transitions**

As anyone who has ever faced the daunting task of dressing for the day knows, the real magic of life often happens in the span of an afternoon specifically, the fine art of taking your look from day to night. In the enchanting universe of fashion, versatility reigns supreme, transforming what was originally devised for playdates into eveningwear worthy of a 'Fancy Mom' award. If you've ever found yourself stuck in the bathroom, frantically re-applying lipstick while debating if it's too early for a glass of wine, welcome to the chaotic chic club! After all, isn't it marvelous how you can gleefully juggle tasks like toddler wrangling by day, and then switch gears to an evening of dazzling adult conversations with your friends (hopefully over wine and not soggy apple slices)?

Let's start with the basics - layers! Ah, the deliciously complicated world of layering. The pièce de résistance for any mother on the go— first, it's your daytime companion, then, in one dazzling swoop, it becomes the night's star attraction! A cozy oversized cardigan, for instance, is perfect for the morning hustle, battling the forces of tiny tots racing to the nearest trampoline. But as evening rolls in, add a cinched belt, and voila! You've just elevated your style quotient without losing a beat. You may have snuck in some extra snugness during the day (hello, snack-crusted knees), but in the glorious haze of night, you're a fashionista with an aptitude for style transformation.

## PAJAMAS TO PARTY: DRESSING UP AND DOWN

Next, let's chat about colors because, darling, nothing screams "I've got my life together!" quite like a color palette maneuvering from latte to bubbly. In the light of day, soft pastels or bold choices can create a relaxed vibe, showcasing your inner 'Mama Bear'. But when the sun sets, swap that cheerful ensemble for a much bolder hue. A striking red (or, let's be honest, anything that is not smeared with fruit puree) conveys "I am fierce and ready to conquer the night." Remember, you don't need to re-invent the wheel; simply work those colors to your advantage. After an afternoon of crayon disasters, emerging from the chaos in vibrant shades serves as both a distraction from potential juice stains and a declaration that you are living your best life!

Another delightful fashion trick lies within the enigmatic world of accessories. Think of them as the fairy godmothers of fashion — without needing to wave a wand or risk losing a shoe. By day, a dainty little pendant may do just the trick. However, by evening, you need to unleash your inner drama queen. Swap the simple piece for a chunky statement necklace that declares, "I am a sexy superhero wearing heels, in case you missed it!" The joys of accessorizing are immeasurable, yet I sometimes find it akin to a balancing act while on a tightrope-over-do it with a cocktail ring the size of a grapefruit, and you may inadvertently knock a few toddlers off course while holding an enthusiastic conversation about the art of finger painting.

And let's not forget fabric! During the day, soft and stretchy materials are divine, courtesy of the demands of motherhood. But you deserve more than just leggings and T-shirts! Don't shy away from materials that ooze glamour, like silk or satin, that can shift your silhouette from 'mommy on a mission' to 'glamazon swanning around.' Sure, large fluctuations in temperature due to kid-induced chaos might lead to small bouts of sweat, but throw a structured blazer over those loose-fitting clothes, and you instantly have achieved an aesthetic that would make even the toughest fashion critics give you a standing ovation (even if they are judging you from the confines of their living rooms).

Finally, one cannot venture into the evening without a nod to your magnificent mane. A quick tousle or a sleek ponytail can elevate your look in an instant. Just don't forget that, sometimes, crafting your hair requires a magical incantation as well! I'm convinced that fairies oversee the business of untangling four-year-old-inspired knots. The key to evening magic is simplicity — because we all know that spending three hours flat-ironing hair before a night out is not a viable option when your toddler is wrestling the couch pillows like wild animals.

In conclusion, embracing versatility from day to night is an art form, but one that can undoubtedly be mastered through practice and comedic grace. At the end of the day (pun intended), it's about channeling that inner drama queen and owning every outfit you stepped into, whether it was chased by children or serve classy cocktails. Remember, you're a fabulous mama — it's all about the transition! So, grab your tea, chuckle at spilled snacks that once were, and step out knowing you can dazzle at any moment because, darling, you absolutely can dress like the superhero you are!

## Wardrobe Wizards: Key Pieces for Transformation

The wonderland of wardrobe wizards-those magical pieces that can transform your look faster than a toddler can down a juice box. Just when you thought fashion was complicated, let me assure you, all you need is a sprinkle of creativity and a few key pieces that do all the heavy lifting while you manage to juggle life, work, and your adorable little tornadoes (also known as children). If my crystal ball told me anything, it's that a little foresight in fashion can enchant a simple ensemble into a show-stopping display of mom chic that leaves every soccer mom' on the sidelines gaping.

First up on our magical list is the ever-reliable "little black dress" or LBD if you want to sound a tad cooler. This stunning wonder is oh-so-versatile! Picture it: You're plucked from the chaos of toddler negotiations, and suddenly, as if by magic, you slip into this glamorous garment. With just a quick change of shoes and accessories (and perhaps an infusion of dry shampoo), you're

## PAJAMAS TO PARTY: DRESSING UP AND DOWN

speeding off to a dinner party-sans baby wipes and sippy cups—but it's still pretty darn glamorous! This isn't just a wardrobe item, it's like a trusted sidekick ready to save the day. It whispers elegance despite the toddler-apocalypse that might have taken place earlier. Plus, every drama queen knows that confidence is the best accessory!

But, let's be honest, what's a magical wardrobe without a pair of statement pants? Enter: wide-leg pants or those fierce culottes that have taken the fashion world by storm. I mean, who doesn't love a good swish while navigating a grocery aisle? Slip on a pair of these beauties, and I guarantee they'll elevate your appearance from chaos coordinator to chic supreme! Hiding a disaster zone under a billowing fabric? Now that's my kind of magic trick! Kids may toss food around with wild abandon, but with these beauties, you'll scamper around like you own the place while looking terribly sophisticated. And let's be real, fitting snacks through the side pockets is just a bonus!

Now, let's have a chat about the oversized blazer —you know, the one that makes you feel like you're walking down a runway, even if that runway happens to be strewn with toy trucks and crayons. This wardrobe wizard is much more than a clothing item; it's a superhero armor against the world's judgment! Throw it over your day look, and suddenly it's like you've completed a magical transformation. Add some sleek mules or a pair of snazzy sneakers, and you're off to slay another day! Blazer on? Meetings are tackled. Blazer off? You're ready to kid-wrangle like an Olympic sprinter!

Of course, let's not forget about the power of the wrap dress-the ultimate ally in your fashionable quest. It embraces curves, creating a silhouette that shouts, "Hey, I may have toddlers, but my style game is unmatched!" This dress can miraculously convert from a casual day look to an evening stunner in the blink of an eye. The best part? You can chase after your children and still feel like the belle of the ball! And let's discuss the immediate appeal of a wrapped dress that's merely two seconds away from a post-baby bod return —because who says you can't fashionably flaunt your figure?

Don't get me started on footwear, because there is a whole universe of transformation just waiting to be unlocked. Picture this: You're running late for a school drop-off, rocking some snazzy flats that could double as a running shoe. But once the dust has settled, swap those flat gems for some killer heels, and watch as you strut into an evening outing that would make Cinderella jealous! Yet, I implore you to invest in a pair that enables you to sneakily chase after your offspring without sacrificing your newfound sophistication.

And my favorite piece-last but certainly not least—is the magical accessory fairy dust, also known as statement jewelry. A chunky necklace or oversized earrings can transform an outfit from "meh" to "mama's got swag!" in a heartbeat. In a universe where children's laughter and screams often clash with adult conversation, let your accessories be your best conversational weapon. Or you can opt for something more subtle; I've even faked social engagement by wearing a giant pendant that distracts everyone from my over-caffeinated ramblings!

Lastly, magical wardrobe transformations are all about choosing the right key pieces that scream versatility while allowing you to channel your inner stylish diva (even if that diva sprouts from messy toddlers). With the right foundation in place from our best pal, the LBD, to those enchanting statement trousers, you can conquer any adventure life throws your way. So, gather your wardrobe wizards, embrace their power, and take on the world (while occasionally hiding in the bathroom for a quick moment of peace). Remember, you are the enchanting force behind your style journey, enjoy the playful chaos while wearing it fabulously!

**Accessorizing for Day and Night: The Perfect Touch**

Accessorizing! The delicate art of transforming an outfit from "I just rolled out of bed" to "I am the queen of the universe" in mere minutes. Let's be real; accessories are like the trusty sidekicks in a superhero movie, they hold the power to elevate your look and distract from the grim reality that you might be wearing the same yoga pants for the fourth consecutive day.

# PAJAMAS TO PARTY: DRESSING UP AND DOWN

Accessories can take the most casual of day-to-day outfits and whip them into a sparkling evening affair faster than a toddler can hide a crayon under the couch. So, buckle up, because we're about to explore the charming, chaotic world of accessorizing for day and night!

Let's kick things off with the humble statement necklace. You know the one— the chunky, eye-catching gem that can turn your everyday T-shirt into a dazzling ensemble! By day, this brave accessory can sit comfortably above a simple white tee, creating a look that's casual yet chic enough for school runs and playdates. I mean, nothing says "I might not have showered today but look at my accessory game!" quite like a glorious, oversized piece that glistens in the sunlight. But come evening, that same necklace can transform a sundress into something that says, "I'm ready for cocktails, darling!" Without even having to break a sweat. Just be careful, because you want to ensure you're not pulling a muscle when you whip your hair back while walking through a restaurant— you're trying to showcase that necklace, not audition for a pirouette competition!

Let's not forget about earrings— the delightful little adornments that can make or break your look. Daytime calls for understated styles, like classic studs or small hoops that whisper, "Oh, I just happen to have great taste!' as you navigate your way through endless toddler tantrums and snack chaos.

However, as the sun dips and your social commitments start to rise, throw caution to the wind and don a fabulous pair of statement earrings. You know, the kind that dangles like a disco ball and can outshine even the most spirited of toddlers during their "life is unfair" meltdowns. Wearing those beauties introduces an element of fun, even if it means having to explain to your children why their crash landing on the floor will not take out your jewelry. Just remember, with great dangling earrings comes great responsibility (and the occasional side glance from other parents who will either be in awe or debate whether you've lost your mind).

Now let's talk about bags, because darling, they are an essential part of this glorious accessory puzzle. You can never have too many bags, just like you can never have too much coffee— you simply survive on a steady supply!

By day, a cute crossbody or a practical tote is everything. It holds all the essentials: snacks, toys, and that elusive pacifier you're now convinced is a mythical creature. But when the clock strikes "Mom's Night Out," out comes the stunning clutch that can be metaphorically depicted as a wand of charm-it brings an elegance to your ensemble that can even distract from any "I was up all night" bags under your eyes. Just be prepared to swap your kid's 33 snack containers for that single lipstick tube because who needs practicality when you can look fabulous?!

Now we simply must address the impact of belts-yep, the unsung heroes of the wardrobe! During the day, a simple belt can do wonders to accentuate your silhouette and support those mystery sweets you stashed in the pockets of your LBD. It gives you that va-va-voom factor that says, "I've got it all together... sort of." But when the evening party beckons, upgrade to something more daring, a statement belt that cinches the waist and can transform that classic top into something that screams "I am ready to take the world by storm." Just don't forget to exercise caution while bending over to pick up the inevitable wayward toys; the last thing you want is to create a fashion faux pas because you're too focused on toddler survival!

Finally, I'd be remiss if I didn't mention the pivotal role that sunglasses play. They're not just for sunny days; they serve as a powerful tool for both day and night looks. During the day, a pair of stylish sunglasses can elevate your quick coffee run while simultaneously creating the illusion that you've just returned from a luxury vacation. As night falls, donning a chic pair of shades becomes a playful nod to the fact that you're too fabulous for the mundane, even if they're resting atop your head as you maneuver through dinner plans. Plus, they're there to provide a must-have excuse when you're not ready for those post-nap bags under your eyes to make their grand entrance.

## PAJAMAS TO PARTY: DRESSING UP AND DOWN

Last but not least, accessorizing is the true magic behind maintaining style amidst the chaos of motherhood. With the right pieces in your arsenal, you can seamlessly transition from daytime dazzle to nighttime glam without breaking a sweat. Remember, life as a mom may often feel like juggling knives while riding a unicycle, but you can still nail it with the perfect touch of accessories. So go forth, make that fashion magic happens, and embrace your status as the chicest superhero in your toddler's world! Afterall, when you accessorize to the nines, not only do you elevate your outfit, but you also create a delightful distraction, ensuring you remain the undeniable fashionista that you are!

### Fabric Choices: Comfort Meets Glamour

When it comes to the magical world of fashion, the adage "comfort is key" might just be the most overused phrase since the caffeine-fueled rise of toddler parenting. But hold onto your yoga pants, because I'm about to drop a truth bomb: comfort and glamour can exist in perfect harmony! Yes, my fabulous friends, we can revel in the joy of cozy fabrics that don't sacrifice an ounce of style while navigating the delightful pandemonium of motherhood. The right fabric choices can be the fairy godmother of your wardrobe, transforming you from "schlumpy mom" to "goddess who is definitely caffeinated" as you sip your cold coffee after dodging several flying Lego pieces.

First, let's delve into the wondrous world of cotton. This fabric is reliable and versatile, much like the best friend who always has your back during toddler meltdowns. Cotton offers softness that feels like a gentle hug, and let's face it: after being tackled by tiny humans, who doesn't need a cozy embrace? A casual cotton dress can be your best friend during those long days filled with snack time negotiations and impromptu trips to the park.

The fabric breathes, moves, and doesn't cling to your body in all the wrong places, which is crucial when you're chasing after little ones with sticky hands.

Plus, cotton comes in a variety of styles—think prints that can disguise ice cream smudges! So, you'll look as fabulous as a runway model, just with a side of delightful cake frosting sprinkled in.

Next up is jersey fabric-ah, the stretchable magic we didn't know we needed! This wonder material wraps around you like a warm, supportive cloud, allowing you to twist, turn, and dance as you navigate the adorable chaos that comes with parenting. Featuring twist-and-turn capabilities that rival the best acrobats of the animal kingdom, jersey dresses and tunics can effortlessly transition from morning playdates to brunch dates with friends (hello, mimosas, my old friend!). Just be cautioned on those particularly wild days when your mini mess decides that yogurt is a suitable form of body paint, the stretchiness ensures that the fabric won't pull a disappearing act when you least expect it. However, jersey silences that unspoken fear of becoming a "toddler art canvas" through the sheer virtue of its resilience!

Let's not forget about the enchanting texture that is chiffon. If cotton and jersey are your practical friends, chiffon is like that whimsical acquaintance you invite to every party because they spark joy. Drenched in glamour, this floaty wonder fabric has a way of turning a simple outfit into theatrical attire in less time than it takes for your kids to conspire to make a giant mess. With a chiffon overlay, you can transform your daytime look into something ethereal for evening outings! Nobody ever said you couldn't channel your inner fairy queen while ensuring your kids don't devour the last of your lunch. However, a word of caution: chiffon also has a tendency to billow dramatically in unexpected gusts of wind. Just keep that in mind when trying to reenact a dramatic movie entrance-it'll still look fabulous, but the result might end up being something you could send to America's Funniest Home Videos.

Now, allow me to introduce you to the chic versatility of spandex. This magical fabric is the secret weapon of all comfort-loving mamas, seamlessly providing stylish support while you bend over to pick up toys or deftly execute a pirouette while dancing to the latest nursery rhyme. Imagine perfectly fitted leggings with

## PAJAMAS TO PARTY: DRESSING UP AND DOWN

spandex that sculpts and smooth while lovingly accommodating that third round of cookie dough you munched on last night— because hey, life is short, and so are my patience levels sometimes.

Not to be confused with sweatpants, spandex allows you to embrace movement without worrying about awkward adjustments or the dreaded fabric wedgie. Throw on a long, flowy top, and you'll not only look chic but also have the ability to outrun any toddler who thinks sprinting away while making airplane noises is a valid life choice. Speaking of chic, let's have a word on silk- sublimely luxurious, it's the fabric equivalent of plunging into a bubble bath after a long day. Sure, silk might be a tad on the fancier side but hear me out. You can rock a silk blouse while pretending to be calm and collected during chaotic drop-offs. Should any salad-related accidents arise (because at least one toddler will think lettuce is a quality projectile), you'll exude chic confidence while knowing that it's easily washable. Plus, trying to convince your children that you are indeed a stylish queen while they paint the walls with Crayons becomes that much easier with silk; it's like a secret shield against judgment!

Finally, let's all take a moment to applaud linen— the carefree cousin of the fabric world who saunters into the room with a nonchalant attitude that screams summertime chic. Linen allows breathability, ensuring comfort as you wrangle toddlers in the heat. It's perfectly imperfect, slightly wrinkled appearance channels "effortlessly chic" in stark contrast to days spent looking like you've just run a marathon. Because let's face it, wrangling tiny humans can feel like an Olympic sport, and the last thing you want to stress about is maintaining pristine fashion while doing it.

In short, comfort and glamour can coexist beautifully in the enchantingly chaotic life of motherhood. By selecting fabrics that suit both your busy lifestyle and your passion for style, you embrace the art of dressing with fairness. So, go forth, my fabulous fashionistas, and revel in the joy of comfortable fabrics that effortlessly blend into your wardrobe! With the right choices, you can walk into any situation — whether it be playdates or girl's night out and still strut your stuff like the stylish superhero you are!

## Confidence in Every Setting: Owning Your Style

Confidence is a funny thing. Some days you wake up feeling like Beyoncé, ready to conquer the world with your fabulousness, and then other days, you catch a glimpse of your reflection right after a toddler-induced meltdown and wonder if the universe is playing a cruel joke on you.

However, when it comes to style, the juicy secret to owning your look—and by extension of your day— lies in the power of confidence, friends. You could be adorned in the most marvelous couture, but if you wear them with trepidation, you might as well be walking a runway in an inflatable dinosaur costume for all the impact you'll have.

So, let's get real. Owning your style starts from within and it's about nurturing that inner drama queen every single day. Yes, darling, whether you're in sweatpants for the umpteenth day or dressed to the nines for a night out, embracing your unique flair is what will set the tone. The most exquisite outfit in the universe can only shine when you exude confidence; it becomes an extension of your personality, not just a fabric covering.

Whether you prefer a fierce blazer or soft, breezy dresses, the magic happens when your heart aligns with your ensemble, and every twirl in the mirror draws you closer to sheer elation.

And confidence is contagious, too! When you step out in your favorite ensemble and strut your stuff with that invisible crown perched upon your head, you not only light up your path but also inspire those around you to do the same. Whether it's at the school drop-off line, where you try to look chic while secretly indicating to your child that they really shouldn't ride the class pet (again), or at a brunch date where you're convinced you can drink all the brunch mimosas without judgment; owning your style communicates to others that self-love is essential. You'll soon notice that your attire gives others permission to unleash their own fabulous expressions. As unpredictable as motherhood can be, part of owning your style is recognizing that you need to blend practicality with amazing aesthetics.

## PAJAMAS TO PARTY: DRESSING UP AND DOWN

Who says you can't rock your favorite heels while pushing a stroller? The key is a dance-like grace and perhaps some minor acrobatics. Best believe you'll develop confidence in your ability to pull off the impossible. So, wear those bold colors, flaunt those intricate patterns, and wrap yourself in textures that make you feel alive! People will take notice, and if they don't who cares? What you radiate is entirely yours to embrace.

Wielding your personal style also means allowing yourself the freedom to take risks. Fashion isn't just cloth; it's an extension of your soul, and how dull would it be if you played it safe all the time? If you feel spirited and want to try out more vibrant prints or intentionally mismatched patterns, go for it! Fashion is like playing dress-up but without the exhausting need to impress the judgmental doll sitting on the shelf. So, wear that neon-colored jacket with something eclectic! As long as you rock it with absolute belief, you're bound to turn heads rather than be questioned about potential fashion faux pas.

Additionally, remember that owning your style means letting go of comparisons. In a world where social media feeds are overflowing with drool-worthy fashion shots, let's be real, those Snapchat filters sometimes work like actual magic. It's easy to fall into the trap of comparing yourself to someone else's sartorial choices. Instead, focus on what makes you feel fabulous. You may not be leading a runway walk in the latest high-fashion trends, but if you feel incredible in your oversized graphic tee, then who cares if it isn't 'on-trend'? Celebrate your journey and find solace in knowing that your style is as distinctive as the joy (and chaos) of raising children.

Confidence also blossomed through practice. Force yourself to step outside your comfort zone. Maybe trying a kooky new hairstyle or sporting a dramatic red lip when you usually opt for nude can evoke surprising joy! Every new venture becomes a form of personal empowerment. Suddenly, that red lip evolves from a mere color choice to a proclamation that "I deserve to feel fabulous!" It's okay to approach each day as a work in progress because ultimately, style evolves as your experiences shape you.

Finally, confidence in every setting is possible when you own your style. Embrace your uniqueness, take those risks, and remove the pressure to fit into a neat little box. Become your own inspiration, even when you're navigating the whirlwind of motherhood. Remember, you are a captivating force, and wherever you go, let it shine through your style! So, as you face the day, don your stylish armor with flair, lift that imaginary crown high, and strut like the fabulous showstopper you are. The world deserves your gorgeous essence! You have the power to be a trendsetter in your own magnificent life, and once you own that, darling, everything simply falls into place!

## CHAPTER 15
# WARDROBE ESSENTIALS: BUILDING YOUR FASHION FOUNDATION

### Understanding Wardrobe Essentials: What They Are

As I sit here, sipping my cold coffee that I'll probably reheat three more times before the day is over, it dawns on me that my wardrobe essentials are as essential as my sanity. And believe me, with two rambunctious four-year-olds racing through the house like they're auditioning for NASCAR, my sanity is a precious commodity! So, let's unravel the thread (pun totally intended) of what wardrobe essentials really are and why they should hold a place of honor in your closet, right up there with that amazing, oversized mom sweater that somehow always tells a story of spilled juice or chocolate milk.

Wardrobe essentials are those glorious pieces that serve as the backbone of your outfits, the unassuming heroes of your sartorial saga, if you will. They're the reliable friends in your closet who never ditch you for a night out, despite that one time you thought a neon green tutu and glittery fishnet stockings would be an excellent combination for a casual Wednesday. These pieces may not shout, "Look at me!" from the rooftops, but they whisper, "Hey there, sophisticated and effortlessly chic lady! I'll be your stylish best friend today." From the classic white button-up to those well-fitted skinny jeans, these essentials are what help you balance the tightrope of motherhood and style like a pro.

Think of your wardrobe essentials as the foundation of a fabulous home; without sturdy walls, you'll be one misguided sneeze away from a major collapse! Imagine inviting friends over for brunch only for your living room to float away like a balloon in a particularly breezy park. It's a disaster waiting to happen but thankfully, good wardrobe essentials ensure you avoid such catastrophes in the fashion department. They're versatile, timeless, and can be dressed up or down in a pinch like the time you bravely wore those fabulous heels to the park only to find yourself two minutes later knee-deep in sand while trying to convince your twins that the slide is, in fact, meant for climbing and not an impromptu wrestling match.

Blend comfort with style, and voilà! You've unlocked wardrobe magic. Essentials often include wardrobe staples such as the universally flattering little black dress (the 'LBD', as we fashionistas refer to it). You can take that LBD from brunch to date night with one simple accessory switch, proving that practicality can indeed taste as sweet as the most decadent slice of cake— or in my household, the leftover birthday cake that mysteriously vanishes after a toddler nap (which seems more like a sneaky heist within our walls). Not to mention, there's another layer of wardrobe essentials that addresses our secret dream. It's that slinky, flowy number you've hidden away for special occasions (or hiding from the dust bunnies lurking in the corners of your closet). Oh yes, I'm talking about that dress you can wear in family photos while simultaneously dodging squirmy children! Did I ever tell you about the time I decided to wear it at a frenzied birthday party for Maximus and Jaxon? I nearly got that magnificent number tangled in their party favor goody bags, proving that even wardrobe essentials must endure the chaos of motherhood!

Remember, your wardrobe essentials are about YOU! They need to reflect your personality, your lifestyle, and your ability to wrangle tiny humans while still managing to embody your inner drama queen! So, as you dive into creating your essential wardrobe, don't be surprised if it takes shape more like an eclectic gallery full of your unique idiosyncrasies. The comfy oversized shirt you snagged during a midnight online shopping spree or those utterly impractical but deliciously gorgeous shoes that still seem to mock you from the back of your closet.

# WARDROBE ESSENTIALS: BUILDING YOUR FASHION FOUNDATION

Lastly, wardrobe essentials are less about following trends and more about creating a personalized capsule collection that feels effortlessly "you." They allow you to be the fashionable mom grappling with school drop-offs, grocery runs, and toddler tantrums without losing your sense of style and, heck, your sanity. So go forth, fellow fashionistas, and assemble your wardrobe essentials, because when the universe aligns with your fabulous outfits, you're not just dressing up-you're crafting the perfect storm of chic. Who knows? The chaos of motherhood might just become your runway!

## The Must-Have Pieces: Building Blocks of Style

The sacred journey of crafting a wardrobe filled with must-have pieces-the building blocks of style! This is like constructing a fabulous house of cards, only instead of cards, you'll rely on luxurious fabrics and fabulously cut silhouettes. Picture it: a place where you can escape the chaotic whirlwind of tantrums, sticky fingers, and the ongoing battle for snack supremacy that reigns at home. Who knew that being a hot mess could be so fashionable?

Grab your coffee (or your third cold cup, like I so frequently do), and let's dive into the essential staples that every woman should have at her disposal, no matter the frazzled state of her life!

First and foremost, ladies, let's talk about the classic white button-up shirt. This timeless garment is not only versatile, but it can elevate your style game quicker than your toddler can turn a perfectly clean living room into a disaster zone worthy of a reality show. Whether you're tackling a work meeting or a playdate at the park, a crisp white shirt can be easily styled with a pair of skinny jeans or layered under your beloved cardigan. It's the piece that casually says, I'm a professional woman who has it all together," while in reality, you're distracting your child from the grocery store candy aisle with the back of your hand!

Next, let's not forget about the trusty pair of fitted jeans. These magical trousers are akin to that devoted friend who always supports you because let's face it, leggings may be the softest hugs you'll ever experience, but sometimes, you need the reassurance of structure. A well-fitting pair of jeans can seamlessly transition from chasing after toddlers to conquering brunch with mimosas (for you, not them, of course!). Jeans absorb the chaos of life, thrive under pressure, and manage to have your back when your children inevitably choose that moment to launch a snack attack on each other. Now, I must introduce you to the hero of the footwear industry: the chic yet comfortable pair of ankle boots. Whether they are bold and edgy or classic and timeless, ankle boots can whisk you away from the depths of weekend errands to a lovely evening out in the blink of an eye. They bring a certain je ne sais quoi to every outfit, promising to turn a mundane look into fashion magic even while you're dodging spills and nap-time crises. Channel your inner superhero by slipping into these boots because if you're going to tackle the messy chaos of parenthood, you might as well do it in style! But we can't chat about the building blocks of your wardrobe without mentioning the little black dress— a staple that deserves to be serenaded! The LBD is truly the Swiss Army knife of your closet; it can transform from daytime chic (add a cardigan, and voila!) to nighttime fabulousness (those strappy heels better make an appearance!) in mere moments. Its charm lies in its simplicity, as it allows you the freedom to style it with an array of accessories that speak to your unique flair! Just remember, though, to keep an eye on your kids during gatherings— a swift foot-in-the-pants move can turn your elegant look into an "accidental toddler tumble" real quick!

Additionally, we shouldn't overlook the power of accessories as the cherry on top of your stylish cake. A fabulous statement necklace, a vibrant scarf, or an oversized bag can breathe life into your basic outfits, making you look polished and put together without the eight-hour runway prep. And let's be real, who doesn't love that moment when someone comments on your outfit, and you can bask in the glow of "Thank you! I threw this on last minute while my twins argued like they were auditioning for a courtroom drama!" There's something incredibly rewarding about mastering the art of effortless style amidst the chaos of parenthood.

Considering all this, don't underestimate the value of a great jacket! Whether it's a sleek blazer to polish off your work attire or

## WARDROBE ESSENTIALS: BUILDING YOUR FASHION FOUNDATION

a leather jacket to sizzle up your weekend look, adding structure and personality with outerwear can make all the difference. It's like wearing powerful armor, giving you that extra boost of confidence while you are braving the wilds of everyday life because nothing says "I've got this" like rocking a fabulous jacket while running down the street after a rogue toddler determined to escape to the nearest ice cream truck!

In the end, the must-have pieces are essentially the building blocks of fashion sustainability in a life that can feel as chaotic as herding cats on roller skates. Embrace and flaunt these key items and remember: each piece is more than just clothing, it's a storytelling element that can dance to the rhythm of your vibrant, laughter-filled life. So go on, unleash your wardrobe essentials, and enjoy the wild style ride that awaits when you become the architect of your fabulous and fashionable fortress!

### Mixing and Matching: Versatility in Your Closet

The art of mixing and matching: a delightful dance of fabrics, colors, and styles that can turn an ordinary outfit into a masterpiece! This skill is like baking a cake without the mess of flour explosions, toddler tantrums, or questioning your life choices at 3 a.m. while trying to make chocolate dividends appear from thin air. If I've learned anything from my chaotic life as a mother, wife, and fashion aficionado, it's that versatility in your closet can save you from fashion monotony, the dreaded "I have nothing to wear!" meltdown and could even earn you an honorary gold star in the parenting book of life. So, let's shimmy and shake through the wonders of mixing and matching because and I assure you, it's easier than coaxing your twins into wearing matching outfits for family photos (bless my heart, I've tried).

To kick things off, it's vital to recognize that versatility isn't just about having a closet full of clothes that resemble an explosion at a paint factory. Instead, it's about weaving a beautiful tapestry with your wardrobe, one that allows you to transition from coffee runs to school drop-offs and beyond. Think of your essential pieces as a blank canvas waiting for you to splash colors and textures onto it.

Yes, that oversized graphic tee can glam it up with a tailored blazer and a statement necklace, or it can chill out with your favorite pair of leggings while you engage in a riveting discussion about why unicorns don't actually exist during naptime!

Don't fret about clashing patterns like they're fencing opponents at a very dramatic duel. Embrace them with open arms! However, this does require a tiny bit of finesse; it's like a culinary adventure—sometimes you'll whip up an incredible gourmet dish, and other times, well, let's say it's an acquired taste. Dabbling with stripes and florals, or polka dots with plaid, may seem like diving headfirst into a pool of spaghetti sauce, but once you find your rhythm, it can be like the most melodic pop song on repeat, pulling you to dance like no one's watching (even though, let's be honest, your toddler definitely is). One of my absolute favorite ways to achieve versatility is through layering.

Layering is like building the ever-coveted mom taco; start with a base layer, be it a solid-colored tee or a stylish tank, then add some pizzazz with a chic cardigan or a leather jacket before finishing it off with an accessory that has a "pop" louder than your twins fighting over a toy. Suddenly, you'll appear fashionably constructed as if you just stepped off a runway in Paris, while in reality, you're juggling snack pouches and dodging juice spills! In my experience, finding the perfect balance of layers is akin to having a full day's supply of caffeine in your system — absolutely necessary for survival.

Now, let's take a moment to appreciate the magic of accessories. An effective way to switch things up without turning your wardrobe inside out (which, admit it, we've all done) is to play with differing accessories. That black dress? Complete it with a bold belt, a beautiful scarf, and some killer heels for an evening out. Or you can swap out the heels for chic fats and a denim jacket along with your favorite statement earrings for a laid-back brunch with friends. The transformation is instantaneous, and suddenly, you've transformed from a superhero ready to save the day to a relaxed yet chic version of, well, you!

## WARDROBE ESSENTIALS: BUILDING YOUR FASHION FOUNDATION

Don't overlook the importance of color combinations; these are like secret ingredients in the recipe for style! Complementary colors can accentuate your features and uplift your overall look, not unlike the glorious boost from that first cup of coffee. Mixing shades can develop a cohesive look that commands attention without the need for contrived theatrics. So, before you reach for that basic black ensemble for the umpteenth time, why not take a bold step and try pairing colors you've eyed but haven't dared to mix? Who knows? The boundaries of your closet might expand tenfold, just like your patience levels after shouting "please stop!" for the millionth time.

In the end, my fabulous friends, versatility in your closet is akin to assembling an impressive arsenal for the day-to-day battle that is parenting and life. By mastering the mix-and-match mantra, you'll cultivate a collection that allows you to navigate everything from soccer practices to unexpected brunch outings without missing a beat. And let's be real- who wouldn't want to strut their stuff while sporting a trustworthy outfit that can meta morph from playtime to prime time? So go on, unleash your inner fashionista and mix it up with all the flair you possess, it's time to let your style shine as bright as your fierce mom-energy!

### The Importance of Quality Over Quantity

The age-old debate of quality versus quantity— a discourse as timeless as whether or not to have that third cookie while hiding in the pantry from your children. As a CEO and founder of SAM D'MONES, a women's fashion enterprise, I've seen firsthand how the specter of quantity can deceive us into thinking we're building a fashion empire when, in fact, we're merely hoarding fabric-based chaos. Ladies, let's lay it all out there: choosing quality pieces for your wardrobe rather than drowning in a sea of fast fashion is not only savvy fashion move but also a route to unrivaled peace of mind (and the potential for wardrobe bliss, of course).

Let's start with the unfortunate reality: when you opt for quantity, that fast fashion frittata or, as I like to call it, "I just bought a pink turtleneck because it's on sale? can quickly turn into a frayed mystery, the fashion equivalent of the old pickle jar in the back of the fridge that you've been avoiding for months. Those five-dollar tops (that often cost the same as a fancy cup of artisanal coffee) might feel like a steal at first, but — spoiler alert—they'll wear out quicker than your patience while waiting for dinner to cook and keeping an eye on the twins epic sibling showdowns. In contrast, investing in fewer, higher-quality pieces that are versatile, durable, and fabulously bad-of-gonzo is akin to assembling a loyal fashion army that's ready to stand up to the test of time (and toddlers). You see, quality fabrics like fine cotton, silk, and linen not only feel luscious against your skin, but they also elevate your overall appearance.

Have you ever put on a high-quality dress and practically felt like you were gliding through life like a fashion runway model? That's rent-higher-quality fabrics drape beautifully and are far less likely to awkwardly cling to your dazzling curves. It's basically an immediate "Hello, confidence!" moment in the midst of the daily chaos that is my life-and I can definitely justify a boost in confidence even if I have to wrestle my twins to get them into their car seats!

Now let's chat about price points. You know that voice in your head that insists you need ten trendy tank tops at a discount, only to discover that they rapidly belong to the "luxury hot mess" category by the end of their first washing? However, investing in just two or three well-structured, timeless pieces not only simplifies your wardrobe but also keeps you oh-so-fashionably poised. So, yes, you may need to strategically save for that beautiful designer handbag you've been eyeing but think of it as a long-term relationship rather than a random fling with a faux-leather bag that has more charm than your toddler's latest art project (and let's be real, that's saying something).

Think of each quality piece as an esteemed member of your wardrobe family. You wouldn't invite people over to your house with a flimsy plastic chair that crumbles under the weight of a tiny toddler, would you? Why bring that same disregard to your clothing? Building your wardrobe with higher-quality staples

## WARDROBE ESSENTIALS: BUILDING YOUR FASHION FOUNDATION

nurtures an environment where every item is a true friend-promising loyalty, durability, and the fabulous potential to earn you compliments from unsuspecting admirers on random coffee runs. This friendship creates options for mixing and matching and lets you create looks that remain polished and chic, even amid the delightful tornado of motherhood.

And let's not forget about the environmental aspect! Prioritizing quality over quantity is like gifting Mother Earth a joyful bouquet while whispering a heartfelt apology for the years of fabric waste caused by hasty decisions.

Fewer but higher-quality items mean less impact on our beloved planet and less regret about the piles of clothes you'll eventually find stuffed into the far reaches of your closet (or heaven forbid, the dreaded "donation box"). You're practically becoming a style superhero while protecting our environment, and let's be honest: it is a dazzling win-win!

In general, it can be said, the importance of quality over quantity in your wardrobe cannot be overstated. There's something so beautifully rewarding about ditching the temptation to amass clothing that would serve best in a fabric landfill and instead curating a collection of well-crafted, timeless pieces that truly reflect your voice-wardrobe that embraces versatility while celebrating quality. As you sift through your fashion choices, remember that investing in quality items is an investment in yourself! So please, let's raise our glasses (preferably filled with the remnants of that third cracker) to embracing quality over quantity. You'll not only look fabulous when you leave your house, but you will also feel empowered by a closet that inspires confidence, longevity, and, most importantly, a stylish roaring "I got this!" attitude. Salud!

### Keeping It Fresh: Updating Your Wardrobe Essentials

The delightful task of keeping your wardrobe essentials fresh. It's like indulging in a rejuvenating spa day for your closet, except there's no cucumber water or comfy robe involved. Just the sweet scent of stylish possibilities! In the whirlwind realm of motherhood and life, where time can fly faster than a toddler zooming on a tricycle, updating your wardrobe essentials is crucial for keeping your style from stagnating like leftovers at the back of your fridge. So, let's channel our inner fashion alchemists and sprinkle a little magic dust over our closets, ensuring they remain exciting, chic, and ready to transform us into the fabulous beings we were always meant to be! First things first —when I refer to "wardrobe essentials," let's remember that this doesn't mean a stale collection of pieces that have lost their sparkle.

No! Essentials should evolve as you navigate through life. You may have loved that cute sundress from two summers ago, but if it starts to smell more like memories of spilled toddler juice than fashion statement, it has reached its expiration date! It's time to open the closet doors and assess what garments still serve a purpose, and which ones have been earning their keep merely by lingering in silence, waiting for a second wave of fashion glory to befall upon them. Spoiler alert: there's nothing wrong with saying goodbye to those irregular pieces that fail to ignite joy (feel free to channel your best Marie Kondo impression).

Next up, let's talk about the power of trends! Now, I know the fashion universe can feel like a cosmic rollercoaster with accessories that change with the seasons, but staying connected to fresh trends is vital for keeping your essentials alive and invigorated. This doesn't mean you should radicalize your wardrobe each month as if you're starring in your own personal fashion reality show. Instead, look for innovative ways to incorporate trendy elements while respecting your curated foundation. A contemporary, statement belt can completely transform a simple dress, lending it a modern edge while still embracing your stylish roots. Think of trends as the whimsical sprinkles on your stylish cupcake—not the entire cake itself!

Shopping is an art form, my fellow fashionistas, and it's time to master the technique of skills that'll ensure you continue to add impactful pieces to your wardrobe. Next time you're on a shopping jaunt, online at www.samdmones.com or in-person at your

## WARDROBE ESSENTIALS: BUILDING YOUR FASHION FOUNDATION

favorite store, think of each piece you're contemplating not as a standalone item, but as a potential teammate for your existing wardrobe. A pair of versatile pants should be able to mingle effortlessly with at least three tops and a couple of jackets! This sacred mixing and matching can breathe newfound life into your wardrobe while reducing the unnecessary chaos of endlessly accumulating items that only match... well, each other. It's like assembling your very own stylish Avengers; you want the right combination to save the day!

Moreover, consider engaging in a wardrobe swap with your fashion-savvy friends! Why solely depend on retail therapy when you can expand your collection through camaraderie and fun? Gather a group of stylish pals and host a gathering where everyone brings pieces they're ready to let go of for others to adopt; it's like an empowering cross between a secret Santa and a treasure hunt! You never know what fabulous finds await you — better yet, you'll find yourself raving over how the item that once hung in your buddy's closet looks like it was stitched together with your personality in mind.

And let's address the elephant in the room — a little bit of creativity can go a long way in updating your wardrobe essentials! Take a good look at pieces you haven't worn in eons and reimagine their purpose. That once-amazing summer dress can quickly become a chic, effortless top layered over your favorite jeans or paired with a stylish jacket to ward off climate unpredictability. Channel your inner DIY diva and break out the sewing kit to make alterations — why not transform an oversized shirt into an edgy crop for those sunny days at the park, where your mission, should you choose to accept it, is to reclaim your lost sense of style while juggling the kids? Finally, remember that wardrobe updating is not a one-and-done affair!

It's an ongoing relationship, much like my love-hate connection with my blender that makes smoothies while simultaneously threatening to explode with every use. Embrace the evolution of your wardrobe over time, continually tweaking and refining to reflect who you are in this very moment—your style should scream, "I am fabulous!" even when your life feels like a three-ring circus.

Finally, keeping your wardrobe essentials fresh is as vital as securing a solid caffeine supply (because let's face it, who wouldn't want to sip on a delightful beverage while finally unearthing that treasure from the depths of their closet?) With a little bit of creativity, laughter, and perhaps a glass of wine, you can enable your wardrobe to flourish as the seasons change, adding a dash of spice to your style. So, step into the fabulous adventure of wardrobe renewal— because, my glittering fashionista friends, life's too short to wear uninspired clothing (and that pickle jar in the back of the fridge deserves to be honored by the trash can)! Cheers to freshening up and letting your style thrive!

## CHAPTER 16
# GLAM UP: TRANSITIONING SEASONAL STYLES

### Understanding Seasonal Trends

Seasonal trends! The ever-shifting sands of fashion that somehow dictate my wardrobe choices while simultaneously bickering with my toddler's peanut butter-coated outfit choices. As a fashion-loving mompreneur, navigating the seasonal currents can feel like trying to swim against an ocean of agitated toddlers: exhausting yet exhilarating! So, let's dive into this wondrous world of seasonal trends, shall we?

Understanding seasonal trends is less about obsessing over what the fashion police deem in or out and more about embracing the ebbs and flows of style that suit your unique vibe. Think of seasonal trends as the "crazy aunt" of your wardrobe, she might not always make sense, but she knows how to throw a good party! Each season brings with it a wave of new styles, colors, and themes that can reignite your passion for fashion and, dare I say, even help you express your inner drama queen.

Let's chat about the "big reveals" that typically come with each season. Spring whispers sweet nothings of fresh florals, pastel hues, and light, breezy fabrics. Okay, more like SCREAMS if your four-year-old just spilled grape juice on your "new" floral dress. Summer, on the other hand, brings forth the inevitable linen and cotton rendezvous as you sip margaritas (hopefully while not nursing an infant). Autumn, or as I like to call it, "sweater season," panders to our desire for cozy fabrics, earthy tones, and the pursuit of pumpkin-favored everything. Winter, that merciless fashion battleground, brings layers and layers of clothing that can sometimes look more like survival gear than style! But hey, we call it fashion, right? Let's take a moment to remember that while these trends are exciting, they also have a tendency to recycle themselves faster than my twin boys' toy requests. One moment, it's all about high-waisted jeans, and the next, the fashion gurus (who must be terribly bored) decide that gauchos are chic again. So, when evaluating these trends, it's essential to sift through them like you're hunting for the crème de la crème during a post-holiday sale-you know, the ones where half the customers are fighting over the "Last Pair of Amazing High-Heeled Booties"? Only, instead of fighting dirty, we're going to find what genuinely resonates with who we are, while secretly rolling our eyes at those who embrace the fleeting whims.

Now, here's where it gets slightly serious: understanding seasonal trends doesn't mean you have to morph into a fashion chameleon overnight. Yes, it's fun to try new looks, but ensuring they align with your personality is vital. After all, no one wants a wardrobe that mimics a mood ring! Instead, use seasonal trends as a backdrop for your unique canvas. Add flourishes that speak to your heart: that oversized neon scarf with delightful drama, or the matte red lipstick that elicits compliments even when you're climbing a wall of toys while prying a crayon from your four-year-old's mouth.

But let's face it: keeping up with seasonal trends amidst the noise of cranky toddlers is no mean feat! Those convincing Instagram influencers make it seem like a walk in the park, but let's not forget that they often have a full team and stylists, as myself, hiding in their pockets. For us real-life superheroes, we get it. The only styling teams we have are usually a cadre of colorful foam shapes or half-eaten fruit snacks sticking to our designer shoes. So, here's the key to mastering these trends —don't force them! Rather, find the elements that excite you and weave them into your daily life in a way that instantly makes that beloved pair of leggings feel haute couture.

## GLAM UP: TRANSITIONING SEASONAL STYLES

Overall, understanding seasonal trends is vital to maintaining that delicate balance between style-savvy sophistication and practical mom life chic. Take the trends that make you feel fabulous and shrug off the ones that leave you feeling, well, less than fabulous. Life's too short to be trapped in an outfit that feels foreign to your fabulous self! So, grab that oversized cardigan, put on your favorite statement earrings, and rock your way into the next season with all the flair of a true drama queen! After all, if anyone can juggle toddler tantrums and seasonal trends, it's you, darling!

### Integrating Timeless Pieces

Integrating timeless pieces into your wardrobe is akin to adding secret ingredients to Grandma's famous lasagna; it elevates the entire dish from "Mediocre Monday Night Dinner" to "Appease the In-Laws Feast." These wardrobe workhorses don't just cling to your closet; they become the backbone of your style, allowing you to pair everything from eye-popping statement necklaces to soft, chunky knit sweaters for those cold nights in with the twins. Timeless pieces are pocket-sized treasures in the vast ocean of seasonal trends, and they lovingly whisper (or perhaps shout) to you that you can totally crush it on the style game while savoring snack time.

First, let's talk about the classic white button-up shirt; this chic staple is like the versatile best friend who shows up for all the important moments- weddings, brunches, and even the inevitable "Mom, I have a presentation today" panic. It can go from board meetings to play dates faster than my twins can find the hidden stash of pistachios I thought I'd cleverly hidden. Tuck it into tailored pants for a polished look or throw it on over a pair of jeans for that "effortlessly chic" vibe that says, "I might have had my coffee while simultaneously building the Leaning Tower of Sparkle Crayons, but darling, I'm still fabulous."

Then there's the little black dress (LBD) — legendary and magical in its own right. This hero piece serves as the foundation of your wardrobe and can morph into anything your heart desires! You can wear it to a fancy evening out or check off your to-do list at the grocery store. Pair it with sneakers while dashing after a runaway toddler, or dress it up with heels when it's finally your turn for a date night that doesn't involve explaining why "mommy juice" is not a real thing. The LBD works as your trusty sidekick, it's there for every occasion, even if the occasion is just putting on makeup and taking a photo for social media because that's what we do for cute content, right?

Next up are the denim jeans that fit like a glove and remind you of all the glorious pancake breakfasts you've enjoyed pre-kids. A good pair of jeans has the ability to switch seamlessly from school drop-off to a casual dinner with friends- cue the applause! Select a style that highlights your fabulous figure, whether it's high-waisted, skinny, or bootcut. And hey, let's not forget, with the right fit, they'll probably serve as a disguise against those unsightly fruit snack stains we all seem to collect over time like little badges of honor.

Speaking of fabric, let's discuss outerwear, particularly the classic trench coat. This piece transcends trends like a sartorial superhero, and it's perfect for when you suddenly need to look chic while simultaneously deflecting gooey toddler hands. No more frumpy park jackets: a beautifully tailored trench will amp up your style quotient like-and pardon my French here-like a million bucks! It can easily go from school pick-up to coffee catch-up and, if you're lucky, a spontaneous dress-up moment when you realize your neighbor's party invites always arrive addressed to "The One Who Looks Good in Trench Coats". Now, here comes the tricky part, integrating these timeless pieces with the flashy trends that are popping up every fashion season. The key is to balance those trendy additions with your plot-worthy classics. You can be all about the latest animal print craze while keeping the timeless chic aesthetic alive. Try pairing a statement animal-print top with your sturdy denim and fabulous little black dress. Your timeless pieces provide stability in the storm of ever-evolving trends!

But remember, integrating timeless pieces isn't just about tossing them into the mix, you must wear them like a crown! Strut into brunch with confidence, radiating elegance that shows you're not

## GLAM UP: TRANSITIONING SEASONAL STYLES

just a mom in leggings, but truly a runway-ready fashionista who can tame the wild, unpredictable world of parenthood in style! All it takes is a pinch of effort coupled with a desire to let your personality shine through these classic gems, and trust me, the results will be eclectic, chic, and undeniably you.

So, embrace those timeless pieces, wear them with pride, and let them take center stage. You'll find that they are not just items in your closet; they're the backbone of your stunning wardrobe, a celebration of your fabulous self amid all the chaos. With a solid foundation, you can creatively add trendy flares, ensuring that your wardrobe is timelessly glamorous and utterly unique. Now, let's conquer the world of fashion, one fabulous piece at a time!

**Mixing Textures and Fabrics**

Mixing textures and fabrics-the art form that separates the fashionistas from the "What was I thinking?" crowd! The beauty of a well-mixed outfit can be likened to successfully crafting a gourmet meal: it requires a dash of creativity, a clever selection of ingredients, and a sprinkle of "Who, me?" confidence as you strut out the door, especially when you're juggling toddlers and sanity! So, let's dive into the world of textures and fabrics and discover how we can elevate our fashion game to new heights, even while navigating playground chaos.

First and foremost, let's celebrate the wonders of fabric variety. There's cotton, denim, silk, leather, and knits, just to name a few, each waiting to be pulled into your outfit like eager children clamoring for your attention.

The secret lies in layering these textures because why settle for basic when you can twirl your fabric choices like a fashion-savvy tornado? Picture this: a soft knit sweater paired with structured leather skinnies; it creates a stunning balance that says, "I'm cozy AND fierce!" The juxtaposition is oh so satisfying! Plus, if a toddler manages to launch an errant snack attack your way, you'll look no less fabulous — wool hides stains like a true MVP!

Don't shy away from the plush comfort of mixing textures either! Give a ruffled blouse a robust partner by layering it beneath a tailored blazer, this look instantly shouts, "I could be at a board meeting or an impromptu playdate! Who's ready?" And let's not forget about accessories: a chunky knit scarf can add layers not just of warmth, but also of style! Just imagine wrapping yourself in that fabulous softness while maintaining the poise of a quiet queen. "Oh, this old thing," you say while secretly basking in the admiration flowing your way. Fashion magic, I tell you!

Color plays a significant role in mixing textures and fabrics, so let's paint a picture! When you leap into the world of textured wonders, think about how colors interact with those materials. I'm a firm believer that you can mix prints, patterns, and textures to create a visual feast for the eyes. A bright floral skirt paired with a muted, chunky sweater balances a sense of femininity and strength, while adding sensational intrigue to the eyes. Make your outfits a reflection of your mood! Channel your inner artist and paint joy into your daily attire. You're not just dressing; you're creating an exhilarating masterpiece every day!

But beware of the "too much" trap-mixing textures and fabrics is akin to mixing cake and toothpaste; while both are delightful on their own, together they spell disaster! Avoid reaching for every piece in your closet that has a stitch or a sparkle; curate wisely, my fabulous friend! The trick lies in creating a structured ensemble where a statement piece stands at the forefront, complemented by your favorite supporting textures. Think of your outfit as a theatrical performance where your textures take center stage with style and choreography!

Consider the current popular trends too, like athleisure! Who'd have thought that joggers could be elevated to fashion royalty? Pairing an elegant silk blouse with chic joggers and a tailored blazer will have friends and neighbors questioning whether you've truly found the secret to fashion enlightenment! "Oh, this raggedy look!", your casual response while you channel the inner queen mother, ready to take on anything life throws at you! Those combinations send a message that says, "I have children, but they do NOT define my

## GLAM UP: TRANSITIONING SEASONAL STYLES

style!" And let's talk dimension! Incorporating different textures- and this is vital-adds depth to your look! A suede skirt shimmies fabulously against a cotton tee. We get variety, energy, and an eye-catching ensemble all working in concert. When my kids grab my leg, desperately seeking attention, I give a little twirl, and VOILA! Unapologetic glam! Just like that, we create a whirlwind of fabric brilliance that captures all the attention!

To conclude, mixing textures and fabrics is an exhilarating dance of creativity that welcomes you to express your fabulous self, regardless of those wild, sticky-fingered interruptions by the kids. It's all about balance, confidence, and embracing that inner figure-flattering rock star! Layer that fuzzy cardigan over those tailored pants, sparkle in those bright shoes, and welcome adventure! Remember, if the day ever becomes too chaotic, just throw on an oversized scarf and declare that you're "boho-chic"! Your fabulous self is waiting to emerge; let's celebrate that style tenfold - because every fabric counts in this whimsical game of fashion!

### Color Palettes for Seasonal Transition

Color palettes for seasonal transition —the mystical land where hues and shades gracefully intertwine like a dance party gone right! As summer fades and autumn arrives with its glorious coat of colors, or when winter begrudgingly yields to spring's vibrant blooms, we find ourselves presented with the eternal question: how do we ensure we don't look like a walking kaleidoscope gone rogue? Fear not, dear friends! I'm here to help you decode this intricate tapestry of colors while ensuring you have a chuckle or two amidst the colorful madness.

Let's begin with the beauty of understanding the seasons and what colors naturally thrive during each. Summer often brings that fierce brightness— think coral, sunshine yellow, and vibrant turquoise! It's like a fruity salad party at your local beach! But as the leaves start to change and the air becomes cooler, we begin to crave something a little softer and earthier, an enchanting transition that speaks to the soul. Enter warm terracotta, deep burgundy, and rich olive green; each has a way of making you feel like you've just stepped into a cozy cabin while simultaneously promoting the delightful notion of pumpkin spice everything, if you find yourself donning something in summer shades well into fall, you might just look like a confused beachgoer who stumbled into a harvest festival-and trust me, that's not the vibe you're going for!

Now, let's tackle the autumn to winter transition. As those vibrant leaves flutter down, it's time to swap out your bright yellows and cheerful oranges for deeper jewel tones. Emerald greens, royal blues, and plummy purples emerge like the sophisticated cousins at a family reunion! These shades embrace warmth like a cup of hot cocoa on a snowy day, and they allow for a smooth passage into the cold that lies ahead — sans the risk of looking like a festive ornament! When it comes to winter, don't think drab and dreary; incorporate jewel tones that magnify your fabulousness while keeping you cozy and chic!

But we can't forget about layering— and I'm not just talking about throwing on a fuzzy sweater over those tank tops! Incorporating textures is crucial during seasonal transitions, so pay attention to your fabrics!

A cream cashmere sweater paired with a silky olive-green slip skirt flows seamlessly into autumn, while the rich textures of wool complement the palette beautifully. You can strut into that pumpkin patch while rocking a color scheme straight out of a fall catalog— package it with fleece-lined combat boots, and suddenly, not only are you fashion-forward, but you'll also be ready for any sneaky toddler who requires a piggyback ride when they tire of wandering.

As spring approaches, we witness yet another ensemble rebirth! Out come the pastel palettes: soft pinks, dreamy lilacs, and airy blues come into play like a breath of fresh air, evoking floral gardens bursting with life and hope. These shades are the serene lullabies to sweeten the transition from winter's hibernation to spring's vibrant awakening. Pairing pastel colors can be a match made in heaven but be mindful to avoid the dreaded "Easter Egg" look! One moment you're missing your brunch date, and the next, you're getting mistaken for a walking decoration!

## GLAM UP: TRANSITIONING SEASONAL STYLES

Now, how do we integrate color palettes with our personal style without looking like we staged a fashion show at a thrift store? It's simple, pick a color palette that resonates with your mood. If you love the dramatic flair, channel deep jewel tones! If you're more the lighthearted, whimsical type, allow the pastels to sing a love song to your vibe! One tactic to strut confidently through the seasons is to invest in versatile pieces that complement your chosen palette. For instance, an adaptable trench or an oversized knit can quickly take on a new personality depending on which color combination you choose underneath! Just picture it: you in a brilliant mustard-yellow trench paired with a snug, ivory turtleneck while waiting for your coffee... now that's a picture for the 'gram!

In wrapping up this colorful journey through the whims of seasonal transitions, remember that there's no one-size-fits-all when it comes to color. Embrace your unique flair through your chosen palettes and allow them to empower your magnificent self. Let the colors work together like a symphony and know that confidently wearing what makes your heart sing is always in vogue. So, whether you're contemplating jewel tones as winter rolls in or delighting in pastel dreams as flowers bloom, dress like the fabulous drama queen you are and strut your way through each season like the gorgeous whirlwind of color you were destined to be!

### Creating Seasonal Capsule Wardrobes

Creating seasonal capsule wardrobes is like a fashionable game of Tetris, where the goal is to align your style pieces into a cohesive masterpiece while simultaneously combating the ongoing chaos of toddler life! Imagine stepping into your closet and feeling like a sartorial genius rather than a frazzled mom battling mismatched socks and last week's fruit snacks lurking like trolls in the corners of your wardrobe. The concept of a capsule wardrobe empowers you to streamline your closet, turning panic dressing into effortless chicness, all while adding that flair of joy and humor we all crave.

First, let's define what this magical capsule wardrobe entails: think of it as a rotating cast of characters that work harmoniously together! We're talking about essential, versatile pieces that can be mixed and matched to create endless outfits. This eliminates the dreaded morning conundrum of "What on earth will I wear today?" So, let's banish the "clothes explosion" that often resembles the aftermath of a toddler tantrum and curate pieces that make sense for the season ahead.

When creating your seasonal capsule wardrobe, the first step is to assess your current closet like the fashion detective you are. Scour for items that inspire joy, confidence, and —let's be real —self-love! It's time to bid adios to those clothes that scream "What was I thinking?" or "Who do I think I am?" because if they don't evoke a sense of fabulousness, there's simply no room for them in your champagne-sized dreams! The goal is to create a wardrobe that sings to you, igniting excitement for each day ahead, and banishing those moments of hideousness that make you cling to your cozy pajamas!

Next, let's carefully select those crucial pieces to form your capsule wardrobe. Aim for around 20-30 items, depending on your unique style and lifestyle. Start with timeless classics: a tailored blazer, a couple of well-fitting jeans that hug your curves nicely (not like an overripe banana, thank you very much!), and a versatile little black dress that can go from playdates to date nights faster than it takes to diaper a toddler! For every category—tops, bottoms, dresses, outerwear, and even footwear— pick items that feel like they've been sprinkled with magic fairy dust. They're the kind that you'll wear on repeat and still feel fabulous doing it.

Now, here's where the fun begins: selecting seasonal colors to weave throughout your capsule! As we discussed earlier, each season invites its own palette to play with, so embrace that luscious word! If it's fall, lean toward muted rust tones, rich greens, and soft taupes. Winter brings jewel tones and cozy neutrals, while spring breathes life into pastels and floral prints. You can even mix these seasonal colors to create a unified theme that radiates clarity and style! Nothing brings a mother joy, quite like knowing that every piece can play nicely together. Trust me, I've witnessed many closet wars amidst the mess of parenting!

## GLAM UP: TRANSITIONING SEASONAL STYLES

Accessorizing your capsule wardrobe is where you can truly express your individuality! It's your opportunity to shine like the superstar you are. Accessories can elevate your basic pieces to new heights while giving them different personalities. One day, a tailored blazer can offer you a sophisticated look; the next day, drape it over a graphic tee with bold statement earrings, and voilà! You just transformed your entire outfit. Your style is a delicate dance where personality meets practicality -it's about embracing versatility with fair! Here's the kicker: creating a capsule wardrobe is not done in isolation! It welcomes collaboration with creativity! As you build your seasonal aesthetic, feel free to embrace thrifted gems from that quirky shop down the street or swap outfits with girlfriends for fresh additions without the spending spree. It's a fabulous financial strategy, akin to discovering extra cookie dough in the freezer when you thought you had used it all — nothing but joy!

And let's not forget the all-important goal of making your seasonal capsule wardrobes work for your lifestyle! It should empower you to feel fabulous as you go about your daily adventures. Whether you're sprinting through the playground, attending meetings, or unwinding during a much-deserved date night with your partner, let your capsule wardrobe make you feel like the confident drama queen you truly are.

In summary, creating seasonal capsule wardrobes is all about strategic planning and dynamic style! Celebrate your wardrobe transformation, let laughter mingle with style, and revel in the confidence of knowing that your closet can be a sanctuary of fabulous fashion. So, grab that bling, layer up those textures, and create a wardrobe that's not just functional but fabulously fun! Welcome to the wonderful world of capsule wardrobes, where less truly becomes more, and stylish genius reigns supreme. Here's to embracing every seasonal change like the empowered fashionista you are!

## CHAPTER 17
# MOMMY AND ME: MATCHING STYLES FOR FAMILY FUN

**Matching Concepts: Why Coordination is Key to Family Fashion**

The age-old question of family fashion: to coordinate or not to coordinate?

In a world where every social media feed is screaming for attention like my kids at dinner time, the answer is a resounding "yes!" Coordination isn't just cute; it's practically an Olympic sport that signifies both love and a level of organization I desperately wish I could channel while wrangling mine. And let's be honest, matching your outfits can be the most therapeutic escape from the daily chaos of parenting. Who doesn't want to feel like they just walked off the cover of a glossy magazine, especially when you're knee-deep in toddler tantrums and leftover mac and cheese?

Now, before you roll your eyes and dismiss the idea of being "that family" (you know, the ones like me who have coordinated outfits for every family vacation), let me enlighten you: coordination is not about being overly matchy-matchy. It's about finding a balance that captures your unique family vibe while still allowing each member to express their individuality. Think of it like a delicious flavor profile in a dish. A pinch of coordination can elevate the entire experience, transforming your family into a visually appealing feast for the eyes — because we all know that just like appearances, families are subject to Insta filters!

## MOMMY AND ME: MATCHING STYLES FOR FAMILY FUN

Imagine this scenario: you're headed to your child's school function, and you're trying to gracefully manage a double stroller while a three-year-old confidently announces he needs to go to the "big potty." You glance at your husband, and he's sporting that same old T-shirt from college with "I'm with Stupid" printed boldly on it. The horror! What if instead, you all dressed in earthy tones, faux-fur vests, and bohemian prints? Suddenly, you look like a fabulous tribe ready to take on the world- or at least the snacks table. Life is too short to wear boring attire, especially when you can coordinate in a way that showcases your uniqueness while avoiding the "who-dressed-these-people" judgement from the other parents.

One of my fondest memories is from a Halloween parade when my entire crew, yes, even the husband with his Pharaoh costume, embraced our Egyptian theme. We strode through the crowd looking like we were the Ptolemaic Dynasty. It wasn't just about the pharaoh-headdress and staff, it was the camaraderie we felt as a family. And you know what? We scored the Best Costume award— child's play can turn into parental glory, my friends! So, my personal philosophy is: if you're going to dress alike, you had better do it with pizzazz and an ample amount of flair.

Now, let's talk practically because we know that fashion must work together with the chaos of family life. Half of the time, I can't find a matching pair of shoes, let alone ensure we all coordinate our outfits. A little pre-planning is crucial. Concepts like color blocking or playing with complementary shades can make outfit coordination relatively straightforward— and frankly, fashionably forgiving! For instance, focusing on shades of teal for the kids, while I rock a stunning emerald dress, enhances the coordination without feeling too forced. It's about harmony, not clashing like a toddler's tantrum at the grocery store.

Finally, let's consider the impacts of coordinated outfits on family interactions. When you rock matching outfits, feelings of cohesion ripple through the family like a community hug on steroids. You'll find you have those "aww" moments captured on camera, making your fridge the pinnacle of family pride and Instagram-worthy content. It also opens the door for compliments that might brighten your day —because let's be real, who doesn't cherish a well-placed compliment amidst the daily grind?

So, whether you're a team of superheroes, a squad of wacky animals, or simply existing in a color palette that brings joy, embrace the possibilities of family fashion! Coordination is not about dictating styles; it's about strengthening bonds and having fun with what you wear. The next time you step out with your crew, remember this: dressing cohesively is the secret to transcending the mundane and elevating your family status from chaotic court jesters to a harmonious style symphony. Just imagine the Instagram likes!

Creative patterns: choosing colors and prints for family outfits. The magical kingdom of fabrics and prints, where stripes waltz with polka dots and florals flirt with chevrons in a dizzying array of colors. Choosing patterns for family outfits is like trying to create a masterpiece while your toddler is simultaneously attempting to color on the walls with a crayon. It's chaotic, unpredictable, and just a tad bit glamorous if you do it right! My philosophy? Life is too short for boring clothes, especially when you can create small walking works of art that will either be admired or cause a social media uproar.

So, let's dive into the world of colors and prints, where the possibilities are endless, and so is the potential for hilarity. First on the docket is the royal drama of clash versus coordination. You may be asking yourself, "Vivian, how do I navigate the treacherous waters of color and print selection without looking like I lost a fight with a paint factory?" Excellent question, my fashion-savvy friend! The secret is balancing bold statements with grounded contrasts. Just like a great comedy routine, keeping the audience

Finally, let's consider the impacts of coordinated outfits on family interactions. When you rock matching outfits, feelings of cohesion ripple through the family like a community hug on steroids. You'll

## MOMMY AND ME: MATCHING STYLES FOR FAMILY FUN

find you have those 'aww' moments captured on camera, making your fridge the pinnacle of family pride and Instagram-worthy content. It also opens the door for compliments that might brighten your day —because let's be real, who doesn't cherish a well-placed compliment amidst the daily grind? So, whether you're a team of superheroes, a squad of wacky animals, or simply existing in a color palette that brings joy, embrace the possibilities of family fashion! Coordination is not about dictating styles; it's about strengthening bonds and having fun with what you wear. The next time you step out with your crew, remember this: dressing cohesively is the secret to transcending the mundane and elevating your family status from chaotic court jesters to a harmonious style symphony.

## Creative Patterns: Choosing Colors and Prints for Family Outfits

The magical kingdom of fabrics and prints— where stripes waltz with polka dots, and florals flirt with chevrons in a dizzying array of colors! Choosing patterns for family outfits is like trying to create a masterpiece while your toddler is simultaneously attempting to color on the walls with a crayon. It's chaotic, unpredictable, and just a tad bit glamorous if you do it right!

My philosophy? Life is too short for boring clothes, especially when you can create small walking works of art that will either be admired or cause a social media uproar.

So, let's dive into the world of colors and prints, where the possibilities are endless, and so is the potential for hilarity. First on the docket is the royal drama of clash versus coordination. You may be asking yourself, "Vivian, how do I navigate the treacherous waters of color and print selection without looking like I lost a fight with a paint factory?" Excellent question, my fashion-savvy friend! The secret is balancing bold statements with grounded contrasts. Just like a great comedy routine, keeping the audience engaged is key. A vibrant floral on mom matched with muted stripes for dad creates interest without sending you spiraling into a fashion fiasco. Think of the floral as the headliner and the stripes as the comedic sidekick—each has its role, but together, they create a well-rounded ensemble!

Let's talk about color choices, because darling, that rainbow isn't just for unicorns and fairy tales; each hue evokes a different vibe. Bright colors scream, "fun, let's party!", while pastels say, "I'm soft and sweet, like cotton candy." But herein lies the rub for families with young children, they can make those bright colors look muddy quicker than you can say, "Oops, I spilled grape juice!" So, moderation becomes your bestie! Choose a vibrant shade to highlight and combine it with more neutral tones to ground the look, all while dodging any potential toddler-related food stains that will make the outfit seem like an abstract art piece.

Speaking of prints, there's so much to explore! Stripes have a quirky quality that tickles my fancy-they elongate your silhouette, perfect for that "I'm not here to choose the kids' snack options, I'm here to take on the world" vibe. Pair them with floral pants for the little ones, and boom, suddenly you've created a delightful visual banquet that's sure to turn heads.

Consider trying in some animal prints; because who doesn't want mini versions of themselves running around dressed like cheetahs while they strap on their sandals? It's a fun way to add a sprinkle of wilderness drama without surrendering your sanity or personal style.

But hold on a second! Think about where you're headed before going pattern crazy. If you're strutting into a birthday bash at a castle-themed venue, bold colors accompanied by whimsical prints can inject a sense of fun into the atmosphere! On the other hand, if you're taking the family to a serious museum exhibit (kids in museums? What could possibly go wrong?), perhaps dial it back a notch with subtle stripes and playful accents to ensure no one wanders off pretending to be a Picasso travelling through art history while loitering in front of a lesser-known painting of a fruit bowl. Then, we can't discuss prints without bringing up the delightful phenomenon known as "the theme". This, my friends, is where you can let your creativity run wild while the kids are still on board. One year, I decided our theme would be "Hawaiian

# MOMMY AND ME: MATCHING STYLES FOR FAMILY FUN

Luau." With the kids clad in adorable tropical prints, I confidently rocked a blue floral dress reminiscent of a stylish Polynesian dancer (complete with a Lei necklace that looked stunning but was promptly discarded after one too many "Mom, I need a snack!" moments). We strutted our stuff together, looking like a beautiful family of Hawaiian tourists—until the kids decided to run into a puddle of sand. Spoiler alert: Tropical chic turned into muddy mayhem faster than you could say "Wipe your hands!" Lastly, dear reader, embracing colors and prints in a family ensemble is about balancing. Allow each person to shine through a fun choice of patterns while tethering it back to a cohesive theme that celebrates your bond. Experiment and let your imagination run wild! Coordination should be a joyful expression rather than a meticulous effort; after all, there's plenty of room for laughter (and the occasional stain) on this fashion journey. So, throw open those closet doors, pick those patterns, and let your family bloom in a kaleidoscope of creativity!

## Mommy and Me Styles: Outfits that Celebrate Your Unique Bond

The enchanting realm of "Mommy and Me" styles! If you've ever glanced in the mirror while standing next to your mini-me and thought, "Wow! We are the modern-day, stylish version of a dynamic duo," you, my friend, are not alone! There's something downright magical about rocking coordinating outfits with your little ones that transcend the ordinary —much like finding a clean shirt in an avalanche of laundry. It's like the fashion gurus smiled down upon you, shouting, "You were meant to do this!" Let me set the scene: You and your daughter, both adorned in matching floral sundresses, stroll into the local café for your afternoon caffeine fix.

You feel the glances, the approving nods, the whispered compliments from fellow patrons. There's a palpable aura of delight surrounding you as if you two have just exited a rom-com where the love of both fashion and family reigns supreme. That's right! You're not just two individuals out for a cup of Jo; you're a beacon of style, a walking Instagram filter, living proof that motherhood can indeed be chic. Literally the poster children for adorable bonding moments!

Now, let's be real. As fabulous as it is to match colors and patterns, there is a very delicate line between being fashionable and downright ridiculous-you know, those "What were they thinking?" ensembles that pop up on social media like weeds in a garden. We're talking about images of mothers dressed as superheroes alongside their kids in cheap capes that scream "Halloween leftovers." Avoid the pitfalls of unintentionally becoming an online joke! Focus instead on outfits that capture a bond while still allowing for genuine self-expression. You want to pose for pictures, not end up in a viral meme.

When creating these dazzling moments, versatility is paramount. Take your timeless classics: white tees! You can never go wrong dressing up a crisp white tee for you and your little fashionista. Add a bright skirt for you and let her twirl in a matching one! Alternatively, denim is a fabulous choice that lends itself well to playful accessories. Picture yourself in a chic denim jacket paired with a vibrant tulle skirt while your daughter sports denim overalls and complement them with a fun graphic tee. Voilà - suddenly, you've unleashed a fashion marvel, radiating joy in tandem with your child!

Accessories, my friends, are the secret weapons in this magical mommy and me wardrobe journey. The right accessories can elevate even the simplest outfits into showstoppers. Think of matching hair accessories or hats (because let's face it, messy hair days are our constant companions). Ever seen a mother-daughter duo with matching headbands? It's like they just emerged from a woodland fairy tale, all sparkles and charm! And don't forget fun jewelry, like colorful bangles or charm bracelets— they can express your unique bond in a way that dulls the everyday reality of fighting over bedtime or negotiating snacks.

However, let's not neglect the underlying truth that these matching moments can erupt into delightful chaos. Imagine the stunning photo moment op while simultaneously battling over whose turn it is to pick the next destination on a day out. Or that moment

## MOMMY AND ME: MATCHING STYLES FOR FAMILY FUN

when your little one hilariously emulates your styling efforts by pairing her matching outfit with mismatched socks! These candid moments are the essence of motherhood.

They remind us that style does not exist in a vacuum; it flourishes in authenticity and the beautifully unpredictable nature of life.

But where do we take all of this? Often, capturing memories leads to special occasions-from birthday parties to family vacations. Finding outfits that align with these moments strengthens the bond that is uniquely yours. However, if there's any advice I can impart, it's this: embrace matching style while adapting to each context. The key is to feel comfortable and confident, blending your personalities together beautifully in whatever scenario life throws your way.

In short, celebrating the "Mommy and Me" style is not just about dressing alike; it's a canvas for expressing your love, creativity, and sense of humor. It's about choreographing the delightful dance of parenting while creating lasting memories —whether those memories are sweet embraces or the hilarity of chasing after your child, both of you dressed as butterflies at a backyard barbecue. So go forth, don your matching outfits, and strut into the world knowing that style is an adventure well worth taking, especially when accompanied by your most fabulous sidekick!

### Inclusive Fashion: Dressing for Everybody in the Family

In the grand tapestry of family fashion, one golden thread holds everything together: inclusivity! Today's world of style should be as diverse and fabulous as the families it dresses. After all, whether you're rockin' a petite size, plus, or everywhere in between, everybody deserves to strut its stuff in flair! Inclusivity, my splendid readers, is the magic ingredient that keeps the fashion pot bubbling over with creativity and love. And let me tell you, it's an essential aspect of family life that resonates far beyond the closets!

Now, if you're anything like me, you've had one of those mornings where a simple family outing feels like preparing for combat.

Picture it: you're rushing through the house, tangled in yesterday's leggings while the twins insist on wearing superhero costumes instead of appropriate attire. It's a comedic battle, a circus without a tent, and somehow, we haven't picked out any adult outfits for mom and dad! This is where the magic of inclusive fashion steps in and saves the day, turning chaos into chic like a fairy godmother! So how do we cultivate fabulous inclusivity for everyone in the family?

First, we must embrace diversity in size, style, and, better yet, the unique personalities of each family member. Let's start with creativity! Curate a wardrobe that celebrates everyone's individual tastes while ensuring that the pieces can mingle together harmoniously. I'm talking about structured blazers for your teenage daughter who's ready to take on the world and whimsical graphic tees featuring unicorns for the toddler — because why not? It's all about intertwining each personality thread to create a mesmerizing tapestry of style.

Now let's not forget about comfort, it's the unsung hero of inclusive fashion! My twin boys are notoriously picky. If the fabric itches, they will rebel like tiny fashion critics wearing identical protest signs declaring, "We hate tags!" Their objections only intensify if we attempt to force them into something they view as even remotely uncomfortable. So, when it comes to choosing clothing, always consider the fabric, the fit, and most importantly, the joy of being able to move freely! Luxurious cotton, stretchy leggings, or breathable fabrics are not only excellent for parents with the agility of sloths but will also keep the chaos contained to the surface of laundry piles instead of snags and tears in clothing.

Speaking of snags, let's address versatility-an absolutely essential element to inclusive fashion! Outfits that transition effortlessly from playdates to family dinners? Yes, please! Think soft, stylish joggers that can be paired with a chic blazer for parents or oversized tunics for the kids that allow for layering and layering freedom like a delicious, well-fitted onion. Imagine your family all at once transforming from a playground crew swinging on monkey bars to a stylish, polished brigade ready for a dinner out

# MOMMY AND ME: MATCHING STYLES FOR FAMILY FUN

with relatives, making everyone question how you manage to combine "mom life" with "catwalk ready."

Inclusivity doesn't just stop at fits or fabric; it also speaks volumes about embracing colors, prints, and patterns that resonate across generations.

When families coordinate outfits, let every member shine brightly in their colors of choice! Injecting vibrant hues that pop-after all, we all have opinions on color turning the whole family into a rainbow of boundless joy. Tying in prints that celebrate personality and cultural heritage is another fantastic way to show pride and individuality.

And let's not forget about those delightful little accessories! Adding a few matching hats, scarves, or funky glasses can create an equal visual spectacle while allowing each person's personality to shine. These whimsical additions can transform any ordinary outfit into something uniquely special, laced with laughter and love!

Ultimately, inclusive fashion in family style isn't about adhering to boring standards or making everyone the same. It's about honoring individuality while inviting personal expression that cultivates self-confidence! It's about embracing your family's distinct rhythm, whether it's about being super matchy-matchy or celebrating the hot mess of mismatched socks across every tiny foot. Because, dear reader, let's be real: life is a beautiful chaos, and our family's style should mirror that delightful reality!

So go ahead! Transform those closets into overflowing treasure chests filled with garments that embrace everyone's unique vibe, making each outing a stunning and inclusive fashion statement. Let your family turn heads, spark conversations, and most importantly — remember to have a blast doing it! Fashion isn't just fabric; it's the beautiful story you weave every single day. So, gather everybody in the family, and may you dress them all in glittering love and infectious joy!

## Special Occasions: Coordinated Styles for Family Events

Special occasions-those delightful moments in time that often come packaged with excitement, joy, and more than a hint of chaos! Whether it's a birthday party, a family reunion, or a wedding where Aunt Ida decides to bring her infamous fruitcake, these events offer the perfect opportunity to showcase your family's coordinated style! Picture this: smiling faces dressed to the nines, looking like you've stepped straight out of a photo shoot. But hold onto your hats, folks, because getting to that magical moment often feels like preparing for a Broadway production!

The first challenge, of course, is deciding what "coordinated" actually means. We don't want to venture too far into the matching outfit territory where you all end up resembling a well-coordinated line of crayons. So, my dear fashionistas, let's talk about concepts. The key here is not to imitate an exact theme but to create a harmonious look across the family. Try selecting a color palette— think soft pastels for spring or rich jewel tones for fall that gives everyone a sense of belonging while allowing for personal flair. Everyone can interpret and express themselves under that umbrella, maybe dad rocks deep green while the little ones dance around in lighter hues. It's all about balance and letting everyone shine!

Next, we move on to the most important question of all: comfort. Listen, no amount of family pride is worth enduring an outfit that makes you feel like you're in a Victorian corset while simultaneously wrangling the kids. Choose styles that feel good and allow you to move freely, so you can either catch a runaway toddler or dive for the hors d'oeuvres without losing your dignity. Fabrics and styles that offer stretch and movement are a must!

Unless, of course, you want to be the main event of the family reunion video as you fall face-first into the snack table while attempting to embrace your inner familia "fabulous."

And let's not underestimate the impact of accessories! I cannot stress enough how effectively you can elevate a coordinated look with carefully chosen embellishments. When it comes to special

## MOMMY AND ME: MATCHING STYLES FOR FAMILY FUN

occasions, accessories are like the cherry on top of your sundae but too many cherries can lead to an awkward moment! Think chic brooches, colorful ties, and those ridiculous yet endearing matching bowties for the boys. And please, consider the Princess Di Gatsby-era hat for your daughter. It's not just a fashion statement; it's an experience! Just imagine all the compliments rolling in as you enter the venue looking like you belong in a glossy fashion magazine.

Now comes the magical moment of selection-choosing the right outfits! Family gatherings often revolve around themes— maybe it's an outdoor barbecue, a formal wedding, or a casual picnic at the park. Dressing for the occasion can completely change the family dynamic, while also functioning as a strategic way to prevent any sartorial faux pas. So meticulously plan those outfits, while balancing middle-of-the-road choices.

You want those family photos to capture everyone's personality without someone feeling slighted. "Why does she always get to wear the polka dots while I'm in plain beige?!" One pair of distracted eyes, and choom! You might lose your ideal snapshot moment. And let's talk about practical tips! Always, always check the weather! Imagine everyone decked out in their picturesque summer ensembles only to find themselves shivering under a rain cloud. Bring snacks for the kids, as hungry children are no good for family harmony. Promise ice cream if they cooperate— they're already being forced into uncomfortable shoes, after all.

Have a "just in case" backup outfit, preferably something dainty for mom that can transform from day to night! Trust me, there's nothing like feeling fabulous without breaking a sweat (or mascara) when Uncle Frank decides to spontaneously grab the karaoke mic!

Lastly, let's reflect on what all this really means. Special occasions are about capturing the memories that fill our hearts long after the party favors have been discarded. By coordinating your family's outfits, you're not just playing dress-up; you're weaving a story that speaks to unity and individuality-the vibrant mix of life's many colors. So, pull your children in close, snag that perfectly staged photo by the cake, and revel in the joy of coordinated style! With a dash of love and a sprinkle of chaos, let your family dazzle at every special occasion, making each one a cherished treasure in the incredible journey of togetherness. The truth is, whether your family is fabulously styled or just flat-out chaotic, it's the memories that matter, blended with a healthy serving of laughter!

## CHAPTER 18
# FASHION FAUX PAS: WHAT TO AVOID

### Identifying Your Fashion Faux Pas

Fashion faux pas! It's like that uninvited guest at a party who shows up, sloshed, and tries to dance the Macarena but instead ends up knocking over your grandma's favorite vase. We're all guilty of committing fashion blunders at some point in our lives, often without even realizing it! Identifying these slips is the first step toward emotional recovery — kind of like admitting that, yes, I did indeed cut my own bangs, and it looks horrifying. Fear not, my lovelies; we're here to clown on the cringe-worthy choices and help you strut in style with confidence while dodging those faux pas like a seasoned matador.

Let's start at the beginning — wardrobe confusion. There's nothing more bewildering than staring at your closet, feeling like it doubles as a time capsule of unfortunate clothing decisions. You know your much-maligned high school cheerleading outfit is lurking somewhere behind a fabulous faux-fur coat you swear you'll wear someday. It's time to drag out those relics from yesteryear and throw them into the fashion graveyard, aka the donation bin. Remember, if you haven't worn it in over a year, it's highly unlikely the reincarnated fashion gods will allow it to come back! No one wants to look like they just emerged from a 90s sitcom-leave that for the reruns!

Next, let's address the meters of fabric that seem to suffocate our outfits. Oversized clothing can work, but not all oversized clothing is created equal. There's a fine line between chic and grizzly bear charm, and you don't want to cross it. Wearing a t-shirt that swallows you whole may seem like a cozy idea while juggling jelly-stained toddlers, but at some point, you need another layer of accountability. Perhaps some structured pieces would help prevent you from looking like you're hibernating for winter. Try to find items that both fit well and give your body some love— dresses cinched at the waist speak volumes about self-appreciation!

Now, let's dive into the treacherous waters of color coordination. This is an area where many often find themselves swimming in the fashion deep end without a life raft. Dress in hues reminiscent of a 1970s fruit salad and you risk becoming a walking meme. On the flip side, wearing nothing but a monochrome outfit may lead to accusations of being stuck in a permanent state of mourning. Remember that colors are your friends but choose wisely! You don't want to step out looking like you just consulted a history book on how NOT to coordinate colors. Find complementary colors that brighten your mood and bile your spirit without making it resemble a bag of cotton candy that exploded in a paint shop. And oh, the patterns! Mixing patterns can be exhilarating, like a coffee-fueled dance party in your closet. But dear reader, let's get real for a moment: just because polka dots and plaids have a moment in your mind doesn't mean they belong together, twirling like some mismatched ballroom dance. If you're attempting pattern mixing, remember the golden rule: find commonalities. They should share a similar color story or vibe to prevent a tumultuous clash that could lead to severe questioning on your fashion choices. If your outfit looks like it belongs in a kindergarten art class, it's time to scale back the exuberance.

Finally, we land on the most delightful yet deadly aspect of accessorizing. Accessories can make or break an outfit— one wrong turn and you could go from fabulous to fashion disaster faster than your children can hide your car keys. More isn't always better! Think of accessories as your cherry on top or, as I like to call it, the proverbial icing on the fashion cake. Too many statement pieces can transform you into a walking jewelry store or, worse, a Christmas

## FASHION FAUX PAS: WHAT TO AVOID

tree. Choose accessories that genuinely elevate your look rather than competing for attention.

So, there you have it, ladies and gentlemen of the fashion court- your guide to identifying those sneaky fashion faux pas lurking in your wardrobe and your consciousness. Laugh at the cringe, learn from the mistakes, and use this lighthearted exploration to power your fashion choices. After all, style is not just about what's trendy; it's about owning your look and getting a chuckle or two along the way. Now let's strut our stuff and show those faux pas who's boss!

### Common Mistakes to Avoid in Outfit Choices

The world of outfit choices rich with endless possibilities, yet notoriously treacherous. It's like navigating a field of landmines while wearing stilettos. One misstep, and you've unwittingly sent your fashion credibility toppling into the abyss. But worry not! We're here to shine a comedic light on common mistakes to avoid in outfit choices, so you can strut like the confident peacock you were born to be. When it comes to fashion, it's not just about what you wear; it's about how you wear it and, most importantly, how you avoid becoming a fashion faux pas casualty. One of the most colossal blunders I've witnessed is misunderstanding the term "casual." Trust me, I'm all for lounging in comfort. But when you're casual is teetering on "I-just-rolled-out-of-bed-and-snatched-my-son's-graphic-T-shirt," we have a serious problem. Blow-off-the-day wear should still make you feel like you've put in some effort! Swap that pajama top for a chic, fitted sweater or a trendy oversized tee that flatters your shape. A quick hairdo, even if it's achieved with sheer desperation, can do wonders. You'd be amazed what a spritz of dry shampoo and a couple of hair cups can do to prevent the mom-hobo look that plagues us all. Your toddler might appreciate you looking less like a walking laundry basket and more like the stylish superhero you truly are!

And speaking of superheroes, let's address dressing from the epoch of your youth. We've all been tempted to roll out that high school ensemble, thinking it will transform us into those teenage glamazons we once were. But folks, unless you're coming down from a time machine, putting on outfits that were too small back then is not a valid excuse to travel back in time. Those acid-wash jeans belong in a museum, not on your legs!

Fashion changes like the climate, and we've got to don clothes that reflect our evolving selves instead of closets full of nostalgia. It's a great idea to keep a couple of "vintage" pieces around but wearing that hideous windbreaker from your eighth-grade gym class should remain a fond memory, not a regular outfit choice.

Next, let's discuss the importance of appropriate attire for different occasions. Nothing screams "fashion disaster" quite like showing up to a baby shower dressed like you just walked off the set of an 80s music video. While I adore a good sequined number, it's crucial to understand the context-after all, no one wants to be the only one looking like an overzealous disco ball while your friends casually sip their organic herbal teas and discuss how little Timmy just learned to use the potty. Guide your outfit choices with a keen understanding of the event! If it's a picnic, stick to breathable cotton fabrics rather than leather pants-unless you want to become an unfortunate meme. Moreover, let's dive into the fabulous world of layering. Ah, layering has been touted as the holy grail of building an immaculate ensemble. And it can be! But make sure you're not layering your T-shirt with a sweater, your jacket, and then a boulder-sized scarf while still boasting about your 7- year-old's denim vest. Unless you're walking the runway in Milan, there's a point where it becomes less "effortlessly chic" and more "frumpy burrito." Find a balance— choose strategic layers that add dimension without making you look like a walking, talking marshmallow, because, frankly, no one wants to be mistaken for a campfire treat.

Let's not forget the oh-so-delicate subject of footwear. It's all about choices, my friends. Opt for shoes that elevate your look, both literally and fashionably! While I absolutely adore a good pair of flip-flops (don't get me started on their beachy magic), wearing them to a semi-formal gathering would surely end your outfit in a regrettable fashion fate. Invest in versatile shoes that cater to various occasions. A chic pair of ankle boots can take an outfit

# FASHION FAUX PAS: WHAT TO AVOID

from playdate to dinner confidently! Treat your feet like the stars they are and let them do the talking!

Finally, accessorizing should be an art; a joyous endeavor, not a chaotic tussle. The common error of over-accessorizing leads to disaster, as it can quickly transition your look from "fashionista" to "walking jewelry store." Resist the temptation to pile on the bracelets, necklaces, rings, and earrings all at once! Allow your accessories to be the accent notes in a garment symphony, rather than the entire cacophony. Pick a few standout pieces to harmonize with your outfit— this is your moment to shine, not an orchestra rehearsal gone rogue!

Finally, navigating the world of outfit choices comes with its share of perilous pitfalls. Knowing the mistakes to avoid is crucial in this sartorial journey. Let's simplify it: dress for the occasion, remember your body's evolution, layer strategically, choose appropriate footwear, and accessorize wisely. Armed with this knowledge, you can confidently dance your way through life, dodging fashion faux pas left and right while still embracing your inner drama queen. Let's strut and sparkle like no one is watching —because frankly, they may not be, and that's the glory of it all!

## The Role of Fit: Tailoring is Your Best Friend

Fit! The elusive holy grail of fashion that many of us overlook as we leap into the wild and wonderful world of online shopping. You might stumble across something labeled as "one size fits all" and be lulled into a false sense of sartorial security, thinking you can perfectly channel your inner supermodel. Spoiler alert: If you don't happen to be a human pretzel, it likely won't fit you quite right! Let's take a minute to unravel the crucial role of fit in fashion and how tailoring can literally transform a garment from 'meh' to magnificence-like a fairy godmother with a sewing machine!

First things first, I want to address the way clothes are often portrayed in stores. They hang there, like golden promises of perfection, beckoning you with their siren songs. But herein lies the catch: even that fabulous little number that looks perfect on the rack may turn into a fabric nightmare when it graces your body.

Oftentimes, you'll find yourself wrestling with sagging sleeves, a waistband that defies gravity, or a hemline that seems possessed by vengeful spirits. Enter tailoring - your trusty sidekick in this fashion saga. A well-fitted outfit is worth its weight in gold and can take your ensemble from average to extraordinarily faster than you can say "let's go shopping!" Just imagine, you slip into a dress that's been perfectly tailored to your shape and size, hugging all the right curves and leaving just enough room for dessert. It feels like a hug from an old friend — with none of the awkward small talk! Good fit means confidence. When your outfit has been tailored to flatter your silhouette, it shifts the dynamic in the room.

Suddenly you walk taller, smile wider, and feel like you can conquer the world (or at the very least, not spill your coffee down the front of that tailored blouse). Finding that fit can make all the difference in how you view dressing up, and it may very well save you from the dreaded meltdown that comes when your outfit fails to keep up with your larger-than-life personality!

Now, let's get to the nitty-gritty: investment! Yes, I'm talking about throwing down a bit of cash for tailoring, and I want you to think of it as giving your fabulous finds the royal treatment they deserve! Sure, you could buy that $15 dress off the clearance rack at the local superstore, but if it looks like you pulled it off a too-short mannequin, is it worth it? I say no! Opt for slightly pricier pieces that speak to you and then bring them to the miracle workers, your local tailors. Your tailor is not just a seamstress; they should be seen as fashion wizards, weaving magic into your garments.

They'll nip, tuck, and somehow even give your waistband a little pep talk about staying up. It's a small price to pay for wearing clothing that feels like it was custom-made just for you!

Don't let the fear of being labeled as "high maintenance" because of your emphasis on fit scare you. Quite the opposite! It shows you take your style seriously and understand that fit is foundational. You wouldn't build a house on a wobbly foundation, so don't throw on an outfit that makes you feel like you're wearing it reluctantly. Tailoring ensures that your clothes have a tailored relationship with your body, therefore exuding confidence and

## FASHION FAUX PAS: WHAT TO AVOID

empowerment. Think of it as the secret sauce that transforms an outfit from a hodgepodge to haute couture! And let's not forget about those life transitions! Motherhood, job changes, and a wardrobe that sometimes seems like it's been through one too many pizza parties can all influence how our bodies shift and change over time. Tailoring is your ally through it all, providing the flexibility to adapt your favorite pieces to your changing shape. It can breathe new life into that dress you once loved but now see hanging in your closet like a sad ghost. A few stitches can spruce it up, making it feel fresh and fabulous once more! Just like that, you've got a dance partner again!

Lastly, as you embrace the magical world of fit, remember that it's your overall vibe that matters most. Tailoring can be a transformative element, and it's the cherry on top of the fashion cake. Wear that tailored masterpiece with pride and strut your stuff knowing that you've bypassed the fashion pitfalls and moved straight into "fashionista" territory! So, get cozy with your tailor, befriend them like you would a trusty hair stylist, and don't shy away from requesting that additional nip and tuck. They've got your back.

Tailoring is your best friend, and together, you'll rule the fashion kingdom!

In short, embrace the pivotal role of fit in your fashion journey, and don't underestimate the power of a skilled tailor. After all, life's too short to wear ill-fitting clothes, especially when the right fit can elevate your style from frumpy to fabulous faster than you can say "new wardrobe!" Now grab your tape measure and let's get sewing— because perfect fit awaits!

### Color Clashes: How to Avoid Shocking Style

Color-the glorious spectrum that adds vibrancy to our lives, transforms mundane ensembles into fabulous spectacles, and sometimes, if mishandled, can leave us looking like rebellious kindergarteners unleashed in a paint factory. Navigating the world of color in fashion is a bit like walking a tightrope; one misstep, and you could send your stylish aspirations plummeting into the abyss of awkwardness. Fear not, dear reader! In this illuminating chapter, we will explore the potential of color clashes and how, with just a pinch of savvy, you can sidestep those shocking style moments like a pro.

Let's face it: color has implications. It can evoke emotions, create moods, and even make statements without uttering a single word. Even as a toddler, I could see my mother's vibrant red dress brighten her mood when she twirled around in it. But as I grew older, the reality hit me that strutting around in rainbow hues doesn't guarantee style genius. Enter the dreaded "clash." You know the type when your beloved mustard-yellow blouse suddenly fights tooth and nail with your emerald-green pants, leading to a wardrobe skirmish that leaves no clear winner. Avoiding color clash is paramount in achieving high-impact style without the loss of fashion credibility!

A great starting point to avoid chromatic chaos is understanding the color wheel. The color wheel is like your stylish BFF; it will never steer you wrong! Let's break down some guidelines with an approachable twist. Complementary colors-those that sit opposite each other on the color wheel-often make for stunning pairings (think teal and coral), while analogous colors, those strutting together like a synchronized dance troupe-create pleasing harmony (like blue, green, and teal). Utilizing these guidelines can help ensure you don't pick up your color palette the way you'd pick a toddler's finger paint. So, before you dive headfirst into your closet, consult the wheel, it's like a roadmap to color confidence.

Of course, while we're on this road of color exploration, it's crucial to take saturation into account. Believe me when I tell you that those brilliant neon hues can be a double-edged sword. Sure, they radiate energy and fun, but paired incorrectly, they can also launch you straight into "too much" territory faster than you can say "color block." If you're leaning into bold shades, balance them out with neutral tones to ground your look.

For instance, wearing a bright fuchsia top? Pair it with classic denim or crisp white pants. This ensures the boldness becomes your statement rather than the entire orchestra suddenly playing a

## FASHION FAUX PAS: WHAT TO AVOID

dissonant symphony. Fabric matters too! The texture of materials can influence how colors interact with each other. A shiny silk can amplify colors, making them appear more vibrant and animated-great for a night out but alarming for a morning meeting. Meanwhile, matte fabrics can help tone down more intense hues. So, if you're sporting that attention-grabbing chartreuse top, consider pairing it with soft, matte trousers to strike a beautiful balance. Think of your fabric choices as the supportive cast in your fashion production, allowing the stars (your bold colors) to shine without overshadowing the art!

Patterns are the colorful confetti of the fashion world. They can add texture, fun, and visual interest—if done correctly. However, mismatched patterns in clashing colors can lead to chaos that would make a modern art exhibit look like a Picasso painting gone rogue. When mixing prints, stick to similar tones to create a cohesive look. For instance, pairing a playful floral patterned top with a striped skirt in muted tones provides interest without turning your ensemble into a visual game of twister! Remember, the goal is to be fashionable, not a walking color wheel catastrophe.

And let's not ignore the importance of personal taste in this colorful escapade. As you traverse your wardrobe jungle, don't forget to lean into what makes you feel fabulous! Sure, color theory is an excellent guide, but ultimately it comes down to how you feel in your outfit. If you resonate with that odd combination of burnt orange and electric blue because it showcases your unique personality, go for it! Confidence is key, and when you feel good, it radiates off you like sunbeams of style. Just remember to temper your adventurous spirit with a splash of awareness to avoid shocking style surprises on your journey.

With this in mind, mastering the art of color and avoiding clashes is about balance, understanding, and a touch of whimsy. With the right knowledge of color pairing, saturation, texture, and personal preference, you can create explosive outfits that captivate without causing confusion. So, let's leave shocking style moments for the fashion fails videos and step out into the world wearing colors that sing harmony rather than scream chaos. You'll not only look fabulous but also feel empowered-after all, life is too short to wear colors that don't resonate with your fabulousness! Let's paint the town not in chaotic clashing colors but in resplendent, harmonious style!

## Accessorizing Wisely: The Fine Line Between Elegant and Overdone

The art of accessorizing! It's the most exhilarating part of getting dressed.

It's like the cherry on top of your sundae, except if you go overboard, it can quickly morph into a sundae disaster that's more ice cream soup than elegant treat! Discovering the fine line between elegant accessorizing and looking like you've raided your grandmother's jewelry box can be a delicate dance. Fear not, my fashionable friends, for in this chapter, we'll navigate the treacherous waters of accessories— learning to achieve that exquisite balance that will have everyone thinking, "Wow, you look stunning!" instead of the awkward "What happened to you?"

Let's start with the classics-the jewelry. When it comes to necklaces, earrings, bracelets, and rings, I have just one mantra: less is often more.

Picture yourself at a glamorous soirée, all dressed up in a flowing gown that makes you feel like a Hollywood star. Now, imagine layering delicate necklaces, chunky bracelets, and oversized earrings like they're a game of fashion Jenga. You might think you've reached ultimate accessory level, but alas, one wrong move, and you're teetering dangerously close to "tacky." Keep it simple, Opt for one statement piece that captures attention, whether it's a bold necklace or an eye-catching pair of earrings.

Let that stunning piece shine while your outfit plays the dutiful support role. Together, you'll create a stunning fashion duet that'll have everyone applauding! Let's talk about the power of balance. Accessories are designed to enhance your looks, not to drown them. Instead of piling on 10 bangles and looking as if you're about to audition for a circus,

## FASHION FAUX PAS: WHAT TO AVOID

consider the silhouette your outfit creates. If you're wearing a dress with intricate designs or vibrant colors, opt for understated accessories to prevent a competing contest of who can outshine whom. Picture an elaborate floral dress; it calls for delicate earrings, a dainty bracelet, and perhaps a simple clutch — a gentle touch rather than an accessory avalanche. Balance will help ensure your accessories complement instead of competing, allowing you to exude that effortless elegance we all crave.

And oh, the glorious world of hats! Hats can say so much about your style-whether you're channeling a chic bohemian vibe or a sophisticated elegance fit for tea with the Queen. However, it's essential to choose hats wisely, as they can quickly veer into the territory of costume. Avoid the temptation to don a massive wide-brimmed hat with feathers that could double as a prop in a wildlife documentary. Instead, opt for hats that flatter your face shape and complement your outfit. A simple fedora or a chic straw hat paired with a sundress can elevate your look from "just rolled out of bed" to "I have my life together."

When it comes to bags, think of them as your sidekicks rather than your families of luggage. Choose styles that work cohesively with your outfit rather than those that scream for attention, like that bright neon travel duffle (we've all been tempted, but don't do it!). The same goes for shoes!

Channel your inner thoughtfulness by considering both style and comfort, my lovelies. A gorgeous pair of stilettos might seem like the right way to elevate your outfit, but if you can't walk in them, it's all in vain. Feeling like you're walking on stilts is the quickest way to morph from fashionable diva to fashion disaster. Choose shoes that flatter your style but also allow you to strut confidently — your feet should thank you in the end!

Don't forget about those "power" accessories — the exquisite finishing touches that can make a statement without going overboard. A striking belt around a fitted dress can accentuate your waist, while a pair of classic sunglasses elevate any ensemble, even if it's just to hide your eye bags from a sleepless night of toddler wrangling. Accessories can be the catalyst for that extra sprinkle of flair, transforming an ordinary outfit into an extraordinary statement-keep it in check, though! One statement ring, an eye-catching scarf, and your best shades can create a personal atmosphere of chic without turning you into a disco ball.

Now, let's dive into the world of colors! Your accessories should ideally complement not only your outfit but also your unique complexion. Avoid overkill with colors that clash drastically unless you're auditioning for a role in a cartoon show. Coordinate your accessories with the hues in your outfit and let those colors adjust to each other like two dancers finding the right rhythm.

In short, mastering the art of accessorizing is about finding harmony and elegance in your choices. Avoid the temptation of excess and remember the do-it-for-the-camera rule: if you wouldn't feel comfortable strutting down a runway in your selections, reconsider your choices!

Embrace the gorgeous pieces while ensuring they play nice together, creating a sophisticated symphony rather than a chaotic cacophony. So, step into the world of accessories with confidence, grace, and a joyful twinkle in your eye to shine uniquely — a sparkle that screams, "I've got this!" But don't forget to leave the circus attire at home!

## CHAPTER 19
# CONFIDENCE IS KEY: OWNING YOUR STYLE

**The Connection Between Confidence and Style**

Confidence and style-the most fabulous duo since peanut butter met jelly, or since I embarked on my quest to juggle motherhood with a fashion business! It's undeniable: the moment that self-assurance struts into your life, your wardrobe begins to sparkle like a disco ball at a '70s dance party. You know, the type of confidence that lets you wear sequins at a playdate without a hint of shame or even manage to wrangle toddlers while rocking a pair of heels. It's time we unpack the glorious relationship between confidence and style, shall we?

Let's start with a little reality check: confidence is not about fitting into the stereotypical "ideal." It's about owning who you are, fluff, flaws, and all. You already know that I'm the proud mom of twin boys who are basically pint-sized tornadoes ready to wreak havoc at any moment! As I dash through my home, dodging Lego landmines, it's not the designer pieces that make me feel powerful-it's the attitude I wear with them. And that's the secret sauce, my fashion forward friends! When I feel good in what I'm wearing, the tornadoes could be flinging broccoli at me, and I'd still walk around as if I'm the queen of a fab kingdom, not just a chaotic mom of two!

Here's the thing: style is an extension of your inner self. When you're dolled up in an outfit that makes you feel like you could conquer the world (or at least survive bath time without losing your mind), your confidence shines brighter than a thousand stars. It's as if you have a built-in spotlight, radiating beyond any frumpy sweatpants- though I secretly maintain a soft spot for those during nap time. The best outfits were born from self-acceptance. Forget about the "rules" of fashion! Who says you can't wear polka dots and stripes as if they're long-lost best friends? No one should be bound by fashion faux pas when your confidence can send them flying out the window faster than toddler tantrums.

But let's be real for a moment— confidence doesn't just magically appear when you snap your fingers. Nope, it takes practice. Think of it as training for a marathon. You wouldn't expect to win the Boston Marathon by merely daydreaming about it as you sip your morning coffee, right? You must put in some sweat, equating to "visibly sweat through pristine white blouse" levels or —gasp! — that fear of wearing white after having kids! The more you wear the outfit that feels true to you, the more you exude a fabulous aura that's utterly contagious. And trust me; people will notice. Expect compliments, unsolicited advice, and even a few jealous side-eyes from those who wish they had the same fearless approach!

One way to boost your confidence level is to create a wardrobe initiative, or, dare I say, a "Personal Confidence Campaign." Scrap that dismal closet filled with pieces that made you wince (yes, that "one size fits all" dress that is now a home for stray socks) and curate a collection of garments that celebrate your individuality. When you put on something that flatters your body type and showcases your unique flair, like a fabulous belt that says, "I've got this!" you'll be amazed at how your posture immediately improves.

I'm talking about that proud, regal stance as if you're walking a runway, instead of the default "I'm about to trip over my child's toys" shuffle.

And let's not forget the power of pampering yourself! Self-care is crucial for confidence, whether it's a long-awaited shopping spree, slipping into a cozy, oversized sweater while binge-watching your favorite show with the aforementioned tornadoes snuggling at your side, of course), or finally mastering the "winged eyeliner" technique that makes you feel like a glam diva. Taking the time for

## CONFIDENCE IS KEY: OWNING YOUR STYLE

you foster the confidence you need to step out and style your way through life, children, and chaos in tow.

When you look good, you feel good; when you feel good, you act like a confident queen! So, buckle up, my stylish friends! Embrace your uniqueness and allow confidence to fuel your fashion choices. Because in the end, life's too short to wear boring clothes and twilight zone levels of self-doubt. Dress your inner drama queen with utmost confidence, and watch the world welcome your sparkle like a glitzy entrance at a glitzy gala.

### Unlocking Personal Style Through Self-Acceptance

Self-acceptance— the holy grail of personal style! It's like finding the last cookie hidden behind a carton of expired milk; once you discover it, you realize life is just that much sweeter! But let's be real for a moment.

Self-acceptance and personal style aren't automatically bestowed upon you by a magical fairy godmother the minute you step into adulthood. No, honey! It's a journey-sometimes paved with sequins and sometimes littered with those terrifyingly confusing adult decisions we all dread.

Imagine trying on pants in a dressing room while struggling not to hiss at your reflection because, how can you be sure they don't come equipped with an internal mirror that's out to sabotage your confidence? Welcome to adulthood!

So, how do you get from "Who am I even?" to rocking the perfect ensemble like the fabulous diva you know you can be? The key lies in embracing every nook and cranny of your unique persona. Your style is a piece of art, a patchwork quilt sewn together with threads of your experiences, dreams, and okay-those questionable fashion choices you made in middle school (we all had that furry vest phase, right?). It's time to stop comparing yourself to the seemingly flawless Instagram stars who look like they just stepped out of a Vogue cover. Spoiler alert: they owe some of that fabulousness to clever filters and a team of stylists who have probably seen more fabric swatches than I have seen toddler tantrums. Seriously! Begin your journey by treating yourself with kindness. Create a self-acceptance mantra! You know, something like, "I am uniquely fabulous and deserving of a wardrobe that reflects it." Trust me; you'll need it while sifting through the piles of clothing in your closet that could make a dramatic comeback in a 2000s-themed party. Let's face it- if you're still clinging onto that one "Classic" outfit that just doesn't fit anymore, it's time to acknowledge that it's probably time to let it go. Besides, holding onto it is like keeping old college textbooks —what purpose do they serve, really?

They just take up space! When you accept yourself for who you are, you open the door to creativity and exploration. Picture yourself experimenting with bold colors, quirky prints, and styles that scream your name! Want to rock those flamingo-patterned leggings while on a playdate? Go for it! Forget about what anyone else thinks and let those legging-loving flamingos fly! After all, true personal style is a reflection of the inner you—flaws, obsessions with donuts, and all. When you embrace who you are, you free yourself from society's unrealistic "norms" that can be as suffocating as a four-year-old giving you a surprise bear hug during a grocery store meltdown.

The beauty of personal style is that it evolves. As we go through different life stages, our wardrobes may grapple with identity crises too! So, if your style suddenly resembles a melting ice cream cone due to chaotic toddler moments, guess what? That's okay! Just like the seasons change, so will your style. Embrace that quirky, glam, or even "sweatpants chic" part of you that emerges when you face the challenges of motherhood or after a too-late-night spent binge-watching your favorite series.

Now, let's talk about the ultimate style confidence booster: knowing your body and dressing for it! We often overlook it, but accepting our bodies is pivotal to unlocking personal style. Try saying goodbye to those rigid rules that govern what you're "supposed" to wear. Rock that oversized sweater that feels like being hugged by a friendly cloud while knowing it pairs perfectly with your favorite skinny jeans (or leggings- your choice!).

## CONFIDENCE IS KEY: OWNING YOUR STYLE

Break the mold, my fabulously fierce friends!

Lastly, surround yourself with positivity. Seek inspiration from sources that uplift you, whether that be fashion blogs, TikTok accounts bursting with personality, or your best friend who never hesitates to remind you that your jeans are, in fact, iconic. Create a community that celebrates diversity in style, where embracing every single eccentricity becomes a badge of honor. Step into the spotlight as the dazzling star you are and remember: self-acceptance is not just a haircut or a trendy outfit; it's your shining essence that fuels every sartorial choice.

By unlocking your personal style through self-acceptance, I promise you'll discover a wardrobe that makes you leap out of bed each morning with the enthusiasm of a child spotting the ice cream truck. It's a beautiful journey, my fashionistas! So, let's soak in the magic of authenticity, toss those bitter comparisons aside, and slip into the delightful world of self-acceptance that awaits. Who knows? You may just unleash the fashionista you never knew existed — and that, darling, is a style all on its own.

### Practicing Confidence: Mindset and Affirmations

Let me tell you something, darling; confidence isn't something you just wake up with, like a perfectly organized closet or wrinkle-free pajamas. It takes practice-like getting used to juggling two energetic toddlers while looking fabulous in your statement earrings! Yes, I'll say it again: confidence is a skill you can develop — an art form as intricately as getting your kids to eat their vegetables without a side of bribery. And the secret weapon in this transformative journey? A combination of a sassy mindset and powerful affirmations!

Picture this: you stand in front of your closet, the fabric tyrants mocking you with their overwhelming colors and patterns. Old insecurities scream louder than your toddler after a nap denial, whispering that you'll never look good in anything. What if I told you to silence those pesky echoes with potent affirmations? I'm talking about those powerful little phrases that you can recite to yourself while squinting at your reflection, as if you're trying to decipher whether the shirt you're wearing was originally a pajama top or an art project gone rogue. When you speak kindly to yourself, you start reprogramming the mental playlist that has been stuck on "I Can'?" for way too long.

Let's dive into the transformative magic of affirmations. They work like a charming spell — though perhaps not one you should expect to be conjured up by a questionable magician at a children's birthday party. I mean, if I had a magic wand, I would zap insecurity into another dimension, and I can only imagine the place would look something like a petting zoo with judgment-free goats. Instead, creating a daily affirmation routine becomes your own personal spellbinding practice. Try crafting affirmations like "I am fabulous and utterly deserving of my unique style!" or "I radiate confidence, even when my hair looks like a bird's nest after a tornado." Repeat them like a mantra, and I promise you'll begin to feel the fabulousness seep into your spirit.

Next upon our confidence-boosting adventure, we need to insist on a positive mindset. Think about it-when everything around us feels chaotic, it's far too easy to let negativity sneak in, just like that friend who always shows up uninvited to the party. Rather than allowing the incessant thoughts of "I can't pull that off" or "What if I look silly?" steer your wardrobe choices, guess what? Kick them out on their stylish behinds! Substitute them with a confident mindset, reinforcing the empowering realization that you can wear whatever drapes beautifully over your fabulous self.

One of my favorite mental gems is the concept of "what would my fashion icons do?" You know those confident, unforgettable icons that strut their stuff, leaving a trail of glitter and controversy in their wake? Picture that fiery diva-perhaps channeling those jaw-dropping outfits while confidently sipping coffee out of a sparkly cup — and before you know it, you're embodying that aura. Carry that energy with you throughout the day, even when you feel like you might trip over your own feet on the way to drop your kids off at school.

And here's where the enchantment elevates: if you catch yourself spiraling into a negative mindset, pause! Take a deep breath and visualize the fabulous person you aspire to be. Imagine walking

## CONFIDENCE IS KEY: OWNING YOUR STYLE

through life, unapologetically rocking your style choices as if you just stepped off the set of a fashion shoot. If strutting boldly works for you, embrace that energy!

Exude positivity, even in the face of laundry piling up or a toddler tantrum showing any semblance of a Broadway audition.

Practicing confidence also involves surrounding yourself with inspiring, uplifting company! Ever notice how a supportive friend can make you feel invincible, as though you've successfully navigated a toddler tornado? Seek out those you admire— other moms, supportive pals, or even that one girlfriend who wears animal-print bikinis while sipping green smoothies.

Create a squad that celebrates individuality, and work together to build a shared arsenal of style confidence! Who knows? You might even inspire one another to make bolder choices, such as, say, stepping out in patterned pants that practically scream "I'm being fabulously extra today!"

Ultimately, loving yourself and your unique style is a lifelong journey, my darlings! Remember to treat it with the relentless enthusiasm of a kid on Christmas morning. As you cultivate your mindset and harness the power of affirmations, you'll realize that confidence isn't a destination-it's a lively dance with every quirky outfit and off-beat song of self-expression.

So, throw on that colorful ensemble, recite your affirmations with guffaws, and prepare to take on the world like the unstoppable force of fashion you truly are. Here's to dialing up the volume of your inner confidence queen!

### The Power of Posture: Walking Like You Own the Room

Let's talk about posture, my fabulous friends! You know, that often- overlooked aspect of our presence that can transform you from "Oh my gosh, I just tripped over my own feet" to "Move aside, everyone! The ultimate fashion queen has arrived!" That's right- how you carry yourself not only impacts how others perceive you; it can even dictate how you feel about yourself! In a world filled with messy toddler tantrums and crash-course mom meetings in mismatched clothes, mastering the art of walking like you own the room elevates you to new heights. Grab your imaginary tiara because it's time to strut your stuff!

First things first, let's get down to the basics: why does posture matter? Well, honey, just like the right outfit can change your entire mood, a solid posture can send ripples of confidence cascading through your being. When you walk tall with your shoulders back, it's as if you're channeling your inner runway model — except, this time, it's not about avoiding your dog's slobbery toys but reclaiming your fabulous energy amid the chaos of motherhood. Good posture instantly exudes a sense of poise and authority, letting the world know you're not someone who just rolled off the couch after a Netflix binge (though we know you might have!).

Now, I can hear you questioning: how do I channel that inner goddess if I feel like an anxious rubber band? As we let our busy lives pull us in every direction, don't forget that awareness is key! Take time to connect with your body. For instance, when you catch yourself slouching while helping your toddler find all seven lost dinosaurs (the things we do!), engage in some quick posture checks- transform yourself into that regal creature you were born to be! Picture this: you enter a room, with shoulders back, chin up, walking with purpose-all while appearing completely unfazed by the disaster brewing at home. Yes, you can walk like a manager on the last day of work before vacation!

Now let's talk about the steps literally! If you want to strut like you own the room, you need to embrace that confident energy as you glide (yes, glide) through the setting. Forget about tiptoeing around like a deer caught in the headlights. No, my friends! Stride! Extend those legs like an elegant galloping gazelle! Each step should be deliberate and buoyant, a flow of grace guiding you. Imagine yourself walking across the living room floor, maneuvering through toys like a champion while suppressing any urge to scream about the ideally executed "Technology-Free Day" you've envisioned.

## CONFIDENCE IS KEY: OWNING YOUR STYLE

Instead, you exude confidence while your child offers unsought entertainment, and others can't help but notice your fabulous aura!

A tangible trick involves finding your center. Engage your core! No, I'm not talking about six-pack abs; I'm referring to that magical part of your body that keeps everything aligned and helps prevent the "Floppy fish" syndrome that has plagued many of us — bonus: it also works wonders during post-naptime snack preparation! By drawing in your tummy and grounding yourself, you are not just taking up physical space-you are sending signals of strength and assertiveness that others will perceive. Don't underestimate the effect of eye contact while strutting your stuff.

Look at people— instead of avoiding eye contact like it's about to unleash a pretentious fashion critique. Embrace it! Connect with others with a warm smile, and suddenly, the air becomes electric! It's as if you've flipped a switch that engages your audience, instantly making you feel more empowered. Friendly eye contact can enhance that magnetic energy, as if you've donned an invisible cape that proclaims your marvelous presence.

Of course, nothing completes your powerful entrance like a sensation of ease. Radiate authenticity and comfort in your chosen outfit, whether it's a pair of stylish jeans that transform you into an avant-garde superhero or a playful dress that encourages you to twirl like a spirited dance instructor. When you feel good in what you wear, it becomes easier to exhibit the kind of unshakeable confidence that commands attention, leaving no room for self-doubt or jealousy to crash your party.

Finally, while you practice these transformative techniques, don't forget to have fun! Confidence is all about enjoying the ride— the "Oops, did I just trip?" moments included. View yourself as a work in progress. Wield the power of posture and walk into that room with the elegance of the queen you are— owning the space as if it were a catwalk and not a chaotic lineup of grocery delivery service mishaps!

So go forth, my stylish companions, and strut your stuff! Remember that cultivating an aura of confidence transforms how you show up in your life and the perceptions others have of you. When you walk with purpose, no toddler tantrum or unplanned mishap can shake the fabulousness of your stride. Get out there and show the world just how fabulous you can be!

Now, where did I leave those sparkly shoes? I have a room to own!

## Overcoming Self-Doubt in Fashion Choices

Self-doubt — every fashionista's not-so-secret nemesis! It sinks into our lives when we least expect it, whispering sweet nothings that can lead us to question our closet choices. One minute you're feeling like the dazzling diva of a fashion runway, and the next, you're standing in front of that full-length mirror looking like a confused penguin. But fear not, my fellow fashion warriors! Overcoming self-doubt in your fashion choices is as achievable as finding the perfect balance between toddler snacks and your chic aesthetic. Together, we'll march forward and conquer the swirling whispers of insecurity, fashionista style.

Let's be real: fashion is subjective, and that makes it both fabulous and overwhelming! You've got the likes of runway models strutting catwalks in outfits that look incredible on a six-foot tall person, and then there's you-wondering how on earth you can make that same look work after a night of interrupted sleep thanks to late-night diaper changing. But remember this: what looks amazing on someone else doesn't automatically translate to every person walking this planet. Authenticity and self-acceptance are your armor. Embrace the fact that you are unique and own that! Discovering your personal style means experimenting and stepping outside the boundaries of the latest trend because no one should put you in a box — okay, except for that time when your child thought they could fit into a toy box, and you have photographic evidence for eternity!

Now, let's talk about that first wardrobe rebellion: the "fear of judgment." It's insidiously tempting to dwell in a bubble of concern about what others might think. What if someone thinks your outrageous crop top is too bold or your sequined ensemble is better suited for a disco inferno? Sweetheart, let me let you in on a

## CONFIDENCE IS KEY: OWNING YOUR STYLE

little secret: people are usually too busy worrying about their own lives (and wondering how to rescue that one missing shoe from their toddler) to focus on what you're wearing. Free yourself from that pressure!

If you want to wear neon-colored shoes that make you feel alive while chugging orange juice at the playground, go for it! Let your boldness shine brighter than any potential judgment; it'll turn those whispers of self-doubt into chants of admiration before you know it.

Speaking of judgments, let's address another roadblock: the infamous comparison game. You know the one—a social media scroll through perfectly curated outfits that could make even a potato feel inferior. But remember, my darlings: these images may often be filtered (and heavily curated) snippets. Everyone has bad days, questionable choices, and wardrobe hiccups! Instead of measuring your fabulousness against an unrealistic standard, invest time in finding your unique style. Use those social platforms as a source of inspiration or follow us @samdmones instead of a breeding ground for doubt.

Are those bright floral prints speaking to your soul? Go wild! Does the sight of a flowing maxi dress make you want to drop everything and twirl? Do it! You're not just aiming for someone else's definition of fabulousness; you're crafting your own. But let's not forget about the power of fashion affirmation when self-doubt tries to sneak in! This is where your inner cheerleader swoops in, ready to elevate your spirits! Stand in front of that mirror, channel your inner Beyoncé, and affirm what makes you beautiful and uniquely you. "I am fierce, fabulous, and ready to rock this outfit!" - repeat, repeat, repeat!

When you speak these empowering phrases aloud, you'll cultivate a mindset that fuels confidence, even when you feel like a deer caught in the headlights of an unexpected dance-off at a family gathering.

As you embark on this journey of overcoming self-doubt, remember to embrace whimsy and playfulness! Fashion should be a delightful playground where you can experiment without fear, like your kids tossing crayons all over the floor. Mix and match with abandon; throw on unexpected accessory combinations and pair that radical printed top with a wild pair of patterned pants. What's the worst thing that could happen? You turn heads, encourage wild giggles, and maybe earn some additional compliments along the way!

Finally, seek solace with your inner circle- those fabulous friends who will tell you that you slay, even when a piece of fabric makes you feel like a frumpy frog. Find motivation in your tribe, and if you get discouraged, turn to your fashion-forward pals for the ultimate pep talk. Revel in each other's uniqueness and celebrate the fashion faux pas with a hearty laugh over a glass of wine or (let's get honest) a generous glass of toddler juice after a long day.

Overcoming self-doubt in your fashion choices is more than just about the clothes you wear; it's about radiating self-love and acceptance. It's time to channel your inner fashion superhero and unleash a wardrobe revolution of self-expression! So, the next time self-doubt tries to creep in, remember your sparkle, put on your favorite necklace, slip into those dazzling shoes, and strut out like the confident queen you are. Because darling, fashion should never stop you; it should uplift you— so let it flourish!

## CHAPTER 20
# YOUR STYLE JOURNEY: EMBRACE AND EVOLVE

**Embracing Change: The Journey of Style Evolution**

Embracing change can sometimes feel like trying to fit into a pair of skinny jeans after a wild taco night-it's a struggle, it's uncomfortable, and sometimes all you want to do is wear sweatpants and curl up with a pint of Häagen-Dazs strawberry ice cream. But whether we like it or not, change is a constant companion in our lives, especially when it comes to fashion. Our style journey is not a straight road, but a winding path filled with surprising detours and interesting pit stops, where each twist reveals another layer of our evolving identities. As the CEO-founder of SAM D'MONES, I deeply understand that our clothing choices reflect our inner selves, which means embracing change is essential for unlocking our ultimate style potential.

Remember those teen years when your biggest fashion worry was blending your neon scrunchy with your jelly shoes? Oh, those were the days! Every fashion faux pas was a badge of honor, signifying your daring spirit while rocking that "I just rolled out of bed" look. But then life happened: you blossomed into adulthood, developed an appreciation for more sophisticated attire, and sauntered into the exhilarating yet terrifying world of "serious" fashion. You traded in your whimsical wardrobe for pieces that claimed to embody maturity. Spoiler alert! They often left you pieces that claimed to embody maturity. Spoiler alert! They often left you looking like an overworked office manager who just survived a nine-to-five marathon - caffeine-stained blouse and all. So, how can we not only embrace these changes, but actually enjoy the journey? Let's strut down this fabulous path together, shall we?

Like many moms juggling life's absurdities, I often find myself stuck in a fashion time warp. One moment I'm shopping for trendy boots, and the next, I'm wrestling my twins into their socks while simultaneously deciding if I'm capable of calling the boy's outfit matching that of a superhero. As our lives morph and grow-hello toddler tantrums and messy spaghetti dinners-our style should, too! You may start with sky-high stilettos and fancy blouses, but sooner or later, you'll find comfortable chic sneakers become your best friends as you dash after your little ones, not to mention trying to negotiate peace treaties over snack time. Fashion evolution isn't about abandoning our past; it's about taking those lessons and working them into our lives. So, when the little ones throw a tantrum and your once-coveted heels seem like an impractical dream, embrace it! Let's hear it for that brave woman who dares to wear practical footwear while channeling the fierce elegance of a runway model in her own living room!

As time marches on, our body shapes, personal tastes, and lifestyles change. One day you might feel fabulous in a body-con dress that drapes your curves (hello, confidence!), while another day you just want to wrap yourself in a comfy oversized sweater and call it a night. And guess what? That's perfectly normal! To become a style icon-of, as I like to call it, a fashionable chameleon-one must be flexible and adapt their wardrobe to match the prevailing winds of change. It may sound like a fashion cliché, but life is way too short to wear boring clothes. After all, if I'm navigating the chaos of parenthood, I might as well do it in something that makes me feel like a million bucks, even if that outfit was a steal from the clearance rack.

In this effort to evolve, allow yourself to experiment. Take risks! Try that outrageous color you would have once sworn never to touch or dabble with that "faux pas" style that you've often shielded away from. Who knows?

# YOUR STYLE JOURNEY: EMBRACE AND EVOLVE

The once demure floral may now express your spicy side like never before.

Fashion isn't about strict guidelines; it's about self-expression- the bright, sassy, and goofy aspects of yourself that you want to amplify. As I sashay around with spray-painting-scented clothes and a wine-stained tee, I can say with confidence that change isn't an enemy; it's a fashion-forward friend ready to party at your next playdate.

Ultimately, the journey of style evolution allows you to celebrate who you are today rather than lamenting who you were yesterday. Embrace that quirky phase! Your fashion evolution tells a story every time you step into the world and trust me when I say that if you're feeling fabulous, your inner diva will shine brighter than a disco ball at a dance-off. Just remember, dear fashionista, that life may throw unexpected style challenges your way, but it's all part of this colorful adventure called style evolution. So, let's embrace the chaos, trade perfect for playful, and remember boldness is the true key to enduring fashion. Now go out there and rock your journey - I mean, come on, those toddlers won't chase themselves!

## Reflecting on Your Fashion Growth: Lessons Learned

The sweet, sweet process of reflection! It's like finding the perfect pair of jeans after a long day of shopping — rewarding, slightly exhilarating, and maybe prompting a little happy dance in the fitting room. As we navigate through the winding roads of our fashion journey, it's essential to pause and reflect on the growth we experience, like looking back on the hideous choices we made in middle school (to this day, I still cringe at my choice of neon leg warmers). Learning from our past fashion misadventures is key to embracing our unique style and navigating the sartorial maze ahead. So, grab that cup of coffee (and maybe a snack) as we dig into the delightful lessons I've learned on my stylish rollercoaster ride!

First and foremost, one crucial lesson I've unearthed is that confidence is the magic ingredient in any outfit. I'm talking about the fiercely unshakeable kind that makes you strut your stuff like you just graduated from the prestigious Academy of Awesomeness.

Trust me, I've had my own crises of faith in the world of fashion: one day I'd feel like Rihanna gliding through life, and the next, I'd be holding up a shirt wondering if it required a PhD in geometry to figure out how to wear it. But what I eventually discovered is that confidence isn't conditional on the price tag of your outfit or whether your shoes come with the latest fashion-approved swoosh. It's a mindset that radiates warmth, like your favorite fuzzy blanket on a chilly night. Trust in yourself, and you could be modeling the most eccentric tutu while revealing your inner diva— because style isn't solely about the clothes we adorn; it's about how we wear them.

Another lesson I've gathered to share is that never underestimating the power of accessories can be a game-changer! Think of them as the cheerleaders of fashion-those adorable pom-pom-waving buddies that elevate your outfit to the next level. Remember the days of running out the door, hair frazzled, and not a care in the world because you opted for the same old jeans and tee? Add a fabulously oversized statement necklace or a pair of stunning chandelier earrings, and voila! Suddenly, that casual ensemble transforms into a fashion moment fit for the red carpet (or at least the school pickup line). It's astonishing how a few carefully chosen accessories can help you channel your inner fashionista and garner compliments faster than you can say, "I totally meant to wear this hat!" With personal style, it's also essential to embrace the idea of wardrobe curation as self-expression rather than feeling the crushing societal pressure to fit into predetermined norms. There was a time when I thought I had to dress according to the seasonal trends, which led to me forking over substantial cash to fit into the "global traveler" aesthetic - spoiler alert: I'm not going to Bali anytime soon! I realized that personal style transcends fleeting trends; it embodies who you truly are. Learning to curate my wardrobe has saved my sanity and wallet while allowing me to celebrate my quirks, like that ridiculously bright floral print that makes me feel like a walking garden party. So, trust me when I tell you, never shy away from wearing something that showcases your fabulous self. After all, passion and authenticity will always outshine any trend of the moment!

As I reflected on my personal journey, I learned to let go of the idea that your closet needs to be filled with only "perfect" items. Much like motherhood, my fashion path isn't about perfection; it's about embracing the beautiful mess it can sometimes be. If we're honest, I've had my share of unfortunate outfits— those days when I wore a questionable top and felt like I was participating in a fashion crime wave. It's essential to remember that not every outfit will be a winner, and that's perfectly okay! Fashion is a playful experiment, and some choices will inevitably lead to regrettable results. But guess what? Those mishaps often provide the best stories to share at parties and once again remind us to take fashion lightly-don't let a wardrobe faux pas ruin your day!

Ultimately, my fashion growth has not only shaped my style but has also profoundly impacted the way I navigate life. Each lesson I've learned has been a vital building block on my journey to self-acceptance and happiness.

It's essential to take each step with an open heart-allowing ourselves the grace to grow, evolve and glow along the way. Whether it's discovering confidence, analyzing accessories like a boss, or simply letting go of the image of perfection, recognizing our growth means owning our fashion legacy.

So here's to you, fabulous friend! Let's continue to boldly embrace the fashion journey ahead. Always remember: growth takes time-and perhaps a few fashion facepalms here and there—but the style reveals our delightfully unique self. Now go forth and strut with pride, making every outfit a part of your wonderful evolution.

## The Importance of Personal Expression Through Fashion

When it comes to fashion, let's all take a moment to embrace the brilliance of personal expression-because, darling, your wardrobe should be as reflective of your unique personality as a mirror is to your face (not that questionable bathroom mirror with the weird lighting, of course). Clothes aren't just pieces of fabric stitched together; they're a canvas upon which we paint our vibrant identities. Every time we get dressed, we make a choice an audacious statement announcing to the world who we are or, let's be frank, who we aspire to be at the moment. This power of personal expression through fashion is essentially our way of broadcasting our inner thoughts, feelings, and many, many moods—and notice I said many! As someone deeply entrenched in the fashion world, I can tell you that embracing your vibrant style is like finding the key to your very own magical wardrobe.

To begin, let's acknowledge that fashion is the ultimate form of self-expression, a silent language that speaks volumes. Have you ever noticed how slipping into a pair of fabulous heels transforms your walk into an unapologetic strut? Suddenly, you feel like you could conquer the world, one over-caffeinated mom at a time. Conversely, tossing on a comfy oversized sweater can usher you into "cuddle mode," complete with spontaneous movie marathons and snuggles with a pint of ice cream. Our clothing selection reflects our mood and our unique personality tapestry. It's that spark of creativity that prompts the bold color choices, wild patterns, and quirky accessories— each piece telling its own story while contributing to the masterpiece that is you. Who knew that what we wear could have such an emotional impact? Honestly, it's easier to express ourselves more often through clothing than to confront how we feel directly, especially when nobody looks good in the "crying in the bathroom" ensemble!

The beauty of personal expression through fashion is that it allows us to communicate our individuality without saying a word. Remember those times when you've seen someone sporting a shockingly bright outfit— like they just emerged from a tie-dye explosion? You can't help but admire their audacity! Those brave souls are the trendsetters who aren't afraid to live out loud, unapologetic in expressing their vivid personalities.

Personal expression allows us to embrace our quirks, our oopsies, and our fabulousness wrapped together in one delightful package. So, what if your closet includes a daringly unique pair of glittery

## YOUR STYLE JOURNEY: EMBRACE AND EVOLVE

platform boots that would make a disco ball jealous? You, my dear, are already on your way to becoming a fashion icon in your very own right!

In an age where fashion influencers abound, and social media is bombarded with fit-spiration and hashtag challenges, it's vital to remember that your style journey should be based on one fundamental principle: YOU. I've seen countless women (and yes, even the occasional husband) grapple with the pressures of conforming to societal expectations of style.

Each of us has cherished memories that stem from clothing that sparked joy, confidence, and — dare I say — fashion ecstasy! Take a moment to reflect on those transformative outfits— those dresses from weddings that made you feel like a queen, the comfy leggings that resurrected your slouching self during a Netflix binge, or the ensemble you wore on your first big date that filled you with an intoxicating mix of nerves and excitement. Each of these experiences showcases the beauty of personal expression— our style shapes our identities and encapsulates our unique stories.

And speaking of stories, let's not forget how fashion can act as a source of empowerment. Think of all those days when we feel like we are living in a whirlwind —between juggling work, kids, and everything in between, it's easy to feel like a mere parent in sweatpants. But dressing with intention can flip that perspective entirely! We have the power to strut into any situation, whether it's an impromptu coffee date or a serious meeting, wearing our armor of fabulousness in the form of our favorite outfits. When we choose pieces that resonate with who we are, we're draping ourselves in a cloak of confidence that radiates throughout our lives. Honestly, who wouldn't want to wield that kind of power?

The important takeaway here is that fashion is not merely a decorative aspect of our lives; it is an extension of our very being. Think of it as an instrument through which we play the symphony of our lives. Every time we embrace our personal expression through fashion-whether we are florals and frills or edgy leather and studs — we declare our individuality and contribute to the vibrant tapestry of existence. So, carve out your niche in this enormous universe of fashion, let your unique essence shine, and don't shy away from embracing that audacious self-because you, my fabulous friend, are a masterpiece waiting to dazzle the world!

As we step out in style, let's remember that every stitch, every button, and every zipper is a reflection of our individualism. So go forth, unleash your inner fashionista, and don't be afraid to paint the world in your colors, patterns, and creativity because life is way too short for drab outfits! Now, strut with flair, and let that cloak of fabulousness guide you — after all, the world is your runway!

## Overcoming Fashion Challenges: Embracing Imperfection

Fashion challenges — the delightful hiccups in our style journey that leave us rolling our eyes at our closets as if they've personally betrayed us! We've all faced those defining moments of sheer horror when - shocker! - that once-beloved dress refuses to zip up, or your favorite shoes give you blisters faster than a toddler makes a mess of their dinner. It's all a part of the stylish rollercoaster we call life, and I'm here to tell you that it's time to embrace those imperfections like a long-lost friend who still owes you twenty bucks!

Let's face it, navigating the tumultuous waters of fashion is like trying to find a matching sock in a sea of laundry-terrifying, chaotic, and sometimes downright impossible. But fear not, my fabulous friends; it's time to embark on a journey toward conquering those fashion hurdles with a blend of humor, grace, and a touch of sass!

To kick things off, let's acknowledge the reality that perfection is not only overrated but is also a lie perpetuated by social media influencers standing on picture-perfect beaches. You know the ones: effortlessly gliding through life in their designer attire, sipping coffee that probably contains unicorn tears. But here's the truth-behind every curated Instagram photo is a story of outfit malfunctions, wardrobe mishaps, and at least one minor catastrophe

## YOUR STYLE JOURNEY: EMBRACE AND EVOLVE

involving the dog and lipstick. The truth is that trying to achieve perfection in our appearance only sets us up for disappointment with every laundry mishap. Something as mundane as a stubborn stain can feel like a betrayal worthy of tears! So, why not liberate ourselves from this unattainable ideal? Instead, let's embrace the wacky unexpected beauty of life-because life isn't a runway, it's more of a wild carnival ride with twinkling lights and cotton candy chaos.

Each of us stumbles through fashion challenges at some point, and this is entirely normal. I've had my fair share, from wardrobe malfunctions that would make the Carol Burnett Show proud to misread a sizing chart while online shopping, and let me tell you, it was an experience! But all of these challenges delivered invaluable learning lessons wrapped in laughter and one too many "remember that time" stories that we now treasure. The secret? Approach each challenge with humor and a playful attitude! After all, who hasn't had to walk the precarious line between a stylish appearance and an embarrassing wardrobe crisis? I'm pretty sure I'm sponsored by the "oops" club, the ones who took five minutes trying to figure out how to put on a blouse inside out before giving up and leaving the house that way.

Rocking that unexpected "I2th dimensional fashion choice" can serve as the perfect icebreaker, after all!

Now, let's talk about embracing imperfection. Picture this: you wake up to a chaotic house with screaming toddlers, your coffee spills all over your shirt, and you're left with two minutes to dress before being ousted from the house. Instead of succumbing to the chaos, how about mixing and matching what's left in your wardrobe to create an outfit that celebrates your stylish chaos? The key is to take that once-fearful "flaw" and turn it into a fun signature look! Maybe it's a mismatched ensemble or combining unexpected patterns— call it an avant-garde statement rather than a fashion "oopsie." Trust me, you'll step outside with a grin, ready to face the world forcefully claiming, "Yes, I chose this!" And when friends (or enemies) give you a curious look, you can confidently declare, "You see, I'm not just stylish; I'm an artist experimenting with chaos!"

Throughout my fashion journey, I've learned that the best pieces I've worn can sometimes come with tiny imperfections, like a loose thread or that single button that threatens to launch into space at any given moment.

Much like life, our clothes come with their quirks and idiosyncrasies. They carry stories, lots of laughter, a few tears, and perhaps even a sprinkle of adventure. So, why would we shy away from adorning ourselves in those prized ensembles simply because they aren't flawless? Instead, let's wear those imperfect garments courageously, turning our quirks into badges of honor little reminders of our beautiful journey through life's ever-unfolding fashion challenges!

On the other hand, let's embrace the power of humor while overcoming those fashion mishaps! After all, laughter is the best accessory-and it pairs beautifully with any outfit. Recall those fleeting moments of embarrassment, those off-beat blunders you can't help but chuckle about well after the fact. If fashion has taught me anything, it's that the best stories come from the moments of chaos, and humor weaves together life's most entertaining memories. Share those stories, laugh about them, and take comfort in knowing you're not alone in the wildest struggle of finding the perfect outfit. Plus, wearing that glorious striped top with polka-dots?

That's the real-life equivalent of adding gummy bears to your popcorn-it shouldn't work, but oh, how it charms!

So, here's the bottom line: embrace your fashion challenges, lean into the beauty of imperfection, and let laughter play a pivotal role in your personal journey. Each time you succeed after facing an unexpected hurdle, you'll find empowerment in resilience and the joy of being unabashedly, perfectly you. Fashion is an adventure, and when we learn to conquer our challenges with humor and grace, we, my fabulous friends, become the true icons of our own style saga! Now, go on and wear your quirks proudly, because remember-only you can rock that dazzling ensemble of beautiful imperfections.

# YOUR STYLE JOURNEY: EMBRACE AND EVOLVE

## Celebrating Your Unique Style Journey

Celebrating your unique style journey! It's like throwing a fabulous party for your inner fashionista, complete with confetti, disco balls, and the undeniable power of self-love. You see, your style journey is an ongoing saga that's rich with unforgettable memories, mishaps that make for great stories, and delightful ensemble discoveries. Just like each twist of a cocktail straw, it wriggles and twirls, creating a delicious blend of self-expression that deserves to be celebrated. So, let's pop open the champagne (or sparkling water, depending on what the toddlers have left in the fridge) and revel in the glorious celebration of you and your ever-evolving style!

To start, let's appreciate the sheer diversity of our individual style experiences. Our fashion journeys are like an extravagant buffet filled with endless choices- some dishes tantalize our taste buds, while others leave us questioning our decisions after a late-night snack. Maybe it's the vivid macrame vest from your college years that was the talk of the town or the catastrophic pair of "what-was-I-thinking" pants you debuted at a dinner party that still keeps your best friends chuckling. Each peculiar piece tells a story about you and the beautiful mess of moments that brought you to where you are today. Instead of lamenting those cringe-worthy fashion choices, it's essential to embrace them wholeheartedly because they've all contributed to the fabulous masterpiece that is YOU.

Moreover, stepping back to celebrate our unique style journey allows us to reflect on the shape of our evolving tastes. Remember when you wore nothing but neutrals? We can safely say that chapter is behind us!

Now, you find yourself gallivanting through life in bold colors and wild patterns — perhaps even channeling your inner peacock. It's fascinating how our personal growth can manifest through our clothing choices, as they often reflect the stories of our lives at any given moment. Fashion is a means of storytelling; it communicates our current state of mind, individuality, and everything we've overcome. So, take a moment to honor those stages of life-because each shift is another feather in your chic, stylish cap.

One of the most beautiful aspects of celebrating your unique style journey is realizing that we are not alone. Each of us may appear as a one-woman show, strutting down the runway of life, but there's a vast community of women who share the same struggles, aspirations, and cringe-worthy moments. Support one another in embracing individuality!

When you spot another fabulous woman rocking her style unapologetically, give a nod of respect, raise your glass in admiration, and celebrate her unique journey too. Fashion is a divine connection that binds us together as we cheer one another on! Wear the empowering mantra, "We are all fabulous!" with pride. Life is so much more fun when we champion one another!

Now, let's address the elephant in the room: the hiccups! Those quirky fashion faux pas that lurk in the shadows, poised to pounce at the most inconvenient moments — think of torn hems at critical meetings or that time you accidentally wore two different shoes. When these blunders happen, the key is to embrace and celebrate them as part of your distinctive narrative!

Your personal style is a kaleidoscope of shimmering successes and fabulously funny fails, and owning those moments with humor enriches the fabric of your fashion story. Often, these sidesteps into the theme of disaster become the best anecdotes, the cherished memories that linger long after the fashion faux pas itself has faded.

As you journey through life with stylish resolve, make sure to relish in the magic that occurs when you discover an outfit that makes you feel invincible! If that oversized vintage sweater transports you back to simpler times and wraps you in cozy joy, then by all means, wear it with pride!

Celebrating those precious moments, be it a "this outfit makes me twirl!" experience or a "grab the cameras, I look fabulous!" moment, feeds your fashion flame and nourishes your self-esteem. These magical instances foster unabashed self-acceptance and contribute to the unique narrative of your style journey!

## YOUR STYLE JOURNEY: EMBRACE AND EVOLVE

Lastly, take a well-deserved cue to reflect on your growth over the years. When you began your style expedition, you might have felt lost in a world of fashion choices that didn't quite align with who you were. Recognizing the evolution— a beautiful metamorphosis is essential! Let the memories of your past divergences celebrate the powerful impact you've had on yourself.

Share your journey with others and illuminate the beauty that unfolds when you fully embrace who you are. Celebrate your confidence, your sense of individuality, and your boundless creativity.

So, here's to you and the unique style journey ahead! Wear your imperfections like accessories on a beautiful, vibrant day, and take pride in every glorious misstep as life spirals toward creativity. Fill your wardrobe not merely with clothes, but with stories, joyful memories, and cherished moments- because that's what style is all about! Dance fiercely, laugh loudly, and let the world bask in the brilliance that is your unapologetic self. Here's to the adventurous road ahead, filled with love for every part of your special style journey! Now get out there and celebrate every fabulous moment, darling, because you, just as you are, are absolutely breathtaking!

www.ingramcontent.com/pod-product-compliance
Lightning Source LLC
Chambersburg PA
CBHW050256010526
44107CB00033B/1401/J